Dear Mom and Dad

A Beautiful Life

written by Jack Rhodes Dauner

edited by Natalie West Dauner

Dear Mom and Dad: A Beautiful Life by Jack Rhodes Dauner

edited by Natalie West Dauner

copyright© 2025 Natalie West Dauner

All rights reserved. No part of this book may be reproduced or transmitted in any form or by any means, electronic or mechanical, including photocopying, recording, or by an information storage and retrieval system, without written permission from the publisher.

ISBN 979-8-218-82745-8

Design services provided by Linden Publishing.

Printed in the United States of America

Contents

Preface. vii
Introduction xii
Editor's Note xv
1. Camp Dodge, Des Moines, Iowa. 1
2. 1031st T.S.S.Flight 153 – Barracks 1832 B.T.C. #5 – A.A.F.T.T.C. Kearns Field, Utah. 4
3. 507th Trng. Group 28th Squadron – Flt. 153-2 B.T.C. #5 – A.A.F.T.T.C. Kearns Field, Utah. 9
4. Training Detachment #2 – Section 12 A.A.F.T.T.C. University of Wisconsin, Madison, Wisconsin 11
5. Sq. B – 25th Trng. Group U.S.A.A.F. Jefferson Barracks, Missouri . 23
6. Co. A, A.S.T. (STAR) SCU. No. 4760, Grinnell, Iowa. 34
7. Co. A - A.S.T. 4763 - Section 211, Colorado State College, Fort Collins, Colorado. 39
8. Co. G - 387 Infantry - 97th Division - A.P.O #445 Fort Leonard Wood, Missouri. 64
9. Co. G - 387 Infantry - 97th Division - A.P.O #445 Camp San Luis Obispo, California. 113
10. Co. B - 3rd Bn - 1st Repl. Regt. AGF Repl. Depot No. 1 Ft. George G. Meade, Maryland 125
11. Camp Miles Standish, Mass., Port of Embarkation. 130
12. Co. K - 60th Infantry - 9th Division - APO #9 c/o Postmaster - New York, N.Y.. 138
13. GFRS - APO 545 c/o Postmaster - New York, N.Y. 166
14. Co. K - 60th Infantry - APO #9 c/o Postmaster - New York, N.Y. 171
15. Det. of Patients- 184th Gen Hospital, 4200 U.S. Hosp. Plant - APO 514 c/o Postmaster - New York, N.Y. 176

16. G.F.R.P - APO 874 c/o Postmaster - New York, N.Y.. 184
17. 161st Reinforcement Co., 131st Reinforcement Bn. (AAF) - APO 652 - c/o Postmaster - New York, N.Y.. 186
18. 2nd Station Compl. Squadron, A.P.O. 557 - New York, N.Y. . . 189
19. 413 Air Serv. Grp - Hdqs. & Base Hdqs. Sqd. - APO 557 - c/o Postmaster, New York, N.Y.. 199
20. 8th Air Force - 365 Bomb Sqd. – 305th Bomb Grp. - APO 557 - c/o Postmaster, New York, N.Y.. 205
21. 9th Air Force - 365 Bomb Sqd. – 305th Bomb Grp. - APO 140 - c/o Postmaster, New York, N.Y.. 229
22. Hqs. & Hqs. 397th Bomb Group APO 140, -c/o Postmaster, New York, N.Y. Point of Embarkation Base A-42. 273
23. Post-War Academic and Professional Life 288
24. Jack's Later Life and the Interment at Arlington 314
Acknowledgments 333

This book is dedicated to my parents: Wilson W. "Bill" Dauner (September 30, 1896, to June 26, 1970) and Pauline Ann Rhodes Dauner (March 26, 1898, to August 22, 2000).

In reviewing the formative years of my life, I was fortunate to have parents who in their own way provided the guiding principles for making me a better person, and the necessary motivation to become whatever success I have achieved. The learning experiences which they provided me at home each day of my younger life seemed to stay in tune with the educational experiences I was having in school. They encouraged my participation in outside activities, praised my successes, and provided consolation in my failures. There was always much love and respect in our family, and that was shared with relatives and friends. As the years have passed, I have come to realize how fortunate I was to have parents like "Bill" and Pauline Dauner. I hope that I have been able to live up to the standards which they implanted in me, and the attainment of those goals which they encouraged me to achieve.

—Jack R. Dauner, PhD

Jack Rhodes Dauner

-Born: March 22, 1924

-Entered military service: February 2, 1943

-Combat: Co. K, 60th Infantry, 9th Division

-Wounded: Dec. 11, 1944, Konzendorf, Germany

-Reassigned to: 305th Bomb Group (B-17 bombers)

Chelveston, England, and St. Trond, Belgium

-Honorable discharge: January 11, 1946

-Died: December 18, 2022

In Memoriam

Pfc. George Baumgartner, 22nd Inf., 4th Div. Med. Corps
June 6, 1944 (D-Day), Utah Beach. Awarded the Silver Star, Bronze Star, and Purple Heart. Killed in action on July 10, 1944.

Pfc. George Baumgartner, 22nd Inf., 4th Div. Med. Corps

-June 6, 1944 (D-Day), Utah Beach, Awarded the Silver Star, Bronze Star, and Purple Heart.

- Killed in action on July 10, 1944.

Preface

In 1939, when Hitler first began his conquest of Europe, I was deeply involved in the normal activities of a high school sophomore. The next two years passed all too rapidly. Then just prior to our high school graduation ceremonies in 1941, many of us were already beginning to recognize the possibilities of impending military service - particularly when it became necessary to register for the draft. However, most of my colleagues agreed with me that we should pursue our plans to enter the university of our choice, and earn as many college credits as possible in order to enhance our position in the military. We felt that this would be beneficial either when our number came up in the draft, or in the event that we decided to volunteer into one of the programs which offered the best potential for officer training.

Immediately following graduation from high school, I made application and was accepted as a student in Dubuque University, located in my home town of Dubuque, Iowa. From the summer of 1941 through December of 1942, I was able to successfully complete 60 semester hours of college work. In the fall of 1942, I received information about the Meteorology Cadet program of the U.S. Air Force, which appeared to offer considerable long-range potential. According to the information which was released by the military, the program would ultimately lead to a commission and at the same time provide college credits from an accredited university. Early in December 1942, I was officially accepted into this program and given orders to report to Camp Dodge, Iowa, on February 2, 1943, for induction into military service.

Because of the title of this book I feel it necessary to provide some background about my early home life. Our family was a closely knit one composed of my father, Wilson Walter (Bill) Dauner, my mother, Pauline Ann Rhodes Dauner, and myself. My father started out as Chief Chemist for the Champlain Refining Company with headquarters in Enid, Oklahoma. In 1923, he was sent to Milwaukee, Wisconsin, to resolve a complaint which had been filed by a customer regarding the quality of a carload of gasoline that had been shipped under the Champlain name. He successfully handled this situation and was told by the company president, H.H. Champlain, to "just stay up there and see if you can sell this stuff since you know as much about it as anyone in the company." As a result, my father remained in sales and/or sales management the rest of his working career.

My mother and father were married in Enid, Oklahoma, in 1923; mother joined dad in Milwaukee after it was determined that he would remain in that location. For several months they lived in the Plankington Hotel, later finding a permanent residence on Cass Street in the Colonial Apartment Hotel. I was born in 1924 and we continued to live in that location until late 1926 when dad accepted a position with Skelly Oil Company and we moved to Dubuque, Iowa. A year later Philips Petroleum actively sought his talents and we moved to Des Moines, where dad became Assistant Division Manager with primary responsibilities for negotiating the purchase of sites to establish service station operations throughout central Iowa.

In 1929, we moved back to Dubuque where my father became sales manager of Morrison Brothers Company (a manufacturer of equipment for the oil industry). In this position, he traveled extensively and, on many occasions, my mother and I traveled with him. This included a 30-day trip by train to the West coast when I was in the ninth grade. We left Dubuque for Los Angeles, where we spent several days; then to San Francisco, Portand, Seattle, Spokane, Missoula, Minneapolis and finally home. Dad was involved in business appointments during the day, but always found time for sight-seeing and family dinners with customers and distributors. These were great

Preface

experiences and broadened my knowledge of the country and customs of different segments of society.

Throughout my early years my mother and father were very supportive of my many activities. Somehow, they always instilled in me the importance of thrift, and of being a good student. As a result of this encouragement and a few monetary incentives based on my grades, I always maintained a reasonably high-grade point (approximately 3.5 or B+) average. When I graduated from Dubuque Senior High School in June 1941, I was in the upper 5% of my class and heavily involved on various committees, dramatic productions, club leadership roles, co-editor of the year book, head cheerleader, and track. In both my junior and senior years, I won top honors for selling the most season tickets to the general public for the high school football games. Throughout all of these activities my mother and father were supportive above and beyond the normal parental call of duty.

It was because of this relationship with my parents, and the fact that I was the only heir apparent, that I felt a very deep responsibility to communicate on a regular basis after undertaking my new life in the military. It almost became a ritual for me to sit down nearly every day and write a quick note home. At times, when I was able to get home on furlough or when my mother and father would come and visit me, they often reported how few letters many of our mutual friends received from their sons. In any event, I accepted letter writing as a personal responsibility to my parents in appreciation for all of the things they had done for me during my younger days.

When I returned home in January 1946, I was amazed to find that my mother and father had retained almost all of the letters. They were safely kept in a specially designated box over the years until my father passed away and my mother moved into an apartment. It was at that time that I found the letters and decided to undertake putting them into some form of book so that they might be preserved as a suitable memento of the life and times of a soldier during World War II.

Dear Mom and Dad

The majority of these letters were preserved just as they were written. After I was shipped to the European Theatre for combat duty, many of my letters were sent by V-Mail. In those days, I tried to switch between regular franked mail, V-Mail and Air Mail to explore which provided the best and quickest service to the States. Often the V-Mail was difficult to read; however, with the aid of a good magnifying glass the contents of these letters could the translated. Historically, I do not feel that these letters are all that significant. However, they do provide an indication of how "G.I. Joes," as so named by Ernie Pile, attempted to survive the rigors of military life, particularly those who served in the infantry.

Ernie Pile, was the enlisted man's most beloved author and cartoonist. He spent much of his writing career up in the front during World War II. and he succinctly captured how the enlisted men whom he classified as "G.I. Joes" lived, played, fought, and suffered the trials and tribulations of military life. Ernie Pile will always be remembered as the enlisted man's hero!

I have often said that one of the greatest things that ever happened to me in my younger days was serving my country during World War II for nearly three years as a washed out cadet who ended up as the holder of the Combat Infantry Badge, European Theater of Operation Medal with three bronze battle stars (for the Ardennes, Rhineland and Central Europe campaigns), Purple Heart for wounds sustained in combat with the 60th Infantry of the 9th Division, American Campaign Medal, Good Conduct Medal, World War II Victory Medal, Distinguished Unit Citation, and two overseas service bars (French Legion of Honor received on June 01, 2022).

I am proud to have served my country as a fighting man in the foxholes of Europe with Co. K, 60th Inf., 9th Division; and then as a control tower operator with the 305th Bomb Group, 8th Air Force, which was later transferred to the 9th Air Force. These memories are still with me. Even today I get a lump in my throat when I see the Stars and Stripes waving beautifully in a soft breeze with the strains of "The

Star-Spangled Banner" in the background. Our flag and the National Anthem have always served as a reminder of my many close friends and the thousands of other fine young men who died for our country, and failed to return home for a family hero's welcome.

—Jack R. Dauner, PhD

Jack, in uniform, with his parents.

Introduction

The idea of taking a series of letters written by members of the military and putting them into a book cannot be considered as innovative. Library records indicate that projects such as this have occurred following nearly every major war. However, it is often through these letters that historians and others who are interested in studying the inner workings of these conflicts are able to better understand the personal side of a particular war.

Since World War II we have watched with a certain amount of anguish America's participation in the Vietnamese War, Korean War, and brief encounters in the Bay of Pigs, Grenada, Panama, Desert Storm and Somalia. For the great majority of the veterans who survived World War II, there has been very little sympathy for the "draft dodgers" and others who sought to avoid military service. Yet, with the aging of our population the leadership of our country appears to have been taken over by a new breed - many of whom were the "flower children" of the 1960s. These are the same people who spoke out so loudly, and who so violently castigated United States military organizations. For those of us who accepted the responsibility at one point in our lives to bear arms on behalf of our great country, there is a shared concern that America may lose its position of leadership as the most important military power with the necessary strength to maintain world peace.

I have often said that one of the greatest experiences in my younger life came when I interrupted my college education and volunteered into military service. Although the opportunity was not only available but readily within my grasp to become a Commissioned Officer, a combination of unusual circumstances ultimately led me into the

Introduction

infantry. This was a tremendous change in lifestyle for me - the regimentation; the discrimination between officers and enlisted men; and the broad range of ethnic, cultural and educational backgrounds that one had to deal with on a day-by-day basis. I recall so vividly my first visit to a military payroll line-up. The soldier in front of me was asked to sign the payroll book. He paused and then quietly told the payroll officer that he could not write. To avoid any possible embarrassment, he was quickly shown how to hold the pen and mark an "X".

In many respects the college-bred soldiers who found themselves in the military as enlisted men during World War II often received the worst assignments from the old line army non-commissioned officers. Many who were regular army at that time were high school dropouts, or men who had just finished high school and had entered the military for some type of job fulfillment. These individuals enjoyed making it as tough as possible for those "smart ass college kids," as we were frequently called. This same group of old line military men also had an equal amount of disdain for the new breed of "30 Day Wonders," as they called the officers who were quickly rushed through Officer Candidate Schools (OCS) in order to cope with the bulging military requirements of a full scale war.

It is the intention of the author to share the day-by-day reactions of a person in the military under good and bad circumstances alike. I still look back on those years from 1943 - 1946 and thank God for this great learning experience, and the fact that I returned home suffering from no long-term physical or mental deficiencies. In fact, I have always taken the position that every high school senior should be required to enter one of our military branches of service (preferably the infantry) for a minimum of two years as a step toward learning something about discipline and team work. Possibly such mandatory service might have helped to minimize the tragedies among young people that we are witnessing throughout our country.

—Jack R. Dauner, PhD
August 2000

Dear Mom and Dad

Selective Service System
Notice of Classification following Service in World War II

Jack's Selective Service card.

Editor's Note

In Memory of My Loving Husband, Jack

It was my pleasure and honor to get the opportunity to edit the book, *Dear Mom and Dad*. The book carries the letters written by Jack to his parents during WWII for a period of almost three years, February 1943 – January 1946. Jack desired to edit and to also include a few more letters which are not in the book, but unfortunately, he could not complete the task due to his ailments. Hence, the edited book includes these letters and also two more chapters on Jack's professional life and his later life, respectively compiled by the editor.

The book talks about the author's early life in the introduction, his military life in chapters one through twenty-two, his academic and professional life in chapter 23, and his later life and interment at Arlington National Cemetery in the last chapter. The book extensively covers Jack's military life right from the day he left home on February 02, 1943, until he returned back to New York on January 07, 1946, with an honorable discharge. The last two chapters spell out the life of a soldier who not only received the Purple Heart and the French Legion of Honour, but who also never gave up and continued to fight till his last days; a man who not only fought for his country, but also immensely contributed to the academic and business world; a man who loved life and people.

Dear Mom and Dad provides an in-depth description of daily military life during the war, especially for those in combat and in the frontlines. Therefore, the book will be of great significance to scholars and readers who are interested to know more about World War II and the

Dear Mom and Dad

life of a soldier who fought in this war. In addition, the book contains published articles by Jack in the area of marketing and business, which will definitely assist students and research scholars of business schools. The book offers lessons learned from war times, with the message that war should never be fought and should be stopped by all means. The book closes with an acknowledgment from the editor.

—Natalie West Dauner Kharkongor, PhD

September 2025

Chapter 1

Camp Dodge, Des Moines, Iowa

(February 2–February 5, 1943)

In early January 1943, I received my military orders to report to Camp Dodge which was located on the outskirts of Des Moines, Iowa. This was the beginning of my military career. I was instructed to report by midnight of 2 February 1943. My orders further stated that I should board the Chicago & Milwaukee Railroad train which ran from Dubuque to Green Island, Iowa. Here, I was to make a connection with the mainline train that ran between Chicago and Denver. At Newton, Iowa, I was to disembark and catch a local train which would take me to Des Moines. After arrival in Des Moines I would proceed by military truck to Camp Dodge.

The train from Dubuque left on schedule at 6.00 PM. It was bitter cold and a heavy snow had begun to fall. The trip to green Island was scheduled to take a little over an hour, and the train consisted of an engine, a mail car, one coach and six passengers.

Upon arrival in Green Island, which was nothing more than a small railroad station and a few houses. I learned that the westbound train from Chicago would be anywhere from one two hours late. Iowa, where I was to catch the feeder line that would take me on to Des Moines. Because of the heavy snow, the main line train was slowed to snail's pace. In fact, we stopped on railroad sidings several times for periods ranging from a half hour to 45 minutes. Needless to say, I

Dear Mom and Dad

could already visualize that my first week in the army would be spent in the guard house for being AWOL (Away Without Leave).

The train finally arrived in Newton and those of us who got off the main line train soon learned that because of the heavy snow our connecting train was still in Des Moines. In the meantime, the train on which we had arrived pulled out of the station and headed on to Denver. A large number of army recruits like myself were left stranded in the depot in Newton to wait for our connection that would take us on to Des Moines. To make a long story short, we finally arrived in Des Moines by noon of the following day and were transported by truck to Camp Dodge, we were exactly 12 hours overdue.

We then began processing which included getting our clothing allowances, signing payroll, and getting our shots. This was a totally new experience in every respect. We had to take off all our clothes, each man was given a quick physical examination, and then a medic would hit you with a tetanus shot on the left arm while another medic hit you with a typhoid shot on the right arm. By that time, you weren't too sure what had hit you, but since the room was cold and drafty, the most intelligent thing to do was to get into some clothes as possible and get out of there. The following day processing and testing. I was scheduled to go to Meteorology Cadet School so I was able to avoid some of these tests. However, I do recall taking a mechanical aptitude test which required you to take a simple crystal radio set apart and then put it back together again. Fifteen minutes after everyone else had completed the assigned test, a sergeant who was the testing supervisor came over and said: "Soldier, you have the lowest mechanical aptitude of anyone that I have put through this test over the past two years. It's a good thing you're heading for something that doesn't require any mechanical intelligence because you're just plain dumb."

On February 6th, I received my orders along with six other fellows who were all about my age. I was designated as the leader. We were given our tickets, trucked down to the train station and soon began our trip to Kearns Field Utah. We were assigned to pullman cars which

Camp Dodge, Des Moines, Iowa

was an unexpected luxury. After spending a few hours in the club car, we hit the sack. We arrived in Denver about noon. We had a little over six hours before we were to board the Denver, Rio Grande Railroad which would take us on to Salt Lake City, Utah. I only recall the name of two of the six fellows who traveled with me. One was Frank from Davenport, Iowa. His father ran a well-known photographic studio. The other soldier was Jim Wasson who hailed from Oak Park, Illinois.

Since I had traveled to Denver a couple of years earlier, I at least had a working knowledge of the downtown area. At my suggestion, we headed immediately for the old Brown Palace Hotel where we spent some time in the Ship's Inn bar. From there we went on over to the Cosmopolitan Hotel for a few drinks before heading to Union Station to catch our train. Once again, we were blessed with pullman cars and a had a reasonably good train ride. We arrived in Salt Lake City and were met by trucks from the base. As I recall it was about a one-hour ride to Kearns Field which at that time was a very new military installation and not too fully developed. My military career really got underway at Kearns Field, and my frequent communications home began to take shape.

Chapter 2

1031ˢᵗ T.S.S.
Flight 153 – Barracks 1832
B.T.C. #5 – A.A.F.T.T.C.
Kearns Field, Utah

(February 10 – March 10, 1943)

February 15, 1943

Dear Mom and Dad:

Everything is okay and another guy and I really had a swell time last night. We went down to the service club and had a dollar dinner. We had a great bi T-bone steak, French fries. Apple pie, salad, milk and later a chocolate sundae. It was excellent!

I got a $10,000 life insurance policy and also have invested $6.25 into war bonds each month. I only get paid $16 this month so I don't know if I'll be sending much cash back. This thing about not sending money is a farce. You're always needing this or that. I think I have about $30 on me right now which isn't too bad.

I'm really beginning to like the life. The weather is bad and the food not so hot, but the fellows are great and even though we all do a lot of yelling about everything, we like it. Started drill yesterday- saw some movies on military courtesy and about two hours of drill. Had a half-hour gas drill today and had to have on the gas masks throughout. They actually walk out and throw tear gas at you. Later on, we'll have to

1031st T.S.S., Kearns Field, Utah

go into a gas chamber and stand there a while in it before "hitting" the fresh air. Tomorrow we have to be ready for drill by 7.45 A.M. We get up at 5.45 A.M. and must dress, eat, make our beds and clean barracks before drill. We have 24 days of basic training and then I don't know what will happen. I should be sent to my school assignment.

Wish you would send me the Kodachrome to look over, also my heavy socks and all of my handkerchiefs. I could also use some vitamins which are good for fighting colds. Ask Doc Pfohl which would be the best and then send me the strongest, I have "Kearns Cough" but it's nothing serious. Am greasing my chest with mentholatum and wearing a towel around my neck. Most of this is purely for precaution because I don't want to come down with anything. I am going to a dance down at the Service Club tomorrow night. It is a military ball, I'll have you know. Nothing more for now except everything is fine and there is no need to worry. Will write later – tell everyone – hello!

Love…. JACK.

February 20, 1943 (Saturday Night)

Dear Mom and Dad:

Well, practically a week has passed for me out here and I'll be darned if I know where time has gone. Went on parade this morning in review for two generals. They only had the rank of Brigadier. However, that represents a few ranks above most of us. So, we marched and marched and then finally got back to the barracks.

As I told you in my last letter, I have started my basic training. Well, about 45 of us did not have our names on the roster, but had been told to drill. Today, after three days of drill, we were told that we would have to go back to the barracks until 150 men were in our group. That means we lose 3 days and must wait until the new group is filled. Until that time, we will be detailed – or put to work. This afternoon, I was "making little ones from big ones" and then piling the rock in order to make a border around some barracks. I really did pull a ream-supreme tonight. Our flight is up for "K.P." tomorrow and when they called out

Dear Mom and Dad

the names there was a Jack R Davies but no Jack R Dauner. I knew that it was supposed to be ME, but the mistake was so great that I decided to run the risk since "K.P." is about an 18-hour steady job- and that ain't hay.

I'm really getting quite adept at making beds, shoveling dirt, scrubbing floors, polishing shoes, etc. I think I ought to make somebody a good wife someday. Had beef stew the last four days, it's getting a habit, but I'm so hungry by the time dinner rolls around that it doesn't make a difference. Please send clippings out of the paper when you see anything interesting. I seldom read a newspaper anymore. To tell the truth, I don't even know how the war is coming along. All they do here is keep us in constant suspense. It's really a great life, no kidding. I don't mind it a bit – in fact, I like it except that I'll be glad when I get into school.

No more news-= - will write later – am okey, so don't worry. It looks as though I'll be fighting "the battle of Kearns Field" for several more weeks. All my love…. JACK.

February 22, 1943

Dear Mom and Dad:

I tried to call you last night at 7.30 P.M. The LD operator said it would take 4 to 5 hours to get the call through. I imagine it will be the same old thing every time I try to make a call. My shoes have been hurting me lately so I took a crowbar and beat them to a pulp. They are really soft now and with a coat of saddle soap on them they look like new. Glad the big celebration went off so well, Dad. I am proud of having such a B.B.M. (Big Business Man) for a father. The guys around here are getting jealous of all the mail I get. I either get no mail at all or about 4-5 letters. Wrote grandma and grandpa yesterday and told everything was wonderful. I made it sound so good, I'm afraid grandpa might decide that if it is such a great life, he might leave his job as County Assessor of Kingfisher County, Oklahoma, and join up.

1031ˢᵗ T.S.S., Kearns Field, Utah

Am on detail this P.M. Take care of yourselves – my cold is much better. Please send me some airmail stamps in your next letter. Thanks and lots of love…. JACK.

February 24, 1943

Dear Mom and Dad:

We moved over to the new barracks today. We are now in Barracks 1938. Have to get acquainted with another bunch of fellows again. The candy arrived today, also your Sunday letter Mom as well as from Dad. All I can say is that I really hit the jack pot in getting a triple header.

Am scheduled for "K.P." again tomorrow, but I'm going to try that same deal I pulled before so keep your fingers crossed. I got away with it like a flash. One thing about the military establishment is that they keep you "lean and mean". Probably will start drilling again this week. I still have my hopes up that I'll be shipped soon.

Stew is becoming too much of a habit. Was surprised to hear that you had received only one letter. I thought I had written more. Maybe they've been delayed in the front office. Some of your mails take 4 days; other letters I get in two, so you can see everything is crazy. Time to turn in so I'll close. Take care of your colds and don't forget that "a clean ear never decays". Love…. JACK.

March 2, 1943

Dear Mom and Dad:

Well, I've been in the hospital for several days. Am feeling fine but I'm coughing up phloem. Spent all my time eating, sleeping and reading. Everyone in here is so darn friendly and nice that it's just like being among old friends. There is one guy who has been here 40 days. He's had everything done from pulling a tooth to curing a cold. Hope to be out by Friday or Saturday, but I can tell right now that this Captain is very thorough just like Doc Pfohl.

Dear Mom and Dad

Everything is okey – I feel fine and am having one big rest. No more news to report. Love…. JACK.

March 5, 1943

Dear Mom and Dad:

I am still a bird n a gilded cage, but I must be okay because they put me to work. I was on "K.P." last night in the ward – only about 40 minutes of it though. Had to get up and push a food cart this morning.

Went up to the Red Cross last night and shot a few games of pool and also some ping-pong. It really felt like good old civilian life to be doing things like that – especially playing pool. Not much news… thanks for the airmail stamps. I was getting very low on them. Hope you and Dad are both feeling okey. Love…. JACK.

March 6, 1943

Dear Mom and Dad:

Well, a week has rolled around and here I sit waiting for the Captain to give me my okey. The ward is packed to capacity and that's one more reason why I want to get out of here. I went to the Red Cross last night and saw the movie, *Young and Willing*, it was funny.

Am enclosing a little match case. I pulled a hose deal. They are supposed to be 15 cents per piece, but I got them for 5 cents so I bought up a few for souvenirs. Hope to get paid soon, but I don't know when. Have a plenty of money, but I'm greedy and want more. I am getting so tight you'd think I drank scotch all the time. I still have $44.35. Must close for now – oh, by the way I received a letter from grandma and grandpa. They sounded okey. Lots of love…... JACK.

Chapter 3

507ᵗʰ Trng. Group
28ᵗʰ Squadron – Flt. 153-2
B.T.C. #5 – A.A.F.T.T.C.
Kearns Field, Utah

(February 18 – March 10, 1943)

March 9, 1943

Dear Mom and Dad:

    Well, it took only 3 days to get your last letter. It should take 1 ½ but it's usually been 4-5 days. Quite disgusting! I wired the University of Chicago on Sunday but no reply. (15 minutes later). Am on fire guard from 8-10 tonight and a big announcement just came out that a large shipping list will be posted for Flight 153 in a day or two. Things really are beginning to look brighter for once. I'll wire on further developments.

    Was on guard duty this afternoon. I was feeling good and just couldn't hold a straight face. The first thing I did was start laughing when my buddy, Chuck Biebershimer told me the order when I relieved him. Then I forget the special orders and top it off, failed to see a Captain and Major – thus they failed to receive one of my smart salutes – thus I got a very dirty look from both of them. What a day! We had a big pitch on war bonds today – I signed up for $6.25 a month. I believed that will be sufficient. Am down to $35 so I hope we get paid soon. I like to have about $50 on hand in case I'd ever have a chance to fly home. Every day I see those big transports fly over and wish I was on one of them.

The candy arrived from Vera Hummel and I wrote her a thank you note. No more for now. Let's keep hearing from you. Lots of love....
JACK

P.S. Word just came that I am shipping out on Wednesday.

March 10, 1943

Dear Mom and Dad:

Well we've been restricted in our barracks the last day and a half because of shipment. Some of 250 men, all but 36 of our flight, are on the list. I'm almost sure we'll go tomorrow. All the boys are going wild, and they can't wait until the final word is out.

We sat around the barracks almost all day. Had a one hour drill this afternoon and had to keep our gas masks on all the time. It gets quite uncomfortable after that long a time. For some silly reason or the other, the food here has been good for a change. The meals have been okey the last 3 days. Of course, it could be that I'm just getting used to it.

Well, I've given up my pen for good. Lost, stolen, or borrowed. It went on the bum so the guy didn't get a very good deal. I am planning on buying the next Parker 52 that I see in the PX. My watch is going to pot too. That's Kearns for you. It's losing time like mad. Everyone's enthused about getting into school and I am no exception. I lost 10 pounds but got about five of it back. I'm up to 137 pounds again and gaining weight daily. I feel fine and I know I'll be in tip top shape when I get out of here.

Will write soon – tell everyone hello. Love…… "The General" – JACK

Chapter 4

Training Detachment #2 – Section 12 A.A.F.T.T.C. University of Wisconsin, Madison, Wisconsin

(March 12 – June 7, 1943)

On March 11, 1943, we boarded railroad coaches for the trip east and our eventual destination- The University of Wisconsin located in Madison. Needless to say, this was a very pleasant surprise since Madison was only 100 miles from Dubuque, Iowa – home sweet home. The trip was reminiscent of the journey back in February when a group of six of us rode in sleepers from Denver to Salt Lake via the Moffett Tunnel Route. The major difference was that this was strictly a troop train we arrived in Denver where the cars were detached and hooked to other trains depending on the final destination of those on board.

The group that I was attached to, rode in three old coaches which were hooked on to the Union Pacific's crack train – The City of Denver. This high-speed train headed north through Nebraska, crossing into Iowa at Sioux City, then passing through Cedar Rapids before crossing the Mississippi River at, Iowa, at Clinton, Iowa, and proceeding on to Chicago. It was a wild ride and at times we wondered if the old railroad cars we were in would be able to handle the speed that The City of Denver achieved on its run into Chicago.

Dear Mom and Dad

From Chicago our railroad coaches were hooked on to a Chicago & Northwestern train and transported to Madison where we were loaded on military vehicles and trucked to our living quarters. The dormitory facilities were very adequate facilities for four persons. After living under the conditions, we all faced at Kearns Field, Utah, this seemed like Paradise. The trip from Salt Lake City to Madison took two full days so our actual arrival in Madison was March 13, 1943. After a day of orientation, we were given our class schedules and began attending classes. The following letters provide some indication of military life on the University of Wisconsin campus during the Meteorology Cadet Training Program.

March 17, 1943

Dear Mom and Dad:

Well, the books all arrived and I'm beginning to get back into the swing of things again. Everything is straightening up okey and I am getting the stuff reasonably well. However, physics is still quite a mystery but Ed, Bob, and Joe are helping me with it. I think I can get it but it is going to be plenty tough. I had exactly four hours of advanced math today; two hours of physics; and an hour of speech plus an hour of military drill. Figure it out how busy I am. It's been bitter cold to boot but we don't mind it.

Not much news – will call Friday to tell you my plans. Everything is coming along okey so don't worry. The food is fine and I'm gaining back all of my lost weight. Gotta run now. Love……. JACK.

March 23, 1943

Dear Mom and Dad:

Just got through 2 hours of study and so far, as I can see, I didn't accomplish anything. I did 3 physics problems and drew a piece of apparatus for an experiment. I'm not consistent enough in any of this stuff. All I can say is that I should have taken basic physics in high school and also loaded up on a little more math which I did not feel I would need for a Business Administration degree.

Sent a bunch of clothes to be cleaned and pressed. I'm afraid they won't be back until next week. Though, and so in case I get a pass this weekend I'll have to wear my flight jacket. Did a few exercises and then took a dip in the pool.

We all quit studying at 9.00 P.M. and now everyone is in here listening to Bob Hope and Red Skeleton. It's kind of a relaxation after the day's work. I've got a good chance of getting home this week. I hope it works out. Enclosed is the letter for Harker (Rhodes). You can send it on. School is okey but if I start to fall too far behind, I'm going in and see what I should do. Will write later and no doubt will call between noon and 3.00 P.M. on Saturday. Love......JACK.

March 25, 1943

Dear Mom and Dad:

Well, Mom, tomorrow is your big day and I wish I was going to be home to help celebrate. Hope the watch is okey and keeping the big business woman on time to all of her meetings. My pen is going strong and I really like it a lot.

Yesterday, we were drilling with our leggings on and when I took off my shoes and socks, my legs were all red and the skin off in several places. I can't figure out what it is since the leggings weren't too tight. I'm beginning to think I have an allergy to the wool sock. Anyway, they ae sending me to a doctor tomorrow to see what causes the problem. Will call you for sure between noon and 3.00 P.M. on Saturday to tell you if I'll be coming home.

Best of wishes on your birthday, Mom, and wish we were all sitting down to a big steak together tomorrow night. Dad, don't forget to give mother a big kiss for both of us. Love......JACK.

Dear Mom and Dad

March 28, 1943

Dear Mom and Dad:

It sure was good to get back in old Dubuque again and see everybody. We arrived safe and sound at 8.00 P.M. and the bus was packed. In fact, by the time we reached Madison, there were three bus loads coming in. Came on out to the dorm - did some work and then hit the hay.

It sure was good to get back in old Dubuque again and see everybody. I'm not going to apply for a 100-mile pass for a couple of weeks. I think we get paid either today or Wednesday so maybe I'll be in the dough again. Hope they won't have any trouble fixing the tire. We didn't hit the curb hard but evidently, we hit a sharp spot.

Gigging started today and they can get us for anything. If you get 8 gigs you have to walk 50 minutes from post to post and 50 more for every following gig. No doubt, we'll be doing some walking unless, of course, we get busy. Bob's shining up the shoes right now and I just finished sweeping the floor. Have to go to class so I'll close. Will write more later. Love……JACK.

March 30, 1943

Dear Mom and Dad:

Well, today is really like summer. The letter from the meteorology commission was just in response to the wire I sent at Kearns before we were shipped. Saw my name in the "Men and Women in The Service" column.

My legs ached like the dickens all day. I guess it was from wearing my oxfords and then going back to the G.I. shoes. A lot of other guys are bothered with the same thing so I guess it's just the change. Talked to Trewartha (Head of Study) today and he said to continue on and that he thought I would get it okay. That is what he has told all of the others. Mechanics continue to be okay in the second class of the day – maybe I'm catching on.

Must close. Love……JACK.

Training Detachment #2, Madison, Wisconsin

April 2, 1943

Dear Mom and Dad:

I have been doing okey I guess – haven't had any "gigs" yet this week. Ed has had one and Bob, none. Ed got his for not brushing the dust off his overshoes. That's how close they inspect. We sure did ride him about the gig.

No doubt we'll get some shots tomorrow before we leave the post. I guess we'll probably burn around downturn. Got paid on Wednesday and now have $50.67. I got robbed somewhere or else they took 3 months insurance out of my pay. That's all I can think of because I should have gotten more. Blew $5 right away for laundry, Red Cross and gym equipment. They hook you for everything.

School is okey. I'm getting the mechanics fine but don't even bother to read the physics if I don't have the time. We have lousy profs for it and I can get just as much out of their lectures by sleeping all period. Start on a physical aptitude tests on Monday. That will be a snap for me, but no doubt many will have a plenty tough time. Will write more later. Love……JACK

April 12, 1943

Dear Mom and Dad:

Well, the big weekend is over and I'm already to start another one. Saturday was a mad house for me. At 3.15 P.M. we fell out for inspection and Sarge Peters got up for announcements. The first thing he did was call me to report for a physical examination at 3.30 P.M. Everyone has to take the same physical exam over. It is the same one we took when we were fist inducted. Well, I got out of that, I think.

We had a calculus test Friday and a mechanics test on Saturday. I worked 9 out of the 10 problems, but have no idea what score I got. Tuesday, we have a geography test and a speech recording today. No more news so I'll close. Hope you had a good trip, Dad, and wish you could have detoured back via Madison. All my love……JACK.

Dear Mom and Dad

April 13, 1943

Dear Mom and Dad:

Another day gone and the old week is getting well on its way already. The Sarge overslept this morning and we didn't have to fall out for revelry. This was one good thing that has happened here.

Also, took the physical which I skipped out of on Sunday. Am okey except my blood pressure I sup a little. Was 128 at Camp Dodge and 132 in this examination. Pulse was a little steadier. Only about 84. Have been wearing my glasses to study but my one eye is showing signs of a little wear and tear. I managed to get 20/40 vision on it. We've been having tests and will eventually have one in each subject.

Haven't had any gigs yet. However, I think it's about time to get a few pretty soon. Today, I walked out of a study and had my haircut at the Union. Even Joe participated. I was quite surprised. I realize this is a pretty lousy letter but I feel like I'm in a daze from cramming in all this damnable math. Hope you are okey and that Puffet isn't overeating her rations. Tell everyone hello and find out how Jack Ruprecht is doing and what his work incudes now. It would be nice to see him again along with a lot of the other members of our old gang. It certainly seems as though we are certainly getting spread out in a lot of different directions. All my love……JACK.

April 14, 1943

Dear Mom and Dad:

Well, I just finished a 20-minute session with Lt. Hastings (commanding officer of this detachment). Decided that I had better find out what was going on. I had full intentions of getting out of meteorology cadets if there was a chance, though – unless I got out entirely from this program. So, I'll keep on here until they throw me out. I think there will be a "C" school begin about May 17 here, but in case I don't make the "B" course, I don't know whether I'd rather go to "C" school or just get back into the army and try to get into O.C.S. All I want is

Training Detachment #2, Madison, Wisconsin

those bars and if I ever get them I'm going to stay right in the army so the sooner the better. Here, no ratings are given at all except at the completion of the course. Then you are an aviation cadet. If you flunk out in the "H" course you keep your cadet rating and are sent to one of six officer schools: navigation, bombardier, photography, pilot, and two others. I'm stumped as to what to do. I'd like to get 30 college credits from the University of Wisconsin.

Applied for a pass for Easter so you can expect me home. I got my request in plenty far in advance. Have to look at my book for a while. All my love……JACK.

April 18, 1943

Dear Mom and Dad:

Well, the weekend is almost over already. Last night about six of us went down and saw "The Moon Is Down". It was a good movie. I bought a new pair of shoes which sent me back on my very slim budget. They are nice looking and of good quality – at least they ought for the price I paid. I planned on getting a new shirt but must wait until the first of next month.

Believe it or not, I went to church this morning. Had breakfast and then played 3 sets of tennis with one of my buddies. Ran in, took a shower, and went to the services. No more news so I'll close. Love……JACK.

April 26, 1943

Dear Mom and Dad:

Well, we finally got back to Madison. The old bus was packed and they had to leave a lot of passengers behind which meant that they had to send another bus out to pick up all of these additional passengers. However, we got in town on schedule, and immediately took off for the dorm. We sat around and ate cookies and cake and Easter eggs before going to bed. Needless to say, we were all dead tired.

Dear Mom and Dad

It was sure good to get home again and I really had a swell time. The new handkerchiefs looked mighty classy and I have them all folded and in my drawer. I guess I am too sleepy to write anymore. I can't think of anything else, so I had better close. All my love....JACK.

April 28, 1943

Dear Mom and Dad:

It was nice here yesterday and it looks like it will be a nice day today. Had a meeting of all meteorologists last night. They've put new restrictions on us pertaining to boating and swimming in the lake. Two guys from Truax Field drowned Saturday about 100 yards from the dorm and two of our fellows tipped over but managed to swim in to shore okey. Also, we may each get $27 a month extra since they're not using the full $2.75 a day. *These guys running this place are doing everything they possibly can to make our outfit as good as possible and have as any of the other outfits.*

Have a bunch of tests this week so I'm hitting the books hard. All of them are departmental jobs and they line up like this; Thursday - physics; Friday – calculus; Saturday – mechanics; and Tuesday – geography. Got an Easter card from Dan and Ora (Dauner), and also got a letter from George Cassat. Well, I better close now. No more news. Love...... JACK.

May 1, 1943

Dear Mom and Dad:

Got the cookies and stationary today and the cookies are swell. Well, quite a bit has happened lately. First, we got a tetanus shot today. It was bad for the first 2 minutes and then there were no effects. Feels fine now. We had the physics quiz and I didn't do too hot, but did get a couple right.

Well, I'm a "B" meteorologist until at least June 19th. We had a big mechanics test today. I studied like mad and I think I got a better

Training Detachment #2, Madison, Wisconsin

grade. Anyway, I worked all period and seemed to know what I was doing. Which is something! Got an 83 in a geography test. I may be here for a while after all.

You don't realize how close you came to having a son in the Air Corps (flying)as a bombardier. They sent out new orders allowing immediate transfers into flying duty so I made application. I couldn't memorize the eye charts fast enough though and they caught up with me so I guess I won't be an aviation cadet bombardier.

I guess we'll all go to a movie tonight. Have a lot of work to do over the weekend. Hope you have a swell time in Chicago and wish I could meet you there. No more news for now. Love......JACK.

May 4, 1943

Dear Mom and Dad:

We had a big inspection of all our clothing last night to see if it was marked. I was writing a letter to Jeanne and Bob was also writing and Ed was just sitting around when the Lieutenant walked in. He stood there for a few minutes, the boys said, before Ed finally yelled ATTENTION! I guess I told you that 1650 gigs were given out last Thursday. Everybody got five gigs for coke bottles being found in the halls. Russ Ladd and Bob (Theisen) got five more from the Detachment Leader, but they went over his head and saw the Sarge, and those extra five gigs were left off for this week. However, we still may be walking guard duty this weekend.

Not much more news. Hope you're having one swell time and that the old nose is okey, mom. Thanks for sending the slide rule, Dad. I've known how to calculate on one for about 4 weeks. I can multiply, divide, find squares, cubes, square roots, sines and tangents on it so far. Quite an accomplishment I'll have you know. Love......JACK.

P/S. Note the change in my address. I am now in Sect. B-12. The B is to distinguish us from the "C" meteorologists.

Dear Mom and Dad

May 5, 1943

Dear Mom and Dad:

Have been doing a lot of work with the rifle. Monday, we go to the range for a little shooting with the Garand M-1. Also, have been learning a little Jui – Jitsuu. I can kill a man "with my bare hands, now". Well, I think I'll turn in for a few winks of sleep. Love……JACK.

May 12, 1943

Dear Mom and Dad:

Today, we took the U.S. Army 30 caliber M-1 rifle apart from head to stern and the put it back together again. That's really quite a little jewel of a rifle. A bunch of "C" meteorologists are coming in and I imagine they'll come "enmasse" this weekend and next. It will be interesting to see if I know any of them and what universities they hail from.

We have a class until noon and in order to make connections, the boys would have to carry our books back and sign us out. Plenty close connections. Pulled a B+ on a physics lab experiment on Monday. Studied 3 hours of calculus last night and I think I'll put in about the same amount of work tonight. No more news, so I better close. Love……JACK.

May 25, 1943

Dear Mom and Dad:

Well, we got the mechanics test back today and I pulled a 65. That's better than I've gotten before, but it just "ain't" good enough. Tomorrow we've got a big calculus test on everything. Monday night we got two physics lab experiments back and I had a B+ and an A- on them. That's the first time that it seemed like my old school days – at least from a grade standpoint.

About 3 big bombers flew over the place today and just skimmed over our heads. None of them were over 500 feet up. They sure looked nice and you can bet your bottom dollar that I wished I was in one of them. No more news so I think I better close and get this in the mail. All my love……JACK.

May 30, 1943

Dear Mom and Dad:

Hope I didn't shock you too much this afternoon when I called, but I figured it would be best if you were prepared in case some bad news did come your way. There definitely is a list of some 50 guys who are failing in 2 or more subjects. My average in calculus and mechanics isn't high enough to get me by, I'm sure. Of course, they may let everyone take the G.I. Tests and then give them all their furloughs, but on the other hand, the way they've talked lately, those 50 men will leave before that time. No one knows anything for sure. However, I'm not practically worried.

I and another fellow went to church today – believe it or not. We couldn't decide where to go so we saw a real new church and decided to go there. It was quite beautiful and turned out to be a Lutheran church. The service was very nice and I think I may go there again. The sermon was very good, short and to the point – quite a bit different from those of Rev. Hugh Dowling Atchison back during his pastoral term at St. Lukes.

My old sunburn is really radiating heat today. I think it will be okey by tomorrow. I'll write if something further comes up. Lots of love…… JACK.

June 2, 1943

Dear Mom and Dad:

Well, your son is on detail and he's mighty happy about it. I was never so glad to get a hammer in my hand in all my life. We're building a pier out into the lake and I'm getting tan as an Indian. You can't imagine what a relief it is not to have a single worry concerning calculus and all that other stuff. We got the Sarge out working with us this

Dear Mom and Dad

afternoon and he accidentally fell into the lake. Was that ever a riot. He was fully clothed and, in an effort, to show us his prowess with a sledge hammer…fell in!

Got paid yesterday and managed to come out with a few dollars left. They had about 5 deals after the pay table where they wanted some of your money: $3.50 for laundry; $2.00 for gym stuff; a dollar here and a dollar there. They hooked us for everything. Don't worry about me, I'll always get along an I'm going to beat all these boys in getting a commission. I'm just out of something I disliked, and whatever I get into now will be alright by me. Time to get this in the mail. All my love…. JACK.

Chapter 5

Sq. B – 25th Trng. Group U.S.A.A.F. Jefferson Barracks, Missouri

(June 9 – July 26, 1943)

On June 8, 1943, a group of ex-meteorology cadets left Madison for Jefferson Barracks, Missouri – just outside of St. Louis. "J.B." as it was known in those days was a famous old military base dating back to World War I days. The trip was made by train from Madison to Chicago (Union Station) where we transferred to another train which brought us into Union Station in St. Louis.

Jefferson Barracks had a reputation for being a monstrosity in the summer primarily because it bordered on the Mississippi River and hence the humidity made the facility almost unbearable. We were housed in 8 – man barracks and although there was some shade, it still proved to be pretty warm – particularly after enjoying the Chamberlin House dormitory at the University of Wisconsin on Lake Mendota.

This assignment to Jefferson Barracks was strictly for the purpose of reassignment of those men like myself to other programs and/or outfits for further training. I was anxious to be where the action was! With my background in photography, I pressed rather vigorously in my interviews with placement personnel to assign me for further training in combat photography.

Following are letters which were sent home during the period from June 9 to July 26., 1943. They provide some insight into life at "J.B." – but even more so – the wonderful reception given to service men and

Dear Mom and Dad

women by the people of St. Louis. Without a doubt, this was one of the greatest "soldier cities" in America, and I will always have a soft spot in my heart for the wonderful treatment I received in restaurants, bars, theaters, the U.S.O. and by all of the people I came in contact with during the five weeks I was stationed at Jefferson Barracks.

June 11, 1943

Dear Mom and Dad:

Well, here I am at the famous J.B. Got here at around 8.30 and then sat around for a while. Finally, they took us up and we get ourselves a place to sleep. The barracks and food are much better than Kearns. I think tomorrow we will get reclassified and I'll just hope and pray I get shipped out in a week. The discipline here is tough and they have got a bunch of radicals with some new ideas on how to run a camp, hence everything here is different from the regular camps.

Didn't get any sleep! We had an old car which was built way back in the 60's and we were all over the track. No pillow, no nothing, just old straight seat. Not much news, will write when something develops.

Lots of love…. Jack

June 14, 1943

Dear Mom and Dad:

This is the first chance I've had to write so here it goes. I have been awfully busy and they have kept us going almost constantly. Had a bunch of lectures today and also 2 hours of drill. Boy, these exercises are murder – especially when you do them in a broiling sun.

The people of St. Louis are really great to service men and the big U.S.O center located in Kiel Auditorium is absolutely magnificent. Haven't been classified as yet. It should come tomorrow. One of the boys pulled some strings and got himself in with some of the "big shots" so I think he is pretty well set.

Sq. B – 25th Trng. Group, Jefferson Barracks, Missouri

Say, I am getting awfully low on cash, and I don't think we are going to get paid this month since we are so new so will you loan me about $5.00 until I get paid. I am almost at the point of hocking my best suit of underwear. AND, by the way – I haven't played any cards – well, almost no card playing. I did play Saturday afternoon for about 15 minutes and won $2.50 – but our food, lunch and dinner cost almost that much in St. Louis.

Will write soon. Hope dad gets along okey in the big trial. Keep me posted, mom, and drop me a note when you get a chance. Love......JACK.

June 15, 1943

Dear Mom and Dad:

Today was really a big one. All day we took aptitude tests and tomorrow we take another bunch. The math test was a snap, but the mechanics was wicked. It included a generator, electrical set up and another contraption. Well, I'm a little slow, so... I don't think I'll be any kind of a mechanic.

I'll probably be interviewed tomorrow so I've got to get on the beam. I'm sure I can get into A.S.T.P. which is some more college education. These courses range from 3-32 months in length. Got your letter and the paper this afternoon, mom, and thanks a lot for the reading material. Will write as soon as I know what's cooking. Until then, I think I'll get a little shut eye. Loads of love......JACK.

P.S. We moved to tents tonight and they aren't too bad.

June 18, 1943

Dear Mom and Dad:

Got reclassified like I told you., but haven't seen the cadet board on A.S.T.P. board. In any case, you can count on me being back to school in a month or so because everything down on my chart leads to schooling.

Dear Mom and Dad

Today, we really put in some good hard work. This morning we had two straight hours of close order drill and then an hour of exercise. Boy I was really worked out and I am not kidding. I am getting browner than an Indian. Thanks so much for the cash. I was down to 50 cents and was beginning to get desperate.

Until then all my love......JACK.

June 20, 1943

Dear Mom and Dad:

Today was a nightmare and I'm not kidding. The whole 25th Trng. Group was turned into an overseas outfit, so all of us guys had to move to another squadron. We've been in the process all day. Took off few minutes to call you this noon.

Started my life off in the 23rd Tang. Group with an A-I boner today. This is a pretty outfit. They are strict but try to give the men a square deal. You can get a pass almost anytime and they are reverie passes – that is – you don't have to be on post until 5.00 A.M.

I am known as "casual" and will be on detail until I am shipped. That means I'll be picking up cigarette butts again, doing K.P. and all of those little duties. I am hoping I'll get shipped out soon, but I know it will be at least 3 weeks. Things move very slowly here at this camp.

Well, I guess I better close. Lots of love......JACK.

P.S. Be sure to note my new address. It is Sq. D – 23rd Trng. Grp. U.S.A.A.F., Jefferson Carracks, Mo.

June 22, 1943

Dear Mom and Dad:

Things are in a general mess here and I've been changed back to a basic trainee again. I really don't mind since if I ever get into O.C.S. all of this basic stuff will help me a lot. Today we went into the gas chamber and got gassed. First, they put us in a room filled with tear gas. It burns the skin but does not blister and boy, how your eyes water. This

Sq. B – 25th Trng. Group, Jefferson Barracks, Missouri

stuff was all without the gas mask. Then we went outside and we went through 4 kinds of gas, Lucite, chloropicrin, mustard, and phosgene. The phosgene was of 100% concentration and one guy got too much of it and went out like a light. We also ran the obstacle course and it was a snap for me. They had us crawling on our stomachs and numerous other things which were plenty tough. I kind of like the stuff, however.

Believe it or not I've been doing some hand washing. It has finally come to that. Your clothes get so filthy rolling on the ground that you have to wash them. Especially undershirts because they demand that every man has a clean one for each exercise period. Think I will also go before the Cadet Board tomorrow – other than that, I don't know anything new. Lots of love……JACK.

June 23, 1943

Dear Mom and Dad:

My status is again changed. I am a "casual" again as of today. They will probably change their minds again tomorrow. Spent a very exciting morning. Went to the Cadet Board and found out I couldn't get into any ground crew cadet school, because they are closed and naturally flying is out. Also did some checking up on when I would appear before the A.S.T.P. Board. They just said – SOON.

Thanks so much for the extra push in the financial line. I signed the payroll today so I ought to get paid in about 10 days or so and then I'll send $10 home as interest on the loan. Had a swell dinner at the service club. No more news for now. Hope everything is okey at home and that you two are feeling fine. Thanks again for the cold hard cash. All my love to you both……LOVE.

June 26, 1943

Dear Mom and Dad:

Well, the worst deal I've gotten since I've been in the army occurred. Last night my buddy and I went over to see George (Cassat) and then

Dear Mom and Dad

headed for St. Louis. Well, sometime on the way by bus to St. Louis somebody stole my wallet. Boy, I was burning up. I had just put the $5 in it that Dad had sent. Fortunately, I had my pass in my shirt. My social security card and driver license were in it so I suppose I'll have to get duplicates. Oh well. I'll just have to start carrying all my stuff in my shirt pocket.

Say, dad, thanks loads for the extra $5 – even though I didn't get any chance to use it. It was really thoughtful. Don't send me any more – I get paid Wednesday and my pal can pay the bills until then. This morning I made the "Looey's" bed and cleaned his quarters for him. He came in and went to sleep so I sat in a chair and dropped off myself. Fortunately, I woke up before he did. Lucky Me!! Better close for now. Will write soon. Hope you two have a pleasant weekend and thanks a lot for the cash. LOVE……JACK.

June 28, 1943

Dear Mom and Dad:

Just came from the A.S.T.P. Board and I was accepted. I will now wait till I am shipped and then will go to either the university of Nebraska or the University of Wyoming. Here, I will take the screen tests, etc., and then be classified for what school to be sent to. I'll be there about a week and then proceed to school I guess. The whole deal hinges on when I am shipped out of here and I hope that will be real soon.

I am going to get into some kind of chemists and see if I can't get on the beam in that department. Other than that, there is no more news. Hope that everything on the home front is okey. Love……JACK.

June 30, 1943

Dear Mom and Dad:

Today is Wednesday and I pulled out a good one. Was scheduled for K.P. but got out of it and legally at that. I went in for detail duty and didn't get assigned any so I will take time and write. Yesterday, I was

Sq. B – 25th Trng. Group, Jefferson Barracks, Missouri

digging drainage ditches and my old hands are really calloused. It was a plenty good days' work!

Last night, I got very domestic and put out a good-sized washing. It sure seems funny to wash clothes. We aren't paid until the 10th of the month for some reason or other, but I think I'll make it okey. It's been chillier than the dickens the last couple of days and the nights have actually been cold. This morning when I got up at 3,00 A.M. to report for K.P. I almost froze.

In case I didn't tell you, will you please get a copy of both my high school and college transcripts. I'll be needing them when I get to the A.S.T.P. Star Center, I wrote the Cassats a note thanking them for the Sunday dinner. George is getting along fine. Better close for now – will write soon. All my love……JACK.

July 5, 1943

Dear Mom and Dad:

Sure, was glad to talk to both of you on Sunday. I'll have to call from that theater again because the connections seemed really good. It is the first time I could actually hear everything you said.

The letter arrived with the $2.00 and I sure appreciated it a lot. Thanks to you both. This has really been wicked – this not getting paid on time. Saturday supposed to be pay day for sure - they say. Last night, we had to G.I. the floors until they almost sparkled. This morning I think it would be a good idea to get out of the area so I am going to exchange some clothing. That will take all morning the way I plan to do it. Yesterday, we had to parade in that boiling sun and I am telling you we were all a mess. Shirts were soaked through and I felt dirty all over from marching in the gravel. Went to see George last night and he is coming fine.

Saw "Stage Door Canteen" on Sunday and it was excellent. Don't miss it because I am sure you'll enjoy it a lot. Will write soon and thanks again for the cash. All my love to you both……JACK.

Dear Mom and Dad

July 6, 1943

Dear Mom and Dad:

Spent whole day exchanging clothes. Got a good looking overseas O.D. cap in place of that old C.C.C. job I had. Also, I got a new pair of khaki pants. Someone puled a little swipe job on the pair of my pants but a staff sergeant fixed me up with another old pair he had so I "G.I.ed" them and handed them in for the new ones. Pretty cagey don't you think? Tonight, I was on detail to clean headquarters. We "G.I.ed" the floors, dusted and then left. I had a pass to St. Louis but I decided I had better save money

A cat and a little kitten got into our squadron somehow so they've been kind of adopted. The little kitten is as cute as can be and very playful. Almost every night some guy finds the little rascal in his bed or around one of the huts. Haven't a thing on when I am shipping put. The boys are getting shipped out slowly and that is the extent of it. Better close for now…Love……JACK.

July 9, 1943

Dear Mom and Dad:

Yesterday, I turned painter and worked in the post paint shop, did some sweeping and then cut out 500 cards and finished off by painting buckets. Today, I am going up to see board of school assignments, and see if I can't push myself up on a shipping list. It seems as though that school has been completely taken over so who knows? I might be sent there too. I will get a Pfc. Rating when I get shipped; however, I don't know for sure when that will be. I better close and get this mailed. Will drop you a note soon. Love……JACK.

July 11, 1943

Dear Mom and Dad:

Here I am back down at the service men's center. Seems like this is my main hangout but it is a pretty good place. Yesterday noon, I had

Sq. B – 25th Trng. Group, Jefferson Barracks, Missouri

a little operation on my left-hand ring finger. A pulled hangnail got infected and swelled up pretty badly. They sent me over to the surgery clinic and the Captain took out his scalpel and slit it open. Anyhow, he made a nice cut and drained some of the stuff out. It's still swollen some but I am okey.

Last night I had 3 hours of guard duty. I was pretty well done from the finger deal but I got through it okey. Came into St. Louis at 10.00 A. M. and had a marvelous dinner at the Statler Rouge Room. The most beautiful roast beef you've ever set your eyes on. Just for eating such a costly meal, I am eating cookies at the U.S. O. for dinner.

Am going to try to get up to see the board of school assignments tomorrow and find out what is cooking. The rumors from that department say that we should ship near the end of the month. Came in town all by myself today and it actually felt good. I am just selfish or too independent or something, but I like to take the town in alone sometimes and not be bothered by anyone by just wander about as I please. Well, guess I better close for now. You two better take care of yourselves and I'll do the same. Love……JACK.

July 14, 1943

Dear Mom and Dad:

Just a quick note in case I don't get a chance to write the next day and a half. A rush call came through that all men of Sq. D who haven't fired at Arcadia would go today. We'll stay a day and a half and fire the 30 calibre M-1 for record score. We will be shooting competition and a chance to pick up a medal so I am hoping that I can get on the beam. It is about a 5 hour ride to the range so we'll probably have a good time.

Came on back to camp and hit the hay. Now I am all ready for a big day. My finger is coming along just fine and doesn't bother me a bit. Got a new deal now. I am stenciling barracks bags. It is a snap and I sat down most of the time. In fact, the calluses are slowly shifting from my feet to my seat. Well, I better close now. In case, you don't hear from

Dear Mom and Dad

me for a day or two you'll know that I can't write out the range so don't worry. All my love……JACK.

July 16, 1943

Dear Mom and Dad:

Well, the big trip is over and here I am back at "J.B.". Wednesday noon, about 35 trucks with some 650 men left for Arcadia – some miles away. The trip down was nice – not so exciting but enjoyable ride. Got there, had a swell dinner, and then an hour of dry firing on the range. Thursday morning, we went on the range to fire for record. Seventy-eight guys fire at the same time and the noise is terrific. In fact, you have to wear cotton in your ears. Well, I started firing and when I finished my 40 rounds I found that I had qualified and was eligible to receive a marksmanship medal. So now, I'll have something to wear on my shirt.

In the afternoon, I worked out on the range figuring scores. At 3.00 P.M. we left and had a wild ride home. Not much else exciting has happened. It sure was fun out at Arcadia. It really is quite a rugged place – tents, water in blisters bags, eating out of mess kits, etc. Haven't heard anything about shipping either, as yet. Will close for now. Lots of love……JACK.

July 23, 1943

Dear Mom and Dad:

Friday and the latest rumor is that we will ship between Saturday and Wednesday. I wish we could get some satisfaction. Have been working over in the day room lettering posters the last few days and it is very enjoyable work. We make these large charts for basic training instruction. Have been restricted the last two nights. I put out a huge washing last night early and then George another guy and I went to the movie and saw "Hit the Ice" with Lou Costello and Bud Abbot. From

Sq. B – 25th Trng. Group, Jefferson Barracks, Missouri

there we went to the service club and had two bottles of ice cold milk and a piece of peach pie.

No more news – will probably give you a call on Sunday. That's all for now…Love……JACK.

July 26, 1943

Dear Mom and Dad:

Well, good news has finally arrived. Last night when I got back I found out that I was on shipment. This morning we had our first clothing check and I am going over this afternoon and get some clothes exchanged.

I imagine I will ship about Wednesday or may be Thursday since I have to be at my destination by Friday. Have no idea as yet where I am going but will find out by hook or by crook before I call you.

No more news. I'll write or get in touch with you as soon as something happens. In the meantime, all my love……JACK.

Chapter 6

Co. A, A.S.T. (STAR) SCU. No. 4760, Grinnell, Iowa

(July 28 – August 18, 1943)

On July 26, 1943, shipping orders came through for transfer to an A.S.T.P. located at Grinnell Iowa. This college had always had an excellent reputation and as a matter of survival during the war, had elected to participate as one of the educational institutions in the A.S.T.P. as these letters indicate this assignment was just like going back into college but in uniform.

Grinnell was a very pleasant small town about 150 miles from Dubuque. It was almost unbelievable that this assignment would be so close to home; however, it did not last too long as all of the courses in my category were filled and for that reason after processing we were scheduled to move on to another campus.

August 2, 1943

Dear Mom and Dad:

Well, I've really been a busy guy today. This morning, I had an all morning session during which I had tests on college algebra, trigonometry, and analytic geometry. They were plenty tough and I had a rough time with all of them. Tomorrow morning and afternoon, I have another bunch of tests. I hadn't planned on calling since I sent the telegram; that's why I didn't call earlier. I'm going to check up on these tourist cabins and will make arrangements.

Co. A, A.S.T. (STAR) SCU. No. 4760, Grinnell, Iowa

It has been very sultry today and I'm sure we're going to get a beautiful storm tonight. Have a head cold but I think it will be okey. Guess the change in weather and riding up on the train with the open windows must have done it. Time to go eat so I'll close. Love to you both......JACK.

August 10, 1943

Dear Mom and Dad:

Guard duty is drawing closer and closer and as yet no word about shipping. About 400 guys came in yesterday and we put up make shift quarters for them to sleep in, they're really crowded here so I'm sure there will be a large shipping order today or tomorrow.

Yesterday, they had us moving beds all morning. At least, it was better than close order drill so none of us complained. In the afternoon, we took some exercise and then drilled a while. My roommate goes up for interview today and the poor kid is scared stiff. Sure, hope he makes the grade okey because he is a swell fellow. There's not much news – got a letter from Fred and he stayed at Jefferson Barracks. He said it hadn't changed a bit since I left. Will write soon – and keep your fingers crossed that I ship before I snag any more guard duty. All my love......JACK.

August 12, 1943

Dear Mom and Dad:

Well, tonight is the night. I've been named as one of the lucky guys who will be on guard duty. I have Post #7 and will be on from 8 – 10.00 A.M. and from 2.40 A.M. Jim and Joe will probably get the duty tomorrow night, and it is really going to be a riot since Jim doesn't even know the manual of arms. Of course, I can't brag about my ability either. Guess what we need is a little more infantry field training. Not a sign of a shipping order has rolled around. I think I'm stranded here for a while and more guys keep coming in. they are starting to send some of the fellows here up to the STAR unit at Lincoln, Nebraska. In fact, that's where the University of Nebraska is located and it is supposed to be a great institution.

My bracelet looks great. It is much nicer than most of them that the fellows are wearing. Think I'll close and get this mailed so you'll get it tomorrow. Right now, my feet are beginning to get soar just thinking about the walking that's in store for me tonight. Love......JACK.

August 2, 1943

Dear Mom and Dad:

Today, I went on sick call and had my athletes foot cleaned and swabbed with some kind of blue solution, I've got a bad case on my right and the funny part is that I've been wearing wooden shower shoes. It ought to clear up after three treatments according to the doctor.

Last night, I was on guard duty and my old luck held true to form. There were seven posts and only six guns. I happened to draw the post where you didn't have to carry a gun. It rained all night and therefore a little damp. Jim is on tonight so we're going to have to get busy and teach him the manual of arms. Joe is lucky and is going to miss guard duty entirely. Am glad the pictures came out so well and will be anxious to see all of them.

It is awfully hot down here and I am dying for a cool Coke so I guess I better close and mail this letter. Will be here for sometime as it stands now, so write to me here. Love......JACK.

August 16, 1943

Dear Mom and Dad:

Another week started and here I sit in the dispensary waiting to have my feet looked at. I'm positive that I'll be here until September 1st at least. In fact, I'm sure that I sent in two suits of khaki's to be washed and pressed. There is also some talk that some furloughs will be given out, but I still have my doubts. Things like that just don't happen here in the army.

Co. A, A.S.T. (STAR) SCU. No. 4760, Grinnell, Iowa

Just having my feet painted so now I'll sit out with the other guys who are waiting for sick call. I think I am going to try and get myself a permanent detail so I won't have to drill. I prefer manual labor to that stuff: so, I guess the Sarge will get a visit from me and maybe I can swing a little deal. There's not much news available at the moment. Thanks for the special delivery. All my love......JACK.

August 18, 1943

Dear Mom and Dad:

I am still here at Grinnell College in the A.S.T. program. Sorry, I didn't get that letter I wrote off sooner to thank you for the $5.00 – also, the oranges arrived yesterday and they sure hit the spot. Thanks for sending them down. Today, I went on sick call and had my athletes foot looked at again. I made sure that it took all morning and then this afternoon we went down to the study hall for a couple of hours. It was an easy day. Tomorrow, a list is coming out as to whom will stay here to go to school. So... I may know something definite.

There's no news that I can think of but may be tomorrow some will come through. Anyway, I hope so. Hope both of you are feeling fine. Love......JACK

AUTHOR'S NOTE: The long-awaited shipping list was posted early August 19th. We boarded a troop train and were transported to Denver where we boarded trucks for the final journey to Fort Collins, Colorado, where we were to be enrolled in an advanced Army Specialized Training Program (A.S.T.P.) at Colorado State College. This proved to be a beautiful little community whose activities centered around the university. Transportation in the town was provided by old fashioned "Tunerville Trolleys" which were about the same size as the San Francisco cable cars. Interestingly enough, they pretty well provided transportation throughout the whole community.

Colorado State College, like most of the state colleges, was heavily oriented to agriculture and engineering. It reminded most of us

Dear Mom and Dad

who had been in Big 10 locations of colleges in our own states such as Iowa State College which had always been recognized nationality for its strong agriculture and engineering curriculums.

Chapter 7

Co. A - A.S.T. 4763 - Section 211
Colorado State College
Fort Collins, Colorado

(August 18, 1943 - March 8, 1944)

August 22, 1943

Dear Mom and Dad:

    Well, we finally arrived here at the fair city of Fort Collins, we pulled in at 10.55 this morning after a breakfast at Denver. We are living in the college Memorial Union and sleeps on the big dance floor. There are rows and rows of beds. It is a nice place, but I sure hate having to have all the company sleeping around me. The campus itself is quite beautiful and the buildings are okay. I got a glimpse of the University of Colorado. Boy, it is a swell school. The food is fine and we eat cafeteria style in the basement of the Union at night, which makes it hard when it rains.

    Already had my first funny experience here. The Capt. gave us an orientation lectures today and he closed it with the suggestion that anyone having any Pullman towels, sheets or pillow cases might find it profitable to slip them in the orderly room!!

    Well, me, having dried my face on Pullman Towels for the last six months thought maybe I'd better turn my three's and so I walked down to the orderly room- towels in hand. Who should be sitting at the desk but the Capt. Himself, so I just hand them to him and says.

Dear Mom and Dad

"Here's a present for the Pullman Co., Sir". He got quite a hangout of it, I guess!! I hope!!

This is quite a town. They have two movies and three trolley cars, also a U.S.O. (where I am now) and few stores. We can see the mountains in the distance and Estes park is only about 15 miles away. All in all, I think it is a nice place and I just hope we get some dorms. No more news, will write soon and keep you posted. All my love to my Mom and Dad- Jack

Author's note: Life at Colorado State College began in mid – August of 1943 and took on the same atmosphere of any university campus. On the other hand, we were always reminded by our superiors that we were under military jurisdiction. In other words, the old bromide – *There is the Right Way, the Wrong Way, and the Army Way* – always applies, and you had never forgotten it, particularly with the type of leadership heading this detachment.

The author must admit that life at Colorado State College was a wonderful experience. The people in the community were an absolute delight and went out of their way to express their positive feelings for those of us wearing military uniforms. It was reminiscent of the wonderful experiences in St. Louis only on a much smaller and more selective scale. Since all of the men in Co. A. of A.S.T. 4763 were formerly college students before joining the military they represented individuals who were reasonably bright and coming from families who were supportive of the need for higher education. In addition, most had come from families who had tried to instill some feeling for the importance of developing certain social graces. This made a difference to the community and its attitude toward all of the men and this detachment

September 4, 1943

Dear Mom and Dad:

Well, it sure was good talking to you last night. That was the third time that I've tried to call. And the call got through in just an hour and

15 minutes. We seemed to have good connections which helped a lot. They post a 3-4hour delay on all calls to Chicago so you can see how lucky I was in getting through.

This morning is the big barracks inspection so we were all hurrying around getting the barracks cleaned and our bunks looking good. We were issued another blanket since it is beginning to get quite chilly. In fact, I think we'll change to our O.D.'s pretty soon and I know I am going to wear a flight jacket up to Estes this weekend. Guess we'll leave as soon as we can this evening and try to catch the 6:05 bus to Loveland and then hitch a ride over from there. I think it will be a nice weekend - anyway I sure do hope so.

This afternoon I imagine we'll go on about a 10-mile hike. I sent a big laundry in yesterday and finally sent my fatigues to be cleaned. They were filthy - so now I'll have to wear a dirty pair of sun tans for hikes and so forth. I'm going to send the Kodachromes - those of you and dad all dressed up are really a riot. In the meantime, Love......
JACK.

September 7, 1943

Dear Mom and Dad:

Monday has passed and here it is Tuesday and I'm so stiff I can't hardly move. Boy, my neck and back are really tightened up. Remind me not to take those four long hours horseback rides again.

They talked over our schedules with us and it looks like I'll be taking two physics courses, chemistry, analytical geometry, history and government. I'm beginning to have a little trouble with physics again. I sure do hate that stuff! We have three new officers around here but the Captain is hard on them, so no doubt conditions will continue to be lousy. We're still living in the Memorial Union and it looks like we aren't going to get dorms at all. It would be very convenient if a small epidemic of the flu would break out and then they'd have to do something!

Dear Mom and Dad

It's almost time to fall out so I guess I better close and run down and mail this. Hope it isn't as cool there as it is here - it is really frigid. Nor more news for now - loads of love to you both......JACK

September 9, 1943

Dear Mom and Dad:

Got the letter with the cash in it and thanks loads. I've got a wicked laundry bill coming up about Monday so I'll be able to use the dough for a good purpose. I'm sending my schedule and a C.S.C. paper - thought you might be interested. There is no school today, I don't know what we'll be doing. I've signed for a pass to Denver, I'd liked to go in and look up Tom Wood north.

We signed the payroll - but I don't know when we'll ever get paid. Most of the guys have back pay coming so I imagine it will be about a $30,000 pay roll - if you can imagine it. That's is a good chunk of money. I'll get $75 and then probably another $35 in about three more weeks. Thanks a lot for the cash and love to you both... JACK.

September 12, 1943

Dear Mom and Dad:

Just time for a note so here goes. We are now on the new system and it is really lousy. This cadet system is really silly – it is just a matter of seeing who can squeal on the other guy first. Went to a study hall last night and we got our first assignment sheet. I can get the work, under ordinary conditions - but they are making it tough by adding a lot of crazy rules. We are not going to get dorms and we do all of our studying in plain classrooms. In other words, we are not going to get out of the Memorial Union building.

They have this war bond drive on and they expect this outfit alone to purchase $13,000 worth of them. Just to spite the rats I don't think I'll buy one. What do you think I ought to do, Dad? Also, about raising my amount from $6.25 up. What should I do about that? I'll try and

Co. A - A.S.T. 4763 - Section 211, Fort Collins, Colorado

write every other day - but time is no longer our own so I can't guarantee it. We are up at 6:00 A.M. and have to be ready for inspection by 6:30 A.M. Then breakfast and on to classes. All morning and afternoon are devoted to school - then dinner and immediately off for a 3-hour study session until ten o'clock. Lights out at 10:30 P.M.

Saturday night several of us crashed three sorority dances and one dorm dance. They were all just for the A.S.T. and no one knew whether we had signed up at the orderly room or not so it looked legal. It was a lot of fun and I had some good dances. Then yesterday morning three of us went to the Methodist church and got an invitation out for a good old home cooked meal - fried chicken and all the trimmings. It was really delicious. Gotta run so I'll close for now. Love......JACK.

September 15, 1943

Dear Mom and Dad:

Well, this is really getting to be a riot! Our new theme song here is "Take Down that Service Star, Mother - your boy is in A.S.T.P." We have been restricted for the weekend!

The Colonel saw some of the boys picking apples from a tree in front of the dorms and there was a continuous passing of the buck from him to the Lieutenant. It started with the Colonel, to the Captain, to the next Captain, to the Lieutenants, to the cadet officers, to the cadet sergeants and finally to the buck privates - like most of us. That's why they call us buck privates - they pass the buck until it finally comes to us and we haven't anyone else to pass it on too.

So, I had to write Woody and tell him not to come up this weekend. Maybe next weekend we can arrange something. The boys are beginning to take the whole place as one big joke. After lights they have been raising hell and the only guy who gets any cooperation is a real swell master sergeant. The guys like him and respect him - but the officers don't get any cooperation. They can hardly court martial the whole 500 guys without causing an investigation by Lincoln, Nebraska (Headquarters for the 7th), so I guess we'll just have to continue like this.

Dear Mom and Dad

School is a snap so far. Physics is tough but I can get it. We haven't been paid yet - maybe it will come through next week. I'm in fine health and have only lost 5 pounds since I've been here. I think I'll start going through the chow line 3 instead of 2 times so I can get enough to eat and gain it all back.

Hope you are both fine.... Love....JACK.

P.S. I'm going to make reservations on the City of Denver for December 5th - and I expect to use it one way or another. Also...I'll call you this Sunday between 3-5:00 P.M.

September 19, 1943

Dear Mom and Dad:

The weekend is over and here I am ready for another week of drudgery. Sure, was swell talking to you on Sunday. There was a 3-4-hour delay on the call, but they managed to get it through in about an hour and one half. So, I was pretty lucky to get it through during the period we had discussed.

Tom Woodnorth came up on Saturday evening by bus. We stayed in Fort Collins then hitch-hiked down to Loveland and then came back to Fort Collins almost right away. We hit the hay at just midnight. Woody had been up 21 straight hours so he was plenty tired. My bunk mate in the lower birth had gone to Denver so Woody slept there and then on Sunday we ate our meals here. After I called home, I took him down to the highway and the first vehicle to come along picked him up. It was a big diesel truck which was heading straight for Denver. I got paid $74.50 and signed this month's payroll, so I'll get another $37 at the end of the month. I am going to buy a $25 bond and then open up a bank account and start putting some money away for Christmas gifts.

By the way, mom, - guess they don t deliver special delivery letters on Sunday so I reckon there is no use in sending them to me. It is chillier than the dickens here and a flight jacket and O.D.'s feel mighty

Co. A - A.S.T. 4763 - Section 211, Fort Collins, Colorado

good. No more news for now…it is time to get on my hobby horse and go to school. Thanks for the slide rule, dad. Love… JACK

September 25, 1943

Dear Mom and Dad:

I just haven't had any time to write so I'll send this one special delivery so you'll have a little surprise for Sunday. This morning we had a history test in which I feel that I came through with a good grade. Then a math exam this afternoon which was okey. Except for a few careless mistakes, I think I got a good grade on it. Spent 3 hours last night on physics. Wrote up an experiment and then had to knock out some physics problems. This morning we started eating out of our mess kits and it was really a mess. We have to do it until Monday. I'm glad I won't be around for the Sunday meals. There are going to be a lot of sick boys if they don't clean their kits really good. It gives you a terrible case of the "G.I.'S" - mine is good and clean though.

I bought a bond yesterday, but I won't be able to pick it up until next Friday so it ought to get back to you about a week from this Monday. Also, started a bank account. I put $30 away as a starter so I have about $21 for the rest of the month and for some things I want to get in Denver. Then I'll get $37.50 more in about a week and I'll lay $30 of that away. Seems good to have some cash again.

Have a total of 5 hours of physics today so I really have to get on the beam. Gotta close now. All my love to you both.… JACK.

September 29, 1943

Dear Mom and Dad:

Just came back from sick call - I developed a real nasty cold, and last night was sicker than a dog. I really "Yo I heaved ho" - with no bottle of rum. I came back from study hall and went to bed. I don't feel really too bad except it has settled in my neck and shoulders so I

Dear Mom and Dad

reckon I'll go out and take some good stiff exercises and a hot shower. Then I should be okey.

Yesterday we had a chemistry test which was really tough and then combined with my thick head - well I guess I'll be lucky to pass. These are the quarter tests - they grade you as passing or not passing. This A.S.T. is really getting to be a crazy deal. As I told you we're on the cadet system. Yet, we aren't called cadets like the other units. Now to top it off we have to salute and "yes, sir", "no, sir" - to the CADET officers. That's pretty lousy when an enlisted man has to show the courtesy due a commissioned officer to another enlisted man. It's thoroughly disgusting.

There's no more news - I still don't like engineering - but I'll swallow it until it chokes me - and it eventually will. Hope you have a happy birthday tomorrow, Dad! Many happy returns for the day.

Love....JACK

October 3, 1943

Dear Mom and Dad:

Here I am after a somewhat dull weekend. I'm tired and wish I could have a week's vacation starting tomorrow. You see, I have two tests tomorrow and I've really got to hit the books tonight. I asked about the furlough on Friday so I could make some definite arrangements and I guess I am "cobbed". Ten percent of the organization will get furloughs and you know who they'll be -- all the Jewish boys and the guys who are eager beavers that hang around the orderly room like "teacher's pets". If they take them by length of service without furlough, I might rate a chance - but they never do the fair thing in this place.

So, I have given up all ideas of a furlough - I am thoroughly disgusted with the set up - particularly now since it means that I won't rate a chance of getting back to see you. In case you two guys were planning on coming out, I frankly don't know which would be best - Christmas or that week I'm supposed to be off.

I got a short-sleeved sweater and like it a lot. It's one of those which are O.D. in color. Time to hit the books for the two tests tomorrow.

Co. A - A.S.T. 4763 - Section 211, Fort Collins, Colorado

Hope you two had a rip snorting weekend, and that Dad had a big birthday celebration on Thursday.

Love...JACK.

October 15, 1943

Dear Mom and Dad:

Hi!! Does this paper look somewhat familiar? Seems to me I've seen letters written on it before. Well, today the first bunch of washouts were called in. For some reason or other I wasn't among the group. They think that some 150 will be leaving. That speaks well for itself on what the boys think of this place and the C.O. They were all given a chance to stay for another month which is a third of a term. About half of them took it - and the other half told them they didn't like the place that well.

We got a new bunch of Cadet officers. I got my tail chewed out by Herr Capt. Walt - head of the gestapo and other un-American A.S.T. 4763 activities. The super-snooper snuck in and saw me with my foot on a chair. For some reason or other - no one knows; including me - I still have my foot on the chair and also a clean sheet on "gigs". I stared him right in the eyes all the time he was talking - who knows, maybe I scared him!!

I am ahead in my work somewhat. I don't know just exactly what some of the stuff they're feeding us is all about, but maybe dawn will break and the light bulb in my handsome head will again show light and pour forth its lumens once again; Right now, I'm starved! We had a fish dinner tonight. I don't know for sure but I think the fish was at least a year old. I fiddled around with the darn thing for a while and then when I saw the stray cat of our unit come by, I slipped it to her. Even she turned her nose up at the sight and smell off my offering. Tomorrow no doubt there will probably be no cat - they'll use her for soup. No animal is safe here, I tell you.

The week has really gone by fast. All the boys are getting anxious to see what Herr Colonel Winton – chief of the Gestapo will do to raise morale. It's really getting funny – no fooling. The guys are becoming mechanical. They even swear in cadence and it has been rumored that Herr Capt. Walt has made the lids on the stools in the latrine grunt in cadence. This letter may be somewhat exaggerated but not too much. I really love this place as you.

As to the World's Series...well, Dad - I only lost 50 cents, 3 chocolate sundaes, and a malted milk. The St. Louis Cardinals sure did do us dirt. Maybe I better send you $10 in case you two need it for a couple of extra meals. Personally, I am disgusted with those local yokels from Saint Looie. I think I'll sick Herr. Capt. Walt down there to haunt them and he could sure do a good job of that. There seems to be a shortage of any more news so I reckon I'll close and get this mailed.

Hope you two have a nice weekend. I'm sure that I will - at least I'll be ready to take up the battle of A.S.T. 4763 when Monday rolls around. Certainly, the cool breezes of Wyoming will prepare me to face the New Order. Will drop you a note as soon as I can find a few more minutes. Bye for now.... Love......JACK.

There's just isn't any more news and class is almost over so I guess I better close and get ready for physics. Will write when I can find some more spare time.

All my love, JACK

November 3, 1943

Dear Mom and Dad:

Sorry I haven't written so regularly, but I am almost snowed under with work. today is the geography test; tomorrow, a killer of a chemistry exam which is to cover about 170 pages; on Saturday we have two tests and two on Friday. I have my notes pretty well organized - now all I have to do is get all that knowledge in my mind. That is the really big problem.

Today and tomorrow I am section leader. That is going to be really rare - no kidding. I am going to have a lot of fun. Got a letter from George Baumgartner. He is in quite a place. His address is an A.P.O. He

Co. A - A.S.T. 4763 - Section 211, Fort Collins, Colorado

isn't actually in that camp but on an island as I understand it. He'll be there until about the first of December - then will get a furlough before going overseas. In a lot of ways, I think he's lucky - it would be nice seeing some action. Maybe sometime I'll get a crack at those boys - but, I still don't want to do it with the infantry. I want it by air - otherwise I'll take A.S.T. and like it.

Here's our latest song which is sung to My Bonnie Lies Over the Ocean:

> *Civilians can do it in 4 years,*
> *A genius can do it in three,*
> *But we are to do it in 18 months,*
> *For we are the A.S.T.P.*

> *Someday I will sail o'er the ocean,*
> *A dirty old Jap I will see,*
> *I'll whip out my slide rule and kill him,*
> *With the Cosine of A - B.*

Can't think of any more news so I better close and hit the books. Hope it is warmer there than here and you both are okey.

Love...JACK.

November 5, 1943

Dear Mom and Dad:

Well - I am glad this week is over. Just about everything has happened. Thursday the whole section got gigged and today we also got the same treatment. I was in charge on Thursday, but not today. Boy they're really laying it on!!

I picked up an infection on my cheek and my jaw is about three times its normal size. I have had it opened twice. The doctor doesn't know whether it is a boil or what. It is quite a sight but doesn't ache. Just sore to push and looks funny. Then today while eating I suddenly felt my tongue slip through my teeth - and imagine my surprise - no tooth. The peg came off my front tooth and I guess I swallowed it. I went to the dentist but he wouldn't take care of it. they want to put gold in or cut it off even. All I want is another porcelain cap so I'll wait till I get home. The tooth doesn't bother me a bit.

I didn't take the physics test because I was on sick call so I'll make it up later. I got through the chemistry and history exams okey. Tomorrow we have a mechanics test and I think I'll get through it okey. Monday is the math exam. Guess what - I took a medical aptitude test today. It cost me a $1 to do it. There were about 30 of us out of 60 who applied that were selected. It is the one given by the American Medical Society and it was about 2 hours long. I banged it out in nothing flat.

It was quite a thorough test, but I didn't seem to have any trouble. Not even with the medical terminology. I think I probably got a batch of them right and generally got a high score. However, with the studying which would have to be put in I'm afraid my eyes would probably go crazy after a while.

Who knows though - I may get a crack at medicine, yet. Well, I am okey and feeling fine so don't worry. Will write when I can. By the way the packages arrived and thanks so much for the stationary and food. Love to you both...JACK

November 21, 1943

Dear Mom and Dad:

Another weekend gone and it sure has been a lazy one for me. Last night I studied until nine o'clock and then went downtown and just loafed for a while at the U.S.O. Had my shoes fixed which cost me a neat $2.15. Don't ever say it doesn't cost dough to have those babies put in shape. It took just 5 weeks to wear them through. I had metal clips put on the heels so that should help conserve leather a lot.

This morning I went to church. The minister gave a fine sermon and the whole program was very nice. It was the Thanksgiving Day

Sunday service. Came back and had dinner and then checked on my railroad tickets. Here's the deal! I have my reservations going - seat assignment and all. I get the tickets on Tuesday. Coming back, I have seat assignments on the Sunday night train - the City of Denver. However, if I take this train I'll report back here 12 hours late. Now then, Dad - what I wonder is if you'll look into the trains that are leaving Sunday morning.

The San Francisco Challenger leaves Cedar Rapids at 1:30 A.M. Sunday morning and puts me in Cheyenne at 8:45 P.M. on Sunday evening. That means I could be in Fort Collins by about 11:00 P.M. which gets me back in time. I think the latter would be the safest thing to do - since over 24 hours grace has been included in the time allotted. Of course, I could wire and say that due to circumstances beyond my control I had been delayed and have gotten reservations on the Streamliner for Sunday evening, but I don't know exactly how they (the Brass) take it.

If we knew the local Red Cross administrator really well - we could work it smoothly since they don't question them a bit. Anyway, please find out about the San Francisco Challenger deal and also see if the local Red Cross President happens to be a good friend of ours. Since I have reservations on the Sunday night City of Denver coming back I would prefer using them.

Three days of classes this week - then Thanksgiving and finally on Friday and Saturday all day - we get the G.I. Achievement Tests. There's no more news so I guess I'll close and get this mailed. Hope you two are both fine.

Love...JACK.

December 2, 1943

Dear Mom and Dad:

Well this will be the last letter until I get home. Everything seems to be shaping up okey. Yesterday we had a two-hour military exam and later a one-hour geography test. I seemed to get through them without

Dear Mom and Dad

too much trouble. Today we have a chemistry test and frankly I don't know what it is all about. However, it doesn't make much difference whether I get an 80 or 100. It won't help my average. I've got an 86 average right now. that guy really reamed me on the last exam or I could have pulled it up to an "A" average. Tomorrow we have a history and math test and I can get through them okey.

Friday night there is no study hall so I can get my packing all done and get everything lined up. There's just no news at all so I think I'll close and get this in the mail. Just about 54 more hours and I'll be on the old train heading home. Love...JACK.

Author's note: The long-awaited Christmas furlough finally arrived but only after mass confusion created by the Commanding Officer who cancelled all leaves. Then, after everyone cancelled their train reservations - the furloughs were reinstated. In my case I went on down to Denver under my original travel plan. Arrived at the Union Station Office in Denver, and it was an absolute mad house with lines of military personnel trying to get space on numerous trains. I took one look and headed for the Union Pacific General Manager's office. After about ten minutes, he came out and I told him my sad tale of having reservations and a seat assignment, and then because of the whims of the Commanding Officer everything had to be cancelled only to have furlough reinstated 24 hours later.

The Union Pacific manager was not only disgusted with the actions of my Commanding Officer, but also was amazed at the initiative I had shown in coming to his office rather than waiting with the "thundering herd". The result was that he reinstated my ticket and then said: "Soldier - get down to Union Station and work your way up as close as you can to the front of the gate for the City of Denver. When the gate opens just get on board the train. You do not have a seat assignment so sit down anywhere after you get on board, and then just keep moving from one seat to another until the train leaves the station. From there on try to get a porter or the conductor to find you a seat or spend the night in the Club Car".

With that he wished me luck and headed back to his office. To make a long story short I followed his instructions to the "T", and though I had some very uneasy moments going from one seat to another, the City of Denver finally pulled out enroute to Chicago with me safely on board. The trip was both challenging and stimulating! Much of my time was spent in either the diner or Club Car; however, the conductor who had apparently been watching my fast-moving seat changes finally met me in the Club Car and said: "Soldier, do you have a seat on this train or did you just bluff your way on board"! I confessed and told him the whole story. He said he thought that was of the best stories he had heard in a long time and volunteered to find me a seat - which he did! Without a doubt this trip was one of my greatest accomplishments so far in the military - strictly a "gutzy" performance, and one which full credit should go to Bill Dauner for the early training he gave me.

December 12, 1943

Dear Mom and Dad:

Well, here I am and sound back in Ft. Collins. The list of guys coming in late is steadily growing. We were about 15 minutes late getting into La Selle and then had to wait there for an hour and a half before the train left for Ft. Collins. Got here at noon and have been getting everything lined up.

It's awfully dead around here. All the guys are struggling in slowly- and none of them can figure out where the weak has gone. It sure did go fast. There's no more news for now. Will write soon. It was great to get out of the army routine. Thanks and again and love…. Jack.

Dear Mom and Dad

December 27, 1943

Dear Mom and Dad:

Well, today is the big day and at 9:15 this morning we take the Medical Exam, the nice part of it is that we get out of a geography test and also a physics lecture. Hope I am on the beam and get good grade on the exam. That would surely be great to get sent to the University of Iowa. Colorado U is the other school that will be open which still wouldn't be too bad. Maybe I can hit it lucky - we'll soon see.

Had a military test yesterday and I hit a 98 on it. Also gave my book report so now that is over with. It wasn't too hot but I got through it okey and that's all that counts. Paul and Lois's package has not arrived as yet. Pull out their card and see what they said on it.

There might even be money in it someplace, but I don't think so. I looked it over carefully. We haven't heard yet whether we're to get New Year's Eve off so it looks like we may sleep the New Year in. Hope you fellows have a nice celebration. I imagine there will be a party or something. Anyway, I'll be thinking about you. Love to you both...JACK

December 28, 1943

Dear Mom and Dad:

I ran out of ink and the only thing around was this nice green stuff so excuse it. It does look kind of pretty, doesn't it? The first day over and what a day. This afternoon my team won our 4th straight basketball game. I dumped in a total of 15 points. We won 37-23. It was a really rough and tumble game. I had three fouls on me - one more and I would have been out. The referee saw me the last time I gave this guy an elbow to the jaw.

Gee, I don't know where the three days went but they sure did fly by. I really enjoyed it a lot. It sure went fast. We've got another military test tomorrow and then I have to get up and give my book report. That ought to be good. I have no idea what I'll say, but you know me – I can always get up and spout off about something for 10 – 15 minutes.

Co. A - A.S.T. 4763 - Section 211, Fort Collins, Colorado

I'm in study hall now - guess who's sitting at our table - none other than the Cadet Colonel. Gee, all the nobility - a Cadet Colonel. We sure do rate - course we are almost the noisiest section. Maybe that is the reason. No more news for now. Oh, a gift and card came from Jocelyn Dauner today - Paul and Lois's didn't come as yet. Love to you both.... JACK

January 13, 1944

Dear Mom and Dad:

There's hardly any news but I'll jot a note off anyway. Today we had a big inspection by the Colonel and it was a sad mess. Everything went off okey except that the whole affair was just so much hooey. Just before he got to us one of the boys started laughing and it looked for a while as if we weren't going to get sobered up before he got to us. Somehow or other we all got to attention and everything was okey. A couple of guys got gigged but not too many.

As far as I know I am just passing everything - I am sure glad the skin on my teeth is thick. Wow...physics is getting worse and worse. I did get an "A-" in a lab write up though which may help. My cold seems to be okey again now - I just have a little cough and my nose isn't running at all.

The weather has been great. Chilly in the morning but warming up around 10:00 A.M. Just hope that no bad blizzards come up. Hope you two are feeling fine. Take care of yourselves - hope you all, Jeanne and the Karberg's had a great time together. All my love, always...JACK

January 25, 1944

Dear Mom and Dad:

Another week getting underway and I started it out right by getting a haircut - and what a cut. It looks like the barber really threw the axe. I am just like a sheep who has lost all his wool. They are getting strict on haircuts so they've sort of hinted to the barbers in town that they should use the clippers and scissors a little more.

I am going on sick call today and make an appointment to go to Fitz-Simmons Hospital in Denver on Thursday and have my eyes tested to see what is cooking. I had a real deep headache yesterday. Got my calculus test back and pulled down an 81. He docked me 15 points on the last problem. I thought I knew how to do it but was short on time so didn't bother. If I would have written it down I would have gotten a 96. Oh well, if I got a 90 in a test in any course it would be a miracle. I think that I am working too hard. I've got a better than "C" average, I think. Guess I'll rest on my laurels for a couple of weeks and sleep. Only five more weeks of this stuff. I'll be mighty glad when it's over.

Personally, I am ready to start taking basic training over again anytime. That test (competitive) to get into the Coast Guard Academy is to be in May. I am not even going to give it a shot - too ignorant or lazy or something. That place is just like West Point. Go to school three years - you sign for 8 years, though. So, I guess I'll look into some other deals. No more news for now. Love....JACK

January 27, 1944

Dear Mom and Dad:

I forgot when I wrote last. In fact, I don't know what date it is or whether this is even Wednesday. What a mad house! Today we had a spot inspection and had to dump everything out of our barracks bag and then put it all back in. The stuff they think of around here is repulsive. That finished...Dick Bodine and I shot a game of snooker, then to a lousy dinner and finally over here to study.

Haven't heard yet whether I go to Fitz-Simmons to have my eyes tested tomorrow or not. I hope so - because next Thursday we'll have a math test and I hate to miss it since it will be the regular 8th week final. Yes, next week we've got a full round of tests so if you don't hear from me, I'm not dead - just half dead.

Co. A - A.S.T. 4763 - Section 211, Fort Collins, Colorado

Another guy from the section is at Fitz-Simmons. He was the Section drunkard and he is in with ulcers. His dad is a full Colonel over in Italy. Thus, we have another empty bed. Sixteen of the flash pictures I took on Saturday, shoe out very good. Only one bad one in the whole batch. That's what I call good shooting. Got a nice long letter from Jocelyn Dauner a few days ago. I guess she is fine from what she says. Must close now - thanks for the box of food.

Love...JACK

February 7, 1944

Dear Mom and Dad:

Tests are all over so maybe I can settle down and start writing a few letters once again. I have neglected my mom and dad last week. I forgot when I wrote last so I'll start with Thursday and the trip to Fitz – Simmons. Went down and they found my one eye was 20-20 and the other eye was 20-70. I think it is better than that. Anyway, I go down this coming Thursday for a recheck.

Got through all my tests and passed okey. Made up the calculus test on Saturday and missed two problems for sure which is quite disgusting. I passed, however, so I am not worried. George Cassat came down last night and we had a good old visit together. His work is coming along fine from what he says and he likes it a lot. We had lunch together this noon and then he left a 1:00 P.M. I went on down and saw a movie and now here I am.

I've made reservations - or I've written to them for March 4th from the Denver office. I should get a reply this week. From what I hear I no longer can get furlough rates to Cedar Rapids so I may have to buy a ticket to Chicago. The fare to Chicago is $26.10. The non-furlough rate to Cedar Rapids is $32.50, so I'd still save some money. When I find out the deal I am going to buy my tickets immediately so I'll have them. The transportation Officer here has been trying to get them all so I don't want to lose out and then I can always get a refund on the tickets in case no furloughs come through.

Dear Mom and Dad

Ten percent of this Basic III Unit is going on to advanced, that leaves me out so 1 am planning on a move. Nothing definite is out as yet. My Kodachromes that I took two weeks ago aren't back as yet. I expect them any day now. Hope Dad is okey and they couldn't find anything wrong with him. Personally, I think we both need a vacation so if you'll get him to go A.W.O.L from Morrison Bros. Co. why I'll do the same here and then we can go fishing up in the mountains. Gotta close - love to you both...JACK.

February 9, 1944

Dear Mom and Dad:

The dawning of another new day and some of the boys are shipping to good old California. Another bunch was called up yesterday - Dick Bodine was among them. they were fellows who were eligible for Electrical Engineering (Advanced). Dick was second highest in that group. I think a total of 11 guys were eligible of all the fellows who applied for Electrical. This pace is getting to be more and more like an army camp. Shipping orders coming out all the time, and no one knows when they will get the cal.

Tomorrow I go to Fitz-Simmons for a recheck on my eyes. I hope it is a nice day because there are quite a few of us going down and we'll probably take a G.I. truck rather than the station wagon. Got reports on my last three military tests and pulled a 91, 95, and 98. Maybe I'll get one "A" - who knows. I have another military test coming up this morning. It seems like that's all they do is give us tests around here.

Should get my railroad ticket today or tomorrow. Here's the deal on my furlough. First, finish the term and get our seven-day pass like the last time. Second, finish the term and ship immediately, but get a delay of a few days enroute; or third, ship out immediately. My ankle is getting along okey. It isn't nearly as swollen as it was and looks a lot better. Also, it feels better. It is all taped up though and I'll probably be limping around for about a week or so.

Co. A - A.S.T. 4763 - Section 211, Fort Collins, Colorado

Got three letters yesterday - one from, George Cassat, you and dad. Glad that dad is coming along okey and that they haven't found anything wrong so far. Time to eat breakfast so I better run. All my love.... JACK.

February 11, 1944

Dear Mom and Dad:

Friday morning and here I sit with nothing to do but write my mom and dad a letter. Well, first, the trip to Fitz-Simmons was really a cold one. The weather took a change on Wednesday to snow and a nice cold wind. So, you can imagine how it was riding in the back of a G.I. truck. They had a station wagon also and I rode half way in each. Got right in and had my recheck. My glasses will come in anywhere from 10 days to 3 months. I seem to have 20-20; and 20-70 vision. I always said studying was no good on one's eyes. However, I could make out the letters on the 20-30 chart so I may be able to pass the Air Corps physical.

All I want to do is get in there long enough to get back in the Air Corps because it looks like we'll be split to go either to the infantry or combat engineers or maybe even amphibious engineers. The nine boys who were passing all subjects and who had Spec. Numbers in radio left yesterday for a P.O.E. in California.

No more news. Hope you are feeling fine, Dad, and that the trip was just one good rest. Love...JACK.

February 13, 1944

Dear Mom and Dad:

Nine o'clock on Sunday morning so here I sit catching up on my letter writing. First on the list - tomorrow I am heading for Denver at 6:00 A.M. to take the 64 physical and go before the Cadet Board. If I get by, it will be pure luck. I don't know just how many of us are going down but I believe it must be quite a few. Oh - another day of school which I get out of.

Dear Mom and Dad

A little later this morning I am going over and have my ankle retaped since it seems a little weak. I talked to Professor Lewis yesterday about furlough. He's the civilian coordinator of our unit of A.S.T. and he said that in all probability the Basic III will not get furloughs since they'll be shipping. I'll be glad to leave this hole!! School is okey - at least I'm not flunking yet. I should be out of here soon. There's not much more to report so I'll close for now. Love…. JACK.

February 15, 1944

Dear Mom and Dad:

Here I am back from my jaunt to Denver. Well, I flunked the physical for Aviation Cadets. Was okey except for my right eye being 20-70. Spent the afternoon in a good movie. I didn't bother to take the mental since I flunked the physical. So, I guess I'll wait and see what happens. Six out of the 43 didn't make it.

Time for me to get to class so I'd better close. Am almost sure we'll not be getting a furlough, but you never can tell in this man's army what they might do. Love for now.... JACK.

February 19, 1944

Dear Mom and Dad:

Here I sit in study hall. I should be studying, but I don't feel like it. Got yours and dad's letters today, mom, and thanks for the buck. It will come in handy. The furlough list was posted and none of us "Basic Three's" are on it. What a sad state of affairs. The sooner I get out of here the better.

This morning I woke up with a start and the outer lights were on so I figured it was almost time to get up. So, I got up and went down and washed and then to my amazement found out it was only 4:00 A.M. and that some of the guys were shipping out early. I went back to bed. Well, then the light did come on and I got up and made my bunk and had everything in order. I sat down and started reading a field manual when up walks this dumb jerk, Lt. Giddings. He asks me if that's all I had to do! Me... not giving a darn, naturally replied NO, nothing but what I am doing at present. So, he said I should dump all the wastebaskets. I let him get out of sight. I don't know who dumped them, but I didn't. All they can do to any of us is kick us out and that time is so close at hand that it isn't worth their effort. I am not kidding anyone. I know I am going back in the army so what is the difference. The latest is that they are cutting A.S.T. down from 140,000 to 35,000. I've come to the conclusion, that the only requirement to being a 2nd Looey is a dumb look on your face and be a dirty, lousy, apple polisher. All I have is the dumb look, so I've given up all hope of ever becoming an ignorant shave tail.

Everything is okey so don't worry. I think I'll call next Sunday. Maybe I'll know what is going to happen by them. Meantime, all my love.... JACK.

February 24, 1944

Dear Mom and Dad:

Sorry I haven't written the last few days but I have been awfully busy. I passed the calculus test I took last week - no marvelous score, but I did pass. I am really worn out tonight. We had all our physical education tests today and it drained every bit of strength in us. I'm pretty sure I'll pull another "A" in there. Also, had a shot gun test in military. Don't know whether I told you or not but Lt. Thomlison has been sent to a replacement pool in North Carolina and Lt. Peacock, the one all of us like so much, and Lt. "The Jerk". Giddings, both have their shipping orders so that means they'll be leaving soon

Oh, by the way - you guys can put the service flag up again. Our new motto is "Put up that service flag, mother, your son is out of the A.S.T.P." I doubt if we'll have study hall on Thursday, Friday or Saturday nights this week - G.I. tests come on both days.

Dear Mom and Dad

Think I'll call you on Sunday - on second thought maybe I'll wait until we know things are more definite. So, don't plan on me calling until sometime late next week. Love to you both... JACK

March 3, 1944

Dear Mom and Dad:

Here's the latest!! This is all straight stuff. About 20 guys are staying here for Med. The few who were selected for the advanced program have no shipping orders as yet. Capt. Maxwell is afraid that they have been reamed. Capt. Walt left for Fort Warren as head of the graveyard and Capt. Maxwell is leaving soon for the same place to be head of a fumigation company. Shook hands with our calculus professor. He was really tops - one of the nicest men I've become acquainted with out here at Colorado State. I enjoyed his course a great deal and most of the fellows felt the same about his capabilities.

I got reamed in military. Went up and took a look at my form 20 - that is my service record. Everything is in order. I was amazed to find myself with a SPEC. number. This is a specialist number and is usually given after completion of an army school course. The funny thing is, it pertains to my previous school. My No. is 411 - chemical laboratory assistant. I just noticed it. I don't know when, where or how I got it. So, that may be my next move - I just don't know. It might be smart if I put in for Chemical Warfare Officer Candidate School.

We get off tonight and I may run down and see "For Whom the Bell Tolls". I hear it is very good. It has been a week since I sent my tickets in and I've received no money or answer as yet. I am slightly worried. Guess I'll write a letter and find out what is cooking. I hate to lose $20 like that. It was beautiful yesterday. Today it snowed. How do you like that? What a place. Time to close as I have to get this in the mail. Love...JACK.

Author's note: By the grace of God and a little luck I was able to get a three-day pass, and took off for Denver. The whole story on this

Co. A - A.S.T. 4763 - Section 211, Fort Collins, Colorado

particular adventure will be told at the beginning of the next chapter. However, I called the folks and told them to pick me up in Cedar Rapids the next morning at 6:00 A.M. when the City of Denver was scheduled to arrive. They met the train and I was able to spend 14 hours in Dubuque before having to head back to Cedar Rapids to catch the City of Denver for the return trip.

Chapter 8

Co. G - 387 Infantry - 97th Division - A.P.O #445 Fort Leonard Wood, Missouri

(March 12, 1944 - July 12, 1944)

Life on the campus of Colorado State College at Ft. Collins, Colorado, finally came to a halt with the impending abandonment of the A.S.T. program. Though no furloughs were given between assignments, an extended pass issued around the first of March at least permitted a quick trip home.

The trials and tribulations of that trip home on the City of Denver have remained very clear even though many years have elapsed. After learning that I would be able to get a "long weekend pass", I left Ft. Collins and headed for Denver. The lines in the Union Pacific station around the City of Denver ticket windows were huge. Recognizing how little time I had before my train's departure and the fact that I did not even have a ticket or reservations, I went to the office of the District Manager of the Union Pacific - was able to see him - and told my story of having had a reservation, tickets, etc. and then turning them in because of the inconsistencies of military communications at Ft. Collins.

He took sympathy - arranged for a ticket - and a dummy seat assignment. He suggested that I go immediately to the City of Denver gate and try to be one of the first to board the train. His last words: "If

Co. G - 387 Infantry, Fort Leonard Wood, Missouri

you get through the gate okey - you're on your own. Just keep moving from seat to seat until the train gets rolling out of the station. You may be able to hang loose for a while in the Club Car - then work with the conductor to get a confirmed seat into Cedar Rapids, Iowa. GOOD LUCK!!! "

I was about the fifteenth person to board the City of Denver and followed the District Manager's instructions to the "T". I grabbed a seat and when the individual appeared who had that seat reserved I simply moved on to the next one. So, it went until things began to get a little tight. At that point, I moved up toward the Club car. Finally, the train began to pull out of the station and when the conductor got to me and asked where I was sitting I told him I needed his help - that I did not have an assigned seat, but that the Union Pacific District Manager said that you (the conductor) would know of any vacancies and would be glad to help me. He did!!

I spent most of the evening in the Club Car but eventually the conductor took me to a vacant seat where I was able to get a few hours' sleep before arriving in Cedar Rapids, Iowa, where the folks picked me up at 6:15 A.M. We left immediately for Dubuque. All total I had 14 hours before we had to return to Cedar Rapids and get me back on the City of Denver. It was a tough trip but at least I was traveling on one of the best trains of the day.

On March 9, 1944, or thereabouts we finally boarded the train for our departure out of Ft. Collins for Fort Leonard Wood, Missouri. This was a long and relatively slow trip since this particular troop train had little, if any, priority on the tracks. We were taken from. Ft. Collins to Denver and then on to St. Louis. Union Station in St. Louis here become a familiar sight as a result of my several months at Jefferson Barracks. From this we were transported on to Ft. Leonard Wood which was out in the middle of nowhere. Its location was ideal for infantry training. The closest town to the base was Waynesville – a real hell hole. Cities of larger size included Springfield and Jefferson City. The trip to St. Louis took about 4 hours by bus and was anything but enjoyable. However, St. Louis was one of the best cities in the country for soldiers, and the U.S.O. and other facilities made it worth the effort whenever passes could be obtained.

For the first time in my life I really began to see what the other side of the world was like, and what a tremendous melting pot of the human race could be found in the army and particularly in the infantry. As a college kid who had come from a home of extremely pleasant surroundings, I now found that life became a matter of "the right way... the wrong way... and the army way".... and to survive you did it the army way.

Military justice was based on "the book" and it constantly hung over your head. It was always a threat which was held over military personnel if they got out of line. Leadership too often was based on how many stripes or what bar you had on your shoulder, and the constant threat of the worst work details, denial of passes or a court martial. In looking back many of us wonder how the war was ever won with the many poor examples of leadership - particularly involving the quality of training conducted in the United States.

Life for the next several months at Ft. Leonard Wood, Missouri, can best be captured through the following letters which were sent home on a regular basis.

March 10, 1944

Dear Mom and Dad:

"This is the Army" and that ain't no lie!! I'll start off from the beginning. We left Fort Collins at 10.00 this morning. It was really a small trip. Believe it or not, we had Pullmans and the cars were spotless. Anyway, the trip was comfortable. We played cards all day and by evening, I had accumulated a total of $18 profit, not bad! Slept firmly well and wake up in time to find us going through Kansas City.

When we arrived and it was about 4.00 in the afternoon, the board was there to meet us all. We ate and had a physical check and classification. They shuffled the cards and dealt them out between three infantry regiments. Dick and I got split up. Time was flying and we still had to get classified by a Regimental Board. We waited until 12.30 for the classification and then three of us were given the same outfit. The food so far is okay. For bedding, we have two blankets, a mattress and a pillow. This is the Army, and we wear an old outfit which has been activated for 14 months. We are going to be pushed through training as fast as possible. So far, the guys seem like an okay bunch. It looks like a lot of A.S.T. boys will be here.

The whole division will not go over as a unit. They just pull as many guys out at a time and we will have to have infantry basics before we go across. I imagine today we will have to get our field packs and rifle. Yes, I'll soon be the proud owner of a Garand M.I. This is a large camp much larger than Kearns in Jefferson Barracks. Right now, I'm sitting in the barracks. No doubt, this will be the last time so I'm taking advantage of it. From now on, I'll either be standing on my two feet or sleeping on my back. No alternative! Sitting has ceased!

Everything is okay and I'm fine. No more news, all my love as always, Jack.

March 12, 1944

Dear Mom and Dad:

Hang on to your hats and listen to my tale of woe. Yesterday Bob Bixby and I were on K.P. (Kitchen Police). Today Bob Smith has it. The three of us are all from Block 5 back at Colorado State. Smitty (Bob Smith), Dick Bodine and I used to run around together. Well, it was rough but it didn't kill us.

I am now the proud possessor of a beautiful Garand M-1 rifle. Gosh, these guys eat, sleep, and date the darn things from what I can gather. I never saw anything like it. They come in at 11 bells and start massaging the barrels of their guns before they even look at their poor feet. What a bunch of sad sacks.

Had breakfast and my noon meal here at the service club. The food is okey at the barracks but I am not taking any chances of getting

Dear Mom and Dad

slapped on detail. Rumor has it that some of the guys are going back to the Air Corps. Five guys are supposed to have been pulled and are to be shipped. We know nothing definite, of course. If they ship a bunch of the guys out in our outfit we'd have a good chance for stripes. However, right now there is hardly a chance at all. I think they're about due to ship them overseas though since most of them have gone through every kind of training.

Will see Dick Bodine this afternoon. I've seen a lot of the boys. Most of them are in rifle companies - a few in heavy weapons and mortars. By the way...maybe you'd better send me one of those tens. I think next week, if we can get passes, five of us are going up to Colombia.

Will probably start working this week and get some rough bounces. So far it has been strictly detailing and that kind of stuff. May try and call you this afternoon (Sunday) and let you know that I am okey. No mail has arrived but that is to be expected. It usually takes about two weeks for it to start coming. Jim Costekis is in my regiment some place. I haven't seen him as yet but will very shortly. Seems like everybody is here. All A.S.T. schools in the 7th Service Command I believe were assigned to the 97th Division. Well, I have to close. Will write when I can.

Love....JACK.

March 13, 1944

Dear Mom and Dad:

Just enough time to write my tale of woes or something! Well, we shall begin with drill. This morning midst rain and Missouri mud we drilled and tore down the carbine and Garand M-1. Then this afternoon we dry fired and took up triangulation. I've had all this before.

I have been very nicely made a table waiter for a whole week. That disgusts me!! It is almost the same as K.P. I might as well bunk in that confounded kitchen. Am now able to tear my rifle down and put it back together. Also, a carbine. Tomorrow we take up the Browning

Co. G - 387 Infantry, Fort Leonard Wood, Missouri

Automatic Rifle (BAR). No doubt we'll be on the range firing soon. They're throwing this stuff at us just as fast as they can.

Boy, I'm not kidding - now your son really looks and acts like a soldier. I tote a rifle all day. - march. - march. -and march some more. The food is still okey and I am eating like a horse. Will no doubt gain some weight. Gotta close now. Will write when I can. Our time is really limited. Am okey so don't worry!!Love......JACK.

P.S. Give my very best regards to the Karbergs and all of our friends who ask about me!

March 14, 1944

Dear Mom and Dad:

I'm dead tired but I'll knock out a short note. We have really been reamed royally. Was on table waiter detail again today as usual and they let the K.P.'s skip off with the result that we did their work. What a sad sack deal.

Today we took a part 4 different pieces: the M-1, Browning Automatic Rifle, the Carbine, and the 45 caliber pistol. Aside from that we drilled and had some dry firing again and then topped it off with calisthenics. They're really pouring it to us new guys. I'll try and write every night but we have no time at all. They are always finding some lousy detail for us. Gotta get some sleep so I better close. Love, always...... JACK.

March 16, 1944

Dear Mom and Dad:

Just got off table waiter detail and feel fit as a fiddle. Ate a big dinner and just now Killed off two milk shakes and a couple of boxes of cookies. Spent most of the day in lectures and then took about a 3-mile hike this afternoon. Tomorrow we start about the roughest training there is. Bayonet training!! We will learn how to cut a guy in the most pieces with the least effort. Interesting!! Something like W.C. Fields

Dear Mom and Dad

and his: "Cutting through a swath of human flesh." No mail today. I've got some very positive vibes that some will come tomorrow.

Am at the service club now and they have a great band which was brought to the base to play for us. Really solid stuff! So far everything is okey except that I almost live in that !?XX=*%$ kitchen on table waiter and K.P. detail. Boy, I'm telling you - the gal that marries this kid is really going to get a good catch! I think I am the most proficient guy in the army when it comes to working in the kitchen.

Time to quit and clean my baby - that's my rifle in case you are wondering. I all but sleep with it now. Must be association with these other infantry guys. Bye now and all my love.... JACK.

March 17, 1944

Dear Mom and Dad:

Well, we marched in good old Missouri mud today up to the ankles. What a mess. My rifle was really in bad shape. Then we worked on some bayoneting and that was followed with a three-mile march. It was really a snap!

Got up at 5:00 A.M. today for no good reason at all. Tomorrow we get up at six o'clock thank the Lord. Everything is fine. I eat like a horse and feel great. Maybe this stuff agrees with me, who knows? Boy, you should have seen me cleaning my rifle tonight. Had her all apart and put her back together just like a professional. I will call you between 2.30 and 5.30 P.M. this Sunday afternoon.

No news in particular - I am fine and don't worry. Signed the payroll today. Guess I won't need the ten bucks since I won't be able to get to Columbia this weekend. If you've already sent it I'll send it back if I don't need it. No more for now. Will write tomorrow if I have an opportunity. Meantime all my love.... JACK

Co. G - 387 Infantry, Fort Leonard Wood, Missouri

March 20, 1944

Dear Mom and Dad:

Just got through calling and was sure neatly cut off. Don't know what happened but something sure as the devil did the job. Maybe they were limiting the time on calls - I don't know!! Anyway, it sure was good talking to all of you. It took three hours to get the call through. It is really quite a problem in this camp to get calls through since they don't have a switch – board, but have to go through a little town known as Waynesville and through the post telephone system. What a place.

It is still sleeting like the devil outside which means we'll be crawling around in the mud of Missouri tomorrow. No news - just wanted to tell you how good it was to hear your voices. Am skipping table waiter tonight so I can see "Cover Girl". No doubt I'll land on K.P. next Sunday but that's the way it goes. I'm not worried. Time to eat so I'll close.

Will write soon...meantime, all my love.... JACK.

March 21, 1944

Dear Mom and Dad:

What a messy day - typical Missouri weather. the snow we had started melting today and it was muddy and sloppy all at the same time. Anyway, we had all of our work in the barracks mostly in the form of lectures with the final result that I all but wore callouses on my seat from sitting so much.

No doubt, tomorrow we will be sloshing our way through mud ankle deep. We have bayonet drill tomorrow for one hour which will be plenty rugged. The rest of the day I'll guess with you as to what will take place. Sometime this week we are going to fire a round on the "Bazooka". No doubt you've heard of it. It is one of these rocket jobs that you fire from your shoulder. They are used against tanks of all sizes and can really knock them for a loop. Thought we'd be going on the range this week but I guess not.

Dear Mom and Dad

Tomorrow our company has guard duty. I'm just hoping I don't draw a post which carries live ammunition. There are two of them - it would be just like me to shoot the Commanding General in cold blood. So, help me, if I yell HALT three times and the guy doesn't stop he'll be a dead cookie. That's one way of getting out of here!! They give you a cartoon of cigarettes and fine you a dollar for funeral expenses plus six cents for the shell and then ship you on your way. Well, it is nice to think about anyway.

Haven't tried the foot lotion but plan to do so tonight. Thanks a lot. Glad everything worked out back in Boston, Dad. Thought maybe you might come back via St. Louis. I can get a weekend pass if you wire ahead and then I could come in and meet you. Am feeling fine and my rifle looks like a little jewel. I've really got her in good shape. Cleaned it up good tonight.

Bet that sounds funny to hear me say I actually clean and take care of something. I've got to stop and think twice myself once in a while. Got to hit the hay as we are getting up at 4:30 A.M. tomorrow for no good reason whatsoever. Will write soon...Love...JACK

March 23, 1944

Dear Mom and Dad:

Here I am 20 years old and don't feel a day over 19. The box arrived and I really thank you fellows a lot. Everything is delicious. Got a box of stationary from Lucile and a big box of everything from Jeanne. So, I am well supplied with food. As far as money goes I frankly don't believe my relatives have any more and if they do they don't believe in the old adage - "It's better to give than to receive". All I've gotten is $1.00 from grandma and grandpa. A batch of my back mail arrived. A lot of my letters were being sent to the wrong regiment with the result that they were greatly delayed. All in all, I got about 15 or 20 letters. Heard from nearly everybody I've ever known. Got a cute card from the Papes and also from the Baumgartners. Today we dry fired and then this afternoon, ah yes, this afternoon we donned our combat packs and rifles and proceeded to clip

Co. G - 387 Infantry, Fort Leonard Wood, Missouri

off a little over 7 miles in just short of two hours. It wouldn't have been too bad if we had been on pavement but no - we took an old country road with mud ankle deep. We were all an ungodly sight to behold.

Tomorrow among other things we are going to have a regimental review which ought to take the cake. That will be good when we all get out there and screw the works up royally. Somehow or other I missed guard duty tonight. Can't figure it out - guess I am just slipping. Thought I might end up as a prisoner chaser.

I've developed the most ravenous appetite you've ever witnessed. This morning I killed off a very meager breakfast of 6 great big sausages; three slices of french toast; two cups of coffee; a bowl of cream of wheat; and a grapefruit... and, I'm still hungry, and it is only nine o'clock in the evening right now. Must close - thanks again for the box... it is really swell. Bye for now and all my love...JACK

March 23, 1944
TO: Mrs. W.W. Dauner
1726 Overview Court Dubuque, Iowa
SUBJECT: Wishes for a HAPPY BIRTHDAY

    1. In that facilities on this post are very poor in regards to getting any kind of presents or cards for a mother's birthday - this commanding officer of the 97th Division wants to express his wishes for a very HAPPY celebration to the above person.

    2. This office also invites the above to a steak dinner on the house collectable on the below signed - if you can ever catch hold of him.

    3. This office hopes you celebrate many, many more HAPPY BIRTHDAYS, and that you take the best care possible of yourself in the coming year.

For the Commanding Officer:
JACK R. DAUNER
Buck Private - Infantry
Enclosures: Love and best wishes.

Dear Mom and Dad

March 26, 1944

Dear Mom and Dad:

Well, I've really been on the move. Last night, I worked steadily from after dinner until lights were out. No time to write even a single letter. Yesterday, we went into firing positions and then we took a two-hour cross-country march with full field pack and rifle. We went up and down hills and tramped through brush and brambles all the whole march. It really wasn't bad at all and I felt like I could have kept on going when we got back. Must have covered about 5 miles in all. Last night we had a G.I. party and then I took my rifle down and really cleaned it good for inspection. She shines like a silver dollar.

Today - in fact - in a couple of hours - we're going out and throw live hand grenades. I've got one lined up who would make a great target. No doubt, he will be out of range. Things are really tough all over these days.

The two five's arrived last night. Thanks so much. I am going to hang on to them until I get paid and then send what I don't need home. My mail is really in bad shape. It has been coming in from all parts of the country. Those letters with the money enclosed and 4 other cards went way down to Camp Wolters, Texas, for no reason at all. I don't know what the problem is with the postal system. Be very careful to include the exact address I give you. Everything has to be on the envelope.

Hope you had a Happy Birthday, Mom, and sure do wish I could have helped you celebrate. Almost time to fall out so I'd better close and run.

Good bye for now and Love......JACK.

March 27, 1944

Dear Mom and Dad:

Here, I sit waiting for my call to get through so I can wish my mom a very happy birthday. They got through once but you were at church.

Co. G - 387 Infantry, Fort Leonard Wood, Missouri

This telephone system here is really sad. Well, yesterday I heaved a live grenade. Some experience. They really sing when they sail through the air. Then, tomorrow, we go on the range and do some firing - in fact, plenty of firing. We no doubt will fire about 100 rounds so it looks like a big day. It is quite an experience and I must admit I enjoy the work on the range.

Last night we all saw a very good movie - "Heavenly Body" - which was quite cleverly done. Guess today we will all go and see "Up in Arms". It is in technicolor and ought to be very good. Got a letter from Skip Free and he is down in San Antonio. Also, Jeanne said that Don Heitzman washed out. That is too bad. Hope he stays in the Air Corps. Must close now, am feeling fine. Send some cookies - just those in a box put out by National Biscuit will be fine. Our rations are being cut and I am hungry most of the time I sometimes wonder if I have a tapeworm or what is causing this tremendous appetite.

Love to you both...JACK

March 28, 1944

Dear Mom and Dad:

Just a note to let you know that I am okey. Don't worry if you don't get a note too often this week. We started firing today and almost the whole evening has to be devoted to getting our equipment lined up for the next morning. Hence, no time for letters.

We fired almost 100 rounds today as practice. I did swell this morning - in fact, I had a high score in one of the positions. All in all, my shooting was excellent. However, in the afternoon I got tired and a little jumpy with the result that I was all over the target. Even got one "Maggies Drawers". That's a total miss and they wave some red flannels at you from the pits.

Tomorrow we fire for record and I hope that I am on the beam. No news. Was sure surprised to hear about Ellen (Mike) Peaslee and Louie Shortell. No more for now - hope you are both fine.

All my love...JACK

Dear Mom and Dad

March 30, 1944

Dear Mom and Dad:

The box of cookies arrived and thanks a lot. Everything is delicious. We've been getting more to eat the last few days - they must have picked up some ration points. Today was really rough. We went out on the range and it was bitter cold. It was damp and a good wind blowing thus making firing tough. I coached all morning - in fact, I didn't fire all day. I'm deaf as a dead dog right now though from being on the firing line so long. I keep hearing bells, bells, and more bells. Who knows - I maybe be going off the beam.

We came in off the range a little early and I got my rifle all cleaned up. Hope it is; on the beam tonight. Old Bix (Bixby) is a mess. He was firing yesterday and didn't have his rifle sitting in his shoulder real well. When he fired it - it kicked and caught his lip and cheek. He's a mess!! There are about four other guys with black eyes and puffed up lips.

Really it is a funny sight.

Tomorrow we fire some more and then I don't know what we'll be doing. One never knows anything until the last minute in this outfit. We change uniforms anywhere from 8 to 10 times a day. Oh - for the uncertainty of it all. This is getting to be boring - no kidding. Go to bed at 10 o'clock and get up at 5 o'clock. No future!!

In other words, I have a day's work done by one o'clock and then turn around and do a whole other day's work. It ought to be illegal to have to do two days' work in one - that means 12 days' work in six - but they don't listen to me up in the front office. They just sit behind the desk and say "we know"!! Guess I better close - I think that ringing in my ears needs the quieting touch of a little sleep. Will write soon.

Love....JACK

Co. G - 387 Infantry, Fort Leonard Wood, Missouri

April 1, 1944

Dear Mom and Dad:

Got paid today and am sending you a little "mazuma". It is enclosed. Hang on to it for me, please, in case I need it. Also, I boosted my bonds up to where I'll be buying a bond a month now. I figured that I might as well try and start saving some cash in case I might want some later on.

Worked all afternoon on my rifle. Took every single working piece off and scrubbed them all down. It passed company and regimental inspection and tomorrow it goes in for divisional inspection. This company has already had 7 company commanders lose their respective commands. So, our captain is really pouring on the inspections. They are really rough on these company inspections.

Got three V-mails from George Baumgartner. One confirmed that letter concerning his location. I really hit that on the beam. He is no doubt near Plymouth, England, in the country (province) of Devonshire. Got a note from Jocelyn (Dauner) today - first for quite some time. Hope I don't hit detail on Sunday. Tonight, we drew cards for a rifle cleaning detail and I drew a high enough card to keep me off. That's my lucky card sense I reckon.

(Thanks, Dad - I got that from you!!)

The weather was swell all day - there is a chance we still may get furloughs - the food is good what there is - and I'm fine. Will write more later. Love to you both.... JACK.

April 3, 1944

Dear Mom and Dad:

Here it is Sunday again and the day is almost over already. Last night, after playing baseball all afternoon we ate and then came up to the service club and guess who I ran into: George Cassat and Gus Gieser. They are now "sad sacks" like the rest of us. I think that George is pretty discouraged but he'll soon get over that. Today Bix and I got up and went to church. It was really a very nice service and I was glad we went. Will go next Sunday also, unless 1 happen to draw K.P.

Had a very delicious dinner at the service club this noon - on the house. I held a rope in my hand and kept all the poor people out of the dining room for 40 minutes and thus earned myself a free meal. Bet they don't do it again. I believe I ate in the neighborhood of 90 cents worth. You son is really developing a terrific appetite. This afternoon we went over in the ERTC (Engineering Replacement Training Center) area and saw the movie "Buffalo Bill". It was in technicolor and was very good. Then back to the service club for dinner and I again ate heartily. I tell you there is nothing like eating.

Really you would be shocked to see the way I look. My clothes are in a terrible state. My shoes aren't shined; my pants have bags in every spot and speaking of spots - the gravy stains on my tie are almost too numerous to mention. I really believe that the infantry does things to one. It isn't a matter of not having the stuff - you just hate to change.

No one knows what is cooking for the coming week. I will guess it will be night problems. On the 23rd we go out in the field for a two- or three-week bivouac. I sure do hope that the weather is somewhat nice - otherwise it will be a mess. Say, last night 1 got a letter from an Audell Cashion who lives at Farmington and is a cousin guess. Anyway, she said that Ora Dauner had told her that I was here and she invited me down if and when I could make it. What's the deal? Do you know her? I was planning on hitting St. Louis next week but I don't know whether to go or not. I'm getting so I hate to spend the dough and I know it would cost between $10-$15.

It is a beautiful day today and I am keeping my fingers crossed that it stays that way. Dick Bodine is here with me and so is Smitty (Bob Smith). All of us are diligently writing home. I wrote Mrs. Howe a note the other day. Her birthday card arrived late and I thought I had better get my new address to her. Also, I got letters from both Louie Shortell and Ellen Peaslee. They are all excited and I believe they will probably get married in June. It sure would be nice to get back for the wedding.

Co. G - 387 Infantry, Fort Leonard Wood, Missouri

I hope my furlough comes about that time. Reckon I had better close and drop a few more lines before the day is over. Just as a check, I sent $30 home that should have arrived by Monday or Tuesday. Please confirm same in one of your letters. Hope you are both fine.

Love........JACK

April 4, 1944

Dear Mom and Dad:

Well this has really been quite a day. This morning the whole division went out on the parade grounds and had a real demonstration on aircraft identification. About nine different planes would zoom down one at a time about 20 feet over our heads. It was really a spectacle. They had an A-20, B-25, B-26, P-39, P-40, P-51, and P-47. They sure were beauties and when they flew so close to our heads it was really a thrill to watch them. Then they flew over in a tight formation and that too looked mighty great. Man, what I wouldn't give to be a pilot in the Air Corps.

Then we went out on the combat firing course. They gave us 3 clips of live ammunition, then each guy would go through a course of wire entanglements and shell holes - moving forward all of the time and firing at targets which suddenly came up in front of you. The targets were in the shape of men and you kept going on and shooting every one that suddenly popped up. I hit 20 out of the 24 on the course. It was really great.

Now I am sitting here waiting for rifle inspection We have one tonight and my rifle is in fine shape. It shines like a silver dollar. I don't have any idea what is scheduled for tomorrow. However, things have been getting much easier around here now since we've joined the older group of men. No more news for now. Am feeling fine. Love to you both...JACK

Dear Mom and Dad

April 5, 1944

Dear Mom and Dad:

We don't fall out for a few minutes so I have just enough time to knock out a quick note. Well, we really had a day of it yesterday. Up at 5 o'clock and out to the carbine transition range where we fired at silhouette targets at various ranges. I was on the beam and knocked down a possible score - 24 out of 24!! Then we put on our packs and hiked about 3 miles over to the infiltration course. Here, we crawled on our stomachs about 100 yards with live machine gun ammunition flying over our heads and smoke screens floating all over the course. It was rough. They even had land mines going off once in a while.

Then we picked up our packs and hiked all the way back to the transition range where we fired the M-1. I didn't do so well on that deal - in fact, I did lousy! Then, after eating, a bunch of us went out to the anti-aircraft range and fired at targets floating through the sky. That was great! I never saw such a bunch of crap in my life.

Then last night we were restricted for the 2nd straight night for another rifle inspection. I pulled a little quickie out on the range and got in about an hour earlier than the rest of the guys so I got mine all cleaned up real fast. Anyway, my rifle passed okey.

A few more new boys came in and they look quite sad. That will no doubt leave their countenance soon - the dirt will take it off. No telling what will happen today. We should be through firing for a while, I hope., Probably will get some bayonet drill. Nothing about furloughs so it looks as though we can quit worrying about them. Almost time to fall out so I better close.

Love, always.... JACK.

April 6, 1944

Dear Mom and Dad:

I've been terribly busy and just now found some time to write. The Easter box arrived and thanks so much. It looks scrumptious or something. We really have been working the last two days. Yesterday we had quite a bit of bayonet drill and then a bunch of lectures. But today – wow! we hiked 7 miles out to what they call the Nazi village. This is a miniature village which represents a town in Germany.

You work in squads and move in with live ammunition and take the building by house to house fighting. My squad was moving in on the right in good form. Then the order to fire was given, so we fired at the Germans (dummies). Then we ceased firing and we started moving forward. Well, I captured two outhouses and a garage single handed... and that isn't all - I bayonetted three dummies sitting in the outhouses - killed them in cold blood. To get the garage I heaved a hand grenade in and then ran in and bayoneted everything in sight. It was great - why I think they might even award me a medal for my fantastic work. A medal to distinguish me as permanent O.K (Outhouse Killer).

Anyway, when it comes to capturing the "out behind the house and barn" leave it to Jack Dauner - he'll come through as sure as Ex-Lax. Tonight, we've been cleaning rifles. Mine, having been fired, was filthy and needed a lot of extra cleaning. Tomorrow our company is on guard duty. I hope I don't draw it! Who knows, I may though, and if I do I'll have to brush up on my general orders.

Got six letters today: one from you; Barb Adams; George Baumgartner, Reverend Hempstead, and Audell Cashion. I may try and get down there this week and see what the deal is. It would be fun to spend Easter in a home. I'll have to wait and see what happens. Not much more news. May have to capture a few more outhouses and stick a few more German dummies with my bayonet. Hope you are both fine and that everything at home is okey. Have a Happy Easter, I wish that I was going to be there with you, but it just isn't in the cards this year. Love...JACK

April 10, 1944

Dear Mom and Dad:

Well, here I am sitting in the guard house. Yep...they finally caught up with me!! My sentence - 24 hours!! Don't get worried I just got

Dear Mom and Dad

guard duty for the day. Have already walked two hours and am now off for four, then go on for two more and then off for four. It isn't too bad. I am carrying an M-1 rifle with fixed bayonet.

Forgot when I wrote last so I'll give you some of the other news. Last night, we had quite a time. After a full day of work, we ate and then hopped into trucks and went out to the infiltration course. When it got good and dark we went down and they started firing tracer bullets just over our heads. It was just like the fourth of July. Really keen!! A confounded land mine blew up a little in front of me and through dirt all over me - otherwise the whole deal was a snap. When we got back they had coffee and coke for us.

Was planning on going to Farmington this weekend until I hit guard duty. I think next weekend I'll go to St. Louis. I'll try to get a pass. We are going on bivouac the 23rd so in case Dad happens to be coming to Chicago and could get down wire me so I can show it in the orderly room and be able to meet him. Got a long letter from Ellen Peaslee and she is all excited about her engagement. Louie has gone on to New York and will return later.

Hope you guys are both fine. I am!! I should be out of the guard house by tomorrow - who knows, they may be having me chase prisoners next. Love to you both...JACK.

April 13, 1944

Dear Mom and Dad:

Here it is Monday and what a day. Blue Monday isn't the word for it. It has rained all day. This morning we went out on a bayonet course It started raining and we really got soaked. There wasn't a dry spot on any of us. And our rifles were a sight. So, we dried off and then went to work on our weapons.

The result is that the day has really been an easy one. About 50 guys are shipping out of our company tomorrow for a P.O.E. (Port of Embarkation). So, the C.O. is throwing a beer party for all of us and I guess we're going to have some entertainment to go with it. Sure, hate to see some of those guys go for two reasons: first, they were swell group of fellows; and second, it means more details for those of us staying here. Boy, that's what we need is more details with less personnel!

Finished guard duty and it wasn't too bad at all. Forgot whether I told you but I did manage to get to church on Easter for the services. Am enclosing a copy of the program. There was a sunrise service and all of the regiment went except those of us on guard duty. Hope the weather clears up - this stuff is terrible to march in when it is so muddy. Have no idea what is going to happen this week. I imagine we are due for a 25-mile march and also a nine-mile forced march. The latter is done in two hours. Am still planning to go into St. Louis this weekend if at all possible. No more news for now. Will write more later.

Love to you both...JACK.

April 14, 1944

Dear Mom and Dad:

Well, here I am in old St. Louis having a swell time on $12. Please send me $5 immediately to tide me over the rest of this month. I am lacking funds. Guess I shouldn't have tried to run the month on $15.

Came in town after getting off at noon. The bus we took was of the 1920 vintage and sputtered like a fuse. Everything was okey for a while - then old Bessie died. So 28 sad sacks got out and pushed her uphill for a block so we could get a flying start for the next foothill. We finally made it in by 5:30 P.M. Then...no hotels!! Smitty (Bob Smith) was to meet his father and I started out to get a room. Everything was filled except for a few doubles so I found a respectable looking soldier who also needed a buddy to get a double room with the result that we got one with twin beds. Great...I sleep tonight. This hotel situation in St. Louis can really get rough on the weekends.

Tomorrow we (Smitty and I will leave at 9:30 in the evening - get back to camp at 1:00 A.M. and then I get up at 4:30 A.M. for K.P. Sounds great, doesn't it? I will be crawling by the end of the day no doubt. What a life! Anything nice - I couldn't get it here before the stores closed and it is impossible to buy anything at camp. Please use some of the money I have sent home.

Sure, is great to be back in St. Louis. Seems like old times. Even the old guy at the reception table recognized me and wondered what I was doing in the 97th Division. No more news for now. Don't forget the $5 and Jeanne's gift. Thanks so much.

All my love always...JACK.

April 15, 1944

Dear Mom and Dad:

Here I sit in the Service Club with Jim Costakis after a very easy day. No kidding we really had it soft for a change. Hope it continues. Last night, we had a big beer party for all the guys leaving and had a swell time. About ten o'clock, the first Sargent came in and put a stop to all the fun. Good thing nobody had any live ammunition or I'm afraid someone of the guys who were shipping out might have put him out of his misery.

There's a rumor on the loose that 500 A.S.T. guys from here will ship to Camp Shelby, Miss. Of course, that is just a rumor. It has been raining an awful lot and the weather is generally miserable. I'm beginning to wonder if there is a sun in the sky any more. I believe we'll be taking maneuvers, but they haven't decided whether it will be Louisiana, Tennessee or out in the desert. I believe I prefer the desert or Tennessee. Never Louisiana! Of course, I really don't have any choice.

News is slim - so I'll close and write later on any further developments. Hope you two are fine - I'm okey - just a little tired. Love...JACK.

April 16, 1944

Dear Mom and Dad:

Well, things are getting hot around here and I do mean hot. A big bunch of the boys are shipping to Camp Shelby, Miss. Some more to

Co. G - 387 Infantry, Fort Leonard Wood, Missouri

Fort Benning, Georgia, and another group to Camp Crowder to join the signal corps. Bixby (one of the boys from A.S.T. with me) is going tomorrow to Crowder. Smitty (Bob Smith) and I are the only two left from Colorado State College in G Company. The company has gone from 186 to 125 in a week. They are really breaking up this outfit. No one knows what is going on. By all rights, Smitty and I should be leaving on the next shipment if and when there is one.

Well - to continue - last night a squad of 12 of us went on a night problem. We were taken out in the country some 10 miles and then dumped out in the middle of nowhere. We were to make a "recon" of a supposed enemy observation post. It was all cross country and naturally everything was carried out by compass. We even blackened our faces just as though it was the real thing. The patrol was about 5 miles. Well, everything was great and we hit every point on the nose - in fact, we got a commendation on it being the best night patrol problem yet carried out. There was a captain from Regional Headquarters following us and he thought we did okey. I believe the corporal who was in charge of us will get a boost to buck Sargent. Not bad... eh?

Tomorrow we have a forced march. Nine miles in two hours. No doubt, I'll look like the Sad Sack but I have to give her all I've got since Smitty and I have been telling these infantry boys that anyone from the Air Corps can put the infantry to shame in anything. Boy, we and our big mouths. So now we do a little backing up of what we said.

Oh - we got in from that night problem at 3:00 A.M. and we ate a huge bowl of hot chili and two cups of cocoa. I never slept better in my life. In fact, I haven't been out of these clothes (including shoes and socks) for over 64 hours. I didn't even bother to undress last night. Just laid down and threw a comforter over me. I'm getting rougher than a team of oxen.

I still laugh at my being in the infantry and so does Smitty. That is all we do and these lol infantry men don't care for it. Yesterday one of the non-coms got a little disgusted and told us we were just play boys! We agreed. I just can't take their training too seriously - I know how to do everything okey - it is just that these non-coms can tell you all this junk and they can't even do it themselves.

Today we were throwing hand grenades for record. I made expert. It was great! I was really on the beam and winged the darn things right where they were supposed to land. Am at the Service Club now and there is a guy playing the piano who used to fill in for Duke Ellington. He is excellent and the place is packed.

I should get a haircut tonight. It has been 4 weeks now, and it already is a half inch over my ears. In fact, I heard rumors that they're trying to do some research on whether might be the missing link to the Theory of Evolution. That is how bad I look. I feel K.P. coming on this weekend which means I won't go anywhere. If I don't get it, I think I'll head for St. Louis. No more news for now... must rest my weary feet.

All my Love.......J ACK.

April 17, 1944

Dear Mom and Dad:

Here I am just about ready to beat it for the bus depot and end my very pleasant week end. Boy oh boy what a time! I got up at 11:30 this morning and then went down in the hotel's very beautiful main dining room and had the most wonderful southern fried chicken you have ever eaten. There were four enormous pieces of chicken; shrimp cocktail; apple pie and all the other trimmings. And, with all the rest, they must have made a mistake on the check because it all came to only 92 cents. Honestly, the food was marvelous and the place reminded me somewhat of that lovely coffee shop in the Hotel Utah at Salt Lake City.

The Lennox Hotel here in St. Louis isn't a bit bad. It is right across the street from the Statler. Went to two movies this afternoon: "Broadway Rhythm" first; and then out to the Fox Theatre to see "Passage to Marseilles". Both were pretty good. Then I headed for a place where Deidrich and I used to always go for food when we were at Jefferson Barracks. It is called Fredericks and I had two huge pork chops with all of the trimmings.

Co. G - 387 Infantry, Fort Leonard Wood, Missouri

I feel like a new man now and I'm even ready for K.P. The old U.S.O. is really humming. It is great to be here - everyone singing and feeling happy. It makes you glad that you're still in a free country where people can do as they please and have a good time. There were a lot of army officers in town this weekend who had seen action. Most of them were pilots. Saw one fellow about my age with the Distinguished Flying Cross and three Oak Leaf Clusters; the air medal with a couple of Oak Leaf Clusters; the Purple Heart and then two Theater of Operation ribbons. Lucky stiff!

Still some A.S.T. patches around and they look silly. I'd be ashamed to wear one of them now that I am in the infantry and have seen what some of the real army is all about. I haven't any more news except I wish you could have gotten down. It's really hard to plan anything though. Gotta run. Love...JACK

April 18, 1944

Dear Dad:

Just got off K.P. and thought I'd drop you the latest news. Here's the deal!! I'm going to get a furlough - maybe in a few days - maybe in a week - or possibly a month! Anyway, I'm going to get it and have no idea just when.

I was thinking it would be fun to surprise mom and everyone and just happen to whip into town. Write me and let me know as soon as you get this! Also send $20 to cover train fare. I don't know when this furlough will come through so I better have the money to be on the safe side. Also, I have no idea of my routing since the Regimental Headquarters makes all of our train reservations.

K.P. was a snap today. Wish I had it tomorrow since we go on a small jaunt of 25 miles. That will be covered in about 7 hours. And me with new shoes!! Pulled in from St. Louis at 3:00 A.M. and got two hours sleep before going on K.P. Don't feel a bit tired! -1 thought I would, but I feel great so I must be in pretty good condition.

Dear Mom and Dad

Well, dad, I have to close. Drop me a note and tell me what you think about just coming in town unexpectedly. Wish I could let you know when I'll be arriving, but that remains one of the mysteries of the military. My guess is a week or two.

Take care of yourself, Dad, and also mom. Write as soon as you can as I don't know when this may finally develop. Love......JACK.

Author's note: Shortly after writing the above letter word came through that I would have a 10-day furlough beginning on April 19th. Needless to say, it was a welcome change of pace and I quickly called home to let the folks know that I was on my way. Fortunately, I was able to get into St. Louis and get a ticket on the Illinois Central "Green Diamond" - one of the streamlined trains running between St. Louis and Chicago. With some luck I was able to transfer from the Illinois Central Station to Union Depot where I picked up the Burlington Zephyr into Dubuque. Thus, started a most enjoyable ten-day period at home.

April 29, 1944

Dear Mom and Dad:

Here I am in St. Louis after a very quiet trip. Landed in Chicago okey and got over to the Illinois Central and boarded my train. Got in at 7:45 A.M. and I am absolutely dead to the world.

Doesn't seem possible that the big furlough is all over already but I guess it is. Ten days is just a drop in the bucket. Will catch the two o'clock bus out of here and then head row- Leonard Wood. I sure hate to go back. Am going to try and pick up some sleep for now - I'm really dead tired. Bye for now and love to you both...JACK.

May 1, 1944

Dear Mom and Dad:

Here we go again on the Dauner Correspondence Course. Guess what. I'm on K.P. That's right and I am really taking this to heart trying to win an Expert K.P. Medal. Last night before I arrived, they had me posted for duty. Guess they were expecting me. Maybe I should have fooled them.

Anyway, everything worked out fine. Got into Chicago okey and after a little traveling around they got me over to the Illinois Central station. The cab situation in Chicago is sad. Got on the train for St. Louis and though it was slow it was fairly comfortable. Got in to St. Louis at 8:00 AM and ate. Naturally!! Then I bummed around the station. Something told me to walk down and watch the trains unload and as I was standing there who should walk up but Dick Bodine. He had just gotten in.

So, we walked all over town and had a marvelous lunch at the Lenox Hotel. I had shrimp and casserole with all the trimmings. Anyway, it was a whole lot of shrimp in spinach and it tasted great. We caught the two o'clock bus, and it took 6 hours to get to camp. They ran four buses and all of them were really crowded.

The boys are all in from bivouac. They were pulled in from the field, and we are now on the alert for flood control detail. Some have already gone. Smitty (Bob Smith from Evanston) was among them. Don't know what I'll be doing but right now I am avoiding the mess sergeant. Only my day will be done. It's a fantastic day - got paid with all the rest. Am sending $20 so you guys can eat this month and keep the wolf from the door. Remember not to put all of your nickels in the same slot machine. Gotta run - I hear the approaching footsteps of the Lord and Master of the Mess Hall. All my love to you both.... JACK.

May 2, 1944

Dear Mom and Dad:

Got both of your letters and am glad you are okey. Me too!! In fact, I had a great honor bestowed on me today. I partook of my meals in the officer's mess hall! By the grace of God and all HELL they slapped me in that damnable kitchen over there. When I wasn't washing their

Dear Mom and Dad

dirty dishes, I was waiting on them saying "Yes, sir - no, sir" and then a few other things under my breath. I got off at 9:00 o'clock tonight

We all got paid $ 0.35 (cents) for 13 hours work. Coolie wages I tell you. I'd rather do it for nothing than get less than $0.03 per hour. However, I consented to take the cash I'm now convinced that I should have stuck it out in Madison and gotten my 2nd Lt. bars.

387th Regiment is still on Flood Control alert which means that we're included. George Cassat is on bivouac. Our regiment will move to the field if we don't go on flood control soon. So, I probably won't see George for quite some time.

I sent $20 home in my letter yesterday. Just wanted you to know as a check to make sure it got there. Well, I am fine - just a little over "K.P.cd" but that's all. Will write soon. Don't worry if you don't hear from me as I'll probably be moving to bivouac or flood areas tomorrow. Bye for now - all my love to you both.... JACK.

May 3, 1944

Dear Mom and Dad:

Tuesday and here I am still in camp. It has been raining on and off but no word as to what we are going to do. Today we were out on the drill field for the whole period. Worked with booby traps and one of the demonstration fire crackers went off on a guy's knee and wrist. Result: he's in the hospital. Nothing serious just a little shocked and some swelling on the knee and wrist. It was a sergeant so he'll no doubt pull through. Other than that, everything went off very well as far as gaining knowledge on booby traps.

Wednesday night we're supposed to go on another night problem so I doubt if I'll be able to get a letter off. I'll try to, however, if I can. This place is in sad shape. No one knows anything and they hardly know what to do with us. A lot of the new guys who just got here are going out on the range. They will bivouac out there until they finish firing. Tough!!

Co. G - 387 Infantry, Fort Leonard Wood, Missouri

Looks like it may rain again tonight. Wonder if the river is still rising. I am not too keen on this flood control business although it doesn't really matter. Can't even let you in on any good rumors because there just aren't any. In fact, there just isn't too much of anything going on around here. Things are really very quiet. I'd best close and do my washing - no more for now. All my love...JACK.

May 4, 1944

Dear Mom and Dad:

Just a note to let you know everything is okey. No doubt you will get a real load of mail from me all in one day. I sent a lot of postcards to give you some idea of what it was like. Those of the various building are quite good and the one of the anti-aircrafts is the real thing. Those various constructions, the engineers were pictured working on I have never seen, but I suppose they take place.

There are only 25 of us left in the company. All the rest are out on bivouac doing technical firing problems. The place looks terribly deserted and no doubt we will really be working the rest of the week. Say, sometime check, just as a double check, to see if either one of those wires I sent with the $10 ever came back. Both of those guys are not on the post and I was just wondering.

Tomorrow I am working over at Regimental Supply. That will be real work since all we do is carry junk and load and unload trucks. Well I reckon I had better close. Hope you two are fine - no more for now - will write soon. All my love.... JACK.

May 6, 1944

Dear Mom and Dad:

Well, your son is taking life easy all morning today and probably will tomorrow, too. It isn't because of any problem. We all went out on a night demonstration and got in at about 2:00 A.M. so they said we could sleep all morning. Ah, what a marvelous feeling to lounge in bed on a week day when you should be out in the field. Nothing like it!

We came in and had our breakfast at 2:00 A.M. I wasn't very hungry - all I had was 2 shredded wheats; three servings of bacon and eggs; two sweet rolls; a slice of bread; and a cup of coffee. Then straight to bed where it took no time to get to sleep.

The problem was a demonstration of sounds at night and was really interesting. It was about a 5 mile hike out and another 5 miles back. So, we got our exercise, too. Sure, was swell that you got to see Tommy Dorsey. Wish I could have been there myself. I didn't get a chance to hear it on the radio.

Tonight, we go out on another problem on compass work. Who knows I may even have to lead a squad. If I do no doubt, well end up miles from nowhere. Why I might even lead them up to old Dubuque - who knows. This is about the last phase of our training. We have 15 hours of night problems scheduled a week. I don't mind them at all if we can sleep the next morning. Will try and keep the letters coming. These confounded problems are taking quite a bit of time. Hope you're both feeling fine - I am! No more for now. All my love.... JACK.

May 8, 1944

Dear Mom and Dad:

Well, Sunday is almost over and it has really been a quiet weekend. Saturday morning, we slept and in the afternoon all we did was lay around the barracks. Smitty (Bob Smith) got in from flood detail so we got cleaned up and went to the movie. Saw "Up in Mabel's Room". It was funny but not much of anything to it. Then we hit the hay. Today we got up and ate; then there was a rifle inspection. and, of course, I got gigged. All that was wrong was a dirty butt plate. No doubt I'll get some extra detail for being so careless.

We had dinner then Smitty and I got a hold of Dick Bodine and we all went to see "Between Two Worlds". It was a very odd movie. Don't know whether you would care for it or not. Then to the service club

Co. G - 387 Infantry, Fort Leonard Wood, Missouri

for dinner and there I ran into Jim Costakis. He had been out on flood control. Didn't see George Cassat any place. Maybe I'll meet him at the service club one of these nights because I still have his socks. By the way those socks were really swell. Don't send any more because I have plenty, but you can recommend them to anyone whose sons might need them.

Got your letter written on Friday, mom. Say, Dad, just in case you ever get a chance to push that transfer deal for me to that Petroleum Laboratory assignment give it another boost. Also, send me that clipping or article - I'm going to try to push it from this end. No doubt I'll get thrown out of the orderly room bodily for even attempting a transfer but it's worth the risk. My sudden interest isn't due to any disliking for the good old "queen of battle" but there are too many guys pulling soft deals by a little boost from here and there so why shouldn't I?

Of course, maybe it would do me good to take this one the hard way - but even this isn't tough. In fact, I haven't found anything in the Army that's too tough, yet, and doubt if I will. Let me know what you deem is advisable, Dad, and if maybe I ought to even produce a copy of your letter and also the article before the C.O. Maybe the actual letter wouldn't be such a good idea, but possibly I could mention that contact had been made through Washington and they replied it would have to be taken through channels in the division.

As for what's cooking in general, things are a mess. They're sending all artillery men over five feet eight inches to the infantry. It looks like I'll have to spend 4 months here - that means about 6 weeks to go. Then they think we'll go on maneuvers which are about 3 months and then...well, it should be time for another furlough, so it looks like my combat days are a lot farther off then was previously calculated. Guess we'll have to wait and see.

Gotta run - will write soon. All my love.... JACK.

Dear Mom and Dad

May 9, 1944

Dear Mom and Dad:

Guess what? I had a little talk with the C.O. tonight at his request. The results: I am restricted to the Company area, which includes three barracks and a day room, for a period of one week. It was all I could do to keep from telling him just what I thought of the deal.

I would have been just as well off with a Summary Court Martial. It was all on account of a little chunk of dirt on the butt plate of my rifle. Anyway, l am restricted so I am in not too good of humor. The dam rifle can rust as far as I am concerned from now on.

For the next three days I am taking some work on the BAR (Browning Automatic Rifle) and then on Wednesday I'll have to fire for record. It is quite a weapon. Automatic in firing like a machine gun. I am sure I'll fire Expert if I try. Haven't decided whether I want to try since it might mean I would be a BAR man and the gun weighs 21 pounds, and is sought after very much by the enemy in combat.

Got the lock today, Dad, and thanks a lot. It is really a good one and just what I need. I hope everything is okey down at the office and that they aren't working you too hard. Not much more news except that if anyone offered me two cents I'd almost be willing to take off for a few days without a leave of absence. Even the weather is disagreeable - in fact there isn't anything that isn't repulsive. Must close - all my love.... JACK.

May 10, 1944

Dear Mom and Dad:

Just a note to let you know that I am not in the CLINK, yet. Broke restriction tonight and got a haircut for the Divisional Review on Saturday. That is a legal break of restriction - it says here). Anyway, I didn't get caught.

Thursday, I fire the BAR for record. We may have night problems the next three nights so if you don't hear from me you'll know that I

Co. G - 387 Infantry, Fort Leonard Wood, Missouri

am on the field for a couple of days. Enclosed is a greeting from the "General" to mom. I thought I'd send it for you to put in the scrap book. Almost time for lights so I'll close. I am fine and will keep out of the brig so don't worry. Love, always......JACK.

May 11, 1944

Dear Mom and Dad:

Your wondering son has returned from his numerous travels to many fields - strictly drill, and now is about to expound his latest latrine rumor. First, I didn't work at all today. Second, I didn't break restriction. I am a good soldier...it says here in fine print. Well, I am now a battle casualty - yep, I was wounded in action today. "Pete" and I were wrestling around in the barracks and one thing led to another. So, we started using bayonets - you know, just a couple of playful boys! Well, I bet him I could sit him down and that he couldn't hit me with the bayonet in his hand using it as a dagger.

Well - so I am a liar. I missed my hold and felt a tap on my lower leg. Didn't think anything of it until we fell out at retreat and I felt this funny trickling down my ankle. So, I looked and by golly there I was bleeding. So, I let her bleed and then washed it off with Listerine and now I am as good as new. Those babies can really cut. With a little pressure the bayonet point went through my pants and almost 3/8" into my leg. I hardly knew it.

George Cassat came over tonight. He is going on furlough on Monday and is bringing back the yearbook and permanent party Air Corps pins. Also, he and Pat are going to get married. Oh my - it is beginning to look as though Walpole (John Poole), Barge (George Baumgartner and me are going to be bachelors at this rate. I think we'll form a club! Well, must close and get some sleep. Am feeling fine and getting lazier every day. It was actually hot today. Maybe summer is here. Bye now - hope you are both fine. JACK.

Dear Mom and Dad

May 14, 1944

Dear Mom and Dad:

Didn't get a chance to write last night because we were browsing around the countryside. I was selected to make up a platoon. This included three full squads of men from our company to help put on a demonstration of a battalion in attack.

Under Secretary of War, Patterson and his staff were supposed to arrive today and this demonstration was to go on tonight but something happened. Anyway, it was really to be something. They had three battalions of artillery firing; 14 heavy machine guns; twelve light machine guns; 14 BAR's; 12, 80mm mortars; and six 60mm mortars. All in all, they were going to fire 150,000 rounds of 30 calibre ammunition besides all the mortar and artillery shells. All the 30 calibre stuff were tracers which would make probably the most spectacular sight I'd ever seen in my life. So, I'm still hoping that the whole show takes place. We act as advancing infantry and capture a hill between the firing on both sides.

Yesterday we practiced the procedure all day. At night we went through a dress rehearsal and they fired 15,000 rounds. It was better than the 4th of July demonstration. So, you can imagine what 150,000 would be like.

Oh yes - we had a big fire. The tracers landed in an old house and set it on fire and she burned to the ground. It was really some blaze - and naturally G Company was detailed to take charge of it. We always get a lousy deal when it comes to picking up details.

Today we cleaned our rifles all morning and then this afternoon had only two hours of drills so it has been an easy day all around. Just got your letter with the pictures in it today. You had put the 389th address instead of the 387th so it went all over. the post.

Got dad's letter today and I think I'll see the C.O. on either Monday or Tuesday. He has been in a very poor frame of mind lately. Just finished a G.I. party on the floors and they shine like new. Gotta close for now. Hope you are both feeling fine because I am. All my love...JACK

Co. G - 387 Infantry, Fort Leonard Wood, Missouri

May 15, 1944

Dear Mom and Dad:

Just got back from church and it was a really nice service. Went to communion service first and then church so I really "did my duty." Enclosed is the program. They certainly have nicely printed programs. Every Sunday they have that type and it certainly enhances the reading material in preparation for the actual service.

George Cassat was supposed to come over last night but he didn't get here. He's bringing the yearbook from Colorado State College. A lot of the snapshot pages have pictures that I took. I noticed where they have the one of the little life guard that I took - maybe you recognize it. On the whole it is a very poor book and not even as good as the high school annual which I edited in 1941. I'm not bragging or anything!

Well, we didn't put on the big demonstration after all. Guess the jerks changed their mind. However, we did have a divisional review and parade and it was murder. and inform was O.D.'s; steel helmets; combat packs; web belts; canteen and first aid kit; and finally rifles with fixed bayonets. The sun was really bearing down and I was perspiring heavily. They gave Patterson and his staff a 17-gun salute. Then they drove around in a command car and reviewed us. Then we passed in review and finally took the longest way possible back to the barracks. You haven't seen anything until you see a divisional review. About 10,000 guys were all standing at attention or at present arms most of the time. It is beautiful to look at, but just ask the guy who takes part in one as to what he thinks about the whole affair. X#%& - (Censored)!!

It is a beautiful day here. The sun is out and I sure wish I could be home. Tomorrow we go into sun tans so I can stow the O.D.'s away until fall. Hmm - I wonder where I'll be by fall!! Maybe by fall the Axis will have fallen, I hope. This war isn't being run right in my opinion. Maybe a Dauner ought to take charge for a while and show them how to do it.

Guess I'll try and call this afternoon. It may take quite a spell to get through, but I might hit it lucky. Let's hope the C.O. isn't on the post - I'm still restricted. The corporal who heads Smitty (Bob Smith) and my squad came in soused last night. He smashed up a car; slugged three M.P.'s; and will have about four M.P. charges against him. If he's lucky he'll just be broken (which he wants). The guy has been trying to get overseas for the last six months and they keep him here on the Cadre so he has been trying to get broken. That means another set of stripes will be open but they won't pass any out. Their T.O. here calls for 18 staff sergeants and they only have seven. See what I mean - and that's the way it is all down the line in Company G. Great organization!!

Two weeks of every month are to be spent out in the field on bivouac so that means next Sunday we will go out again. Hope the weather is good. No doubt my mail will be sad those two weeks. Can't figure out why the letters are taking 4-5 days. Don't worry if you don't hear from me because they'll all come in a bunch.

No more news for now so I'll close. Bye for now - and Happy Mother's Day, Mom. Love to you both…. JACK

May 16, 1944

Dear Mom and Dad:

Just a note to let you know that I am okey and had a real day of it at the range. My firing was pretty good, but I wouldn't brag about it. Tomorrow and Wednesday we'll be firing for record and maybe I can get on the beam. Not that it makes any difference.

Got a nice long letter from George Baumgartner tonight. It was sent air mail and made it in 8 days. Quite good time I thought. Tomorrow night I believe we have a night problem. When we finish we're supposed to be POR qualified and also eligible for a three-day pass. A big shipment came out today, but none of us, ASTP guys are leaving. The weather is really warm and as far as I am concerned it can stay just the way it is. No more news. Will drop a line tomorrow if I can. Love, always……JACK.

Co. G - 387 Infantry, Fort Leonard Wood, Missouri

May 18, 1944

Dear Mom and Dad:

First chance I've had to write so here goes. Well, we finally finished up our firing on the BAR range and I made Expert. I'm not bragging because my score should have been much better, but I still made Expert so I don't care.

We really had a day of it yesterday. Got up at five o'clock and didn't get off the range until 8:45 P.M. Then we had to eat and clean the weapons so I hit the hay at about 11:30 P.M. Then we got up at four o'clock this morning and back to the range where we worked in the pits. It was a good deal for some of us. They didn't fire any orders on mine so I slept all morning. Then this afternoon by a little slight of hand I got back to camp by 3:00 P.M.- took a shower, washed some clothes and rested. Went to the Service Club and there was a bunch of gals from Stevens College. These coeds really have class. They (most of them, that is) dress like a million bucks and are plenty smooth. They're putting on a show of some kind at one of the theaters. I'll have to find out which one and plan to attend.

Have no idea what we'll do tomorrow. I may try and see the Captain if we don't have a night problem. I am still confident we'll get maneuvers so don't worry about any of George Cassat's talk. I got the "in" with a peach of a guy in Company Headquarters. He's a buck sergeant and a nice guy. He is a drummer in the Regimental band so he gives me all the information when I ask for it. That is almost as good a source for information as going to stool #3 in the latrine. By putting two and two together I still believe we'll do some tactical problems around here and then pick up and move out for the maneuvers. Of course, that's still just my guess but it's as good as any. I'm almost sure I'll be the BAR man in the squad. This means I'll be lugging that 21 pound gun around with several bandoliers of ammunition. It is an excellent piece of equipment but it sure adds weight to the existing load you have to carry.

Got your good long letter today, Dad. You're really getting on the beam when it comes to giving out with the news and views. No word

Dear Mom and Dad

as yet whether we go to the field next week. Almost ten "old" men are leaving for POE (Port of Embarkation) in a day or so. That finishes off the last bunch of guys that were here when we first came. Time for me to go so I'd better close. Hope you both are fine. Glad you like the hankies, Mom. All my love.... JACK.

May 19, 1944

Dear Mom and Dad:

I wired tonight for a copy of that letter from Colonel Sills to get more information about the deal when it is presented in the channels. The Captain wanted the reply. He is going to get to ball rolling as soon as we get that letter, and will see what happens. It goes from him to battalion headquarters; from there to Regimental and finally to Divisional headquarters. He thinks it will get to regimental okey, but will be flatly thrown out at that point.

We'll wait and see, however. Have to get up a three o'clock for K.P. so I'll get about four hours sleep. Gotta close and get some shut eye!! Love....JACK.

May 20, 1944

Dear Mom and Dad:

Just got off of 18 hours of K.P. so I am the true picture of the Sad Sack. Almost all the company went out and fired on the transition range so I did miss that. We got up a three o'clock this morning and every dish was washed by six o'clock. I was sure glad to see night roll around.

Went out on the range with mess this noon and served it out there - that was good for it meant no dishes. Mail has been sad the last few days. I got one letter today and it was from Mrs. Steuck. No doubt I'll get a big batch of it all at once again. Heard from both Mrs. Howe and Grandpa Dauner a few days ago. They both were nice long letters. I applied for a weekend pass since we'll be out on the field the next two

Co. G - 387 Infantry, Fort Leonard Wood, Missouri

weeks. I think that Smitty (Bob Smith of Evanston) and I are going to Jefferson City. I have exactly $6.00, but he'll loan me some and I won't need any dough for the next couple of weeks anyway.

In case I didn't explain to you just what all the rush on that letter was - I went to see the C.O. and he said that would make the files more complete. I am very doubtful as to anything happening. I am sure Regimental Headquarters will rip up the application but well, have to wait and see. In the meantime, I am dog tired so I am going to close and start dreaming about pots and pans and dirty dishes. Hope you have a nice weekend. All my love.... JACK.

May 21, 1944

Dear Mom and Dad:

Monday, we go out in the field. I have everything all ready - my full field pack rolled, and my blankets tied up. I sure hope the weather stays nice. It has been raining on and off both yesterday and today which makes it somewhat miserable. Don't worry if you don't hear from me too often for I imagine writing facilities will be poor out in the field. I am taking stationary with me, however. No more news for now so I'll close. Hope you had a nice weekend. All my love to you both.... JACK.

May 22, 1944

Dear Mom and Dad:

Your letter and the Colonel's were waiting for me when I got back. I am afraid the one from the Colonel won't do any good. He doesn't say anything so I am really just starting from scratch. This means I'll get nowhere fast. Tomorrow we get up at three o'clock in the morning and get on the move. Our bivouac area is 13 miles out and we're marching with full field equipment. I will be really "paining with the training." If this keeps up much longer I am also going to get "fed up with the set up." Had a slew of mail waiting for me when I got in tonight so I've got to get on the beam and answer a few.

Dear Mom and Dad

It's raining here which means that it will really be a mess tomorrow. What a time to pick to rain!! I have to hit the hay so I'd better close. Will write when I can. In the meantime - all my love.... JACK.

May 25, 1944

Dear Mom and Dad:

Haven't had a chance to write at all so I'll try now. We're supposed to be cleaning rifles. Mine is all torn down and Smitty is standing guard. Well, here we are out in the field and it is really quite a life. Monday, we marched out with full field packs, gas masks, belts, steel helmets and rifles. It was an easy march - only about 8 miles.

We pitched our tents and then the order to "dig in" came so I started to work on my fox hole. About this time, they came over and told me that I was wanted for a very important mission. I said to myself that it was probably another chance to win the Purple Heart - so I dug latrines the rest of the afternoon. The dimensions were 8 feet long; 18 inches deep; and the width of a shovel.

Monday night we had a night demonstration which lasted until midnight. I had seen it before so I slept. Yesterday was Tuesday, I believe. In the morning I dug a while on my fox hole and in the afternoon, we had to put on a demonstration of a platoon on the attack. It was pretty good. But now let me tell you about last night. That was the deal of all deals. They split us up into 12-man squads for a patrol which was to infiltrate through the MLR (Main line of Resistance) of the enemy. The enemy fired blanks on us and also flares.

Well, we marched about 5 miles over to the point of beginning. Our squad started out as was doing fine. I was the 1st rifle man. After going about 300 yards, the guy just in front of me said he had lost track of the man in front of him. Result: we had lost the rest of the patrol. I made a reconnaissance and saw a couple of guys crouched down about 50 yards away so I crawled up on one of them and asked him if he was assistant BAR man. He turned around there was a first Lieutenant. I got enough dope to get us from there to the finishing point. I started to

Co. G - 387 Infantry, Fort Leonard Wood, Missouri

lead the squad when I saw another guy crawling up, soot so, I crawled and shoved my M-1 in his face. It was Lazore - our squad leader looking for us. Well, we finally made it.

What a sad patrol that turned out to be. We pulled in at three o'clock in the morning and we were all dead. I'm sure most of us were walking with our eyes open and sound asleep. Several times I would come to and find myself wondering off toward the side of the road. Other than that, everything is fine and I am feeling great. Must close now - will write when I can. All my love, always......JACK.

May 27, 1944

Dear Mom and Dad:

Believe it or not we actually don't have a night problem. Allow me to go into the vivid portrayal of last night's activities. We started at 8 o'clock and got back at 2:30 A.M. We had a night compass course of three miles with three different azimuths. The terrain was terrific and it was pitch dark. Almost all of the course took us through dense woods and rocky terrain with plenty of cliffs and hills. We were really dead. It was about a four-mile march; the course was three miles, and then the march back. Count 'em up - my fingers and toes say eleven little jewels.

So, this morning Smitty and I slept in. Ate breakfast and then back to bed where we slept until 10:30 A.M. Then we were called out for early chow and 36 of us marched out to run through a squad combat course. Our squad got lined up at about two o'clock ready to go when all of a sudden, they passed the word that the General was coming. That turned out to be a damn lie. One general would have been enough, but it turned out that there were four of them. They were Lt. Gen. McNair, head of the Army Ground Forces; Brig. Gen Halsey; Brig. Gen. Partridge of the 97 Inf. Div.; and one other Brig. General. Well, they watched us run the problem. There really was a lot of brass present. I was 1st rifle man and had no responsibility, thank the Lord.

Dear Mom and Dad

We each got 32 rounds of ammo which we shot all over the vicinity. The problem was about 2,000 yards long and really a rough deal. Especially in the blazing sun. Ah me - your son is really getting to be a rugged character. Frankly, I'll take overseas duty to all of this crazy fool stuff - but don't tell that to Dave Cassat. Man, today was the first time in years that Jack Dauner made a third track - but my old tail was really dragging - and every other guy was right along with me.

I am writing this by the light of a candle. Hope you get it within a decent length of time. The food is great and I am fine… just a little tired. Much love to you both……JACK.

May 30, 1944

Dear Mom and Dad:

Sorry the letters to you have been coming in slowly but they are working us. Come the revolution and all first sergeants will be shot. I was so aggravated yesterday that I pulled out my bayonet, jammed it on the rifle and started jabbing all the trees in sight. That relieved me of some of my pent-up steam. The boys are all disgusted with everything. We absolutely have no time off. Other companies are sitting around while Co. G. works like slaves.

This afternoon Smitty and I hiked about 3 miles and went swimming. It felt great to get into the water. Had a good chicken dinner this noon. The food in general is really good. Tuesday, we have a 25-mile hike scheduled and I am getting all set. When everyone else has fallen out, Dauner is going to be going strong. I'll crawl before I fall out. I don't think it will be so tough so I am not worried.

We ran a bunch of squad problems the last part of the week. Used blank ammo and simulated all the firing, etc. It was all quite boring. We have been walking anywhere from 15-18 miles a day. Each of these problems is around 1,500 -2,000 yards long and you really work up a sweat running them. This morning I put out a washing and then went to communion and church. It was really nice - the outdoor services and all.

Co. G - 387 Infantry, Fort Leonard Wood, Missouri

Got the dollar, Mom and thanks. It came in handy. I've been running on 20 cents for a week now. We got paid on Wednesday, thank goodness. I think that Smitty, Dick, and I are going to plan a spree to St. Louis when Smitty gets back from furlough. I think he'll leave about Tuesday. Hope everything is fine. I am okey. No more news for now and will try to write often this week. All my love.... JACK.

June 1, 1944

Dear Mom and Dad:

Here I sit under the evening sky; soaking wet; sitting on my steel helmet; and bearing a dumb look on my face. This morning ten of us were selected to take an infantryman's test to represent Co. G. I got all marks of satisfactory. They marked you with either a "U" or an "S". No doubt for this marvelous feat I will merit a sour grapefruit.

The only good thing about being one of those 10 guys was that it kept me from going on a tactical problem last night. It rained something awful and while the others dug trenches out in the field, Dauner lay asleep in the tent. I got exactly 12 hours of sleep for a change which really felt pretty good.

This afternoon I dug latrines. Pretty soon I'll be dreaming of those things. Don't be surprised when I get home again if I go out and dig a slit trench in the backyard so I can take my morning "constitutional." Don't laugh - I'm serious!! This morning I woke up - uncovered myself from all of the blankets and guess what. - I had slept with a mouse. Yep, there it was, a little baby mouse. Surprising what one will find in the same tent these days. I don't know who was the most surprised - me or the mouse!

Smitty and I have to go and get some candy and other snacks so I'd better close. Will try and write soon. Am feeling fine. Love, always.... JACK.

Dear Mom and Dad

June 2, 1944

Dear Mom and Dad:

Just a note to let you know that I am okey and still kicking. Got on a good detail down at the gym and am on again tomorrow which keeps me off drill. Absolutely, nothing new. Ten guys from the 387th are leaving for the Air Corps, but they are all graduates from Air Corps Mech. School. They also are sending 24 to OCS (Officer Candidate School). Only pull could get a guy in there and I don't seem to know any generals around here. It would take at least a major or up to do one any good and he would have to be strategically located. These OCS appointments are all cut and dried - you might say!! There just isn't any more news at this end so I'll close. Hope you fellows are fine. I am doing great.

All my love.... JACK.

June 4, 1944

Dear Mom and Dad:

I have finally come to - at least somewhat - so I'll try and knock out a note to let you know that I am still alive - barely. Yesterday, they announced the 25 miler. Then they called out names of men to put on the demonstration. Smitty and I were on that list which meant that we didn't have to take the hike. They trucked us out to the area and we practiced the deal. It was the same demonstration that we were going to put on for Under Secretary Patterson - the battalion in attack. The others hiked out - then after the show we trucked back and the rest had to hike back to complete the 25 miles. They got in at 5:30 A.M. I am dead tired so I can imagine how they must feel. What a life!!

But that isn't all!! Smitty and I both have guard duty on Saturday night which means we've got to lay around in the guard house the whole weekend. How do you like that?? This afternoon we've got to clean up the area and fill up our fox holes. I think we'll hike into camp tomorrow morning. We ought to be back by 11:30 A.M. tomorrow.

Co. G - 387 Infantry, Fort Leonard Wood, Missouri

(Later). I just got back off a detail and learned that we get up at 4 o'clock in the morning to move out. Then a rifle inspection when we get back. There is also a rumor of a 60-mile compass course in the offing. At this rate I am going to be worn out before I ever see foreign shores. No more news. Will write when I can. Love....JACK.

June 5, 1944

Dear Mom and Dad:

Here it is Sunday and your son is in the guard house once again. If I "ain't" in the guard house - I'm in the doghouse. I can't seem to win. For the last 24 hours I have been on duty and guarding the water tower. It was really monotonous and I'm not kidding.

Dick Bodine is being sent to Fort Benning, Georgia, for 3 months of radio school and then back here. He is a mighty lucky stiff. By the way, I want to congratulate you two guys on your anniversary. I tried to find time to call but couldn't do it. So maybe I'll call next Sunday. I'll start the call coming at about nine o'clock in the morning. I can't get a 3-day pass, I guess, so it would be just a weekend.

I am feeling great after the two weeks in the field. We hiked in but it wasn't bad at all. I had trouble staying awake on guard duty but I made it. Time to fall out for guard so I'd better close. All my love...JACK.

June 14, 1944

Dear Mom and Dad:

Just a note to let you know that we're going out on a five-day march and an associated problem. It will be tactical throughout and I won't see civilization until sometime Friday. Then I can wire you as to whether to come on down or to stay in Dubuque.

My advice would be to have everything packed and ready to go. I'll try and have the wire arrive by seven o'clock. Looks like rain to start this ordeal. No doubt the weather will be miserable. Wish we could plan definitely for this weekend - maybe it would be best to wait until

Dear Mom and Dad

the week following. I'll wire and let you know. Must run - don't look for any letters because I'll have no time at all. Love...JACK.

June 19, 1944

Dear Mom and Dad:

Sure, was glad to be able to talk and wish you a happy Father's Day, Dad. I haven't been in camp at all this week to get anything, but I'll make it up sometime.

Well, last week was rough. We started Monday night on a combination compass course and mock battle. All in all, we marched some 75 miles in, around, and through the Ozarks. They weren't so nice when you see them the way I did. Three of the four nights the non-coms in charge of us got lost. Result: Monday night we arrived at 1:00 P.M. Tuesday night, we arrived at bivouac at 4:30 A.M. On Wednesday, we arrived at 2:00 A.M. On Thursday, night we marched all night and attacked the enemy at 5:00 A.M. Friday morning.

You can readily see how much sleep we got. We ate "C" rations all of the time and carried a full field pack (60 pounds). The "C" rations come in a can and you either heat them or eat them cold. I'll bring some for you to take back. By the way, I have a lot of stuff to go back. I'll buy a little bag at the PX so that I can bring these things to St. Louis. Then you can take everything back to Dubuque. No more news. Hope to see you soon. Love....JACK.

July 2, 1944

Dear Mom and Dad:

Here I am back in St. Louis. Smitty (Bob Smith) and I managed to swing passes and keep off detail. Got here at seven o'clock and had trouble getting rooms. There was nothing left any place so we scouted around and grabbed a couple of our old buddies from Colorado State University and got a suite at the Jefferson Hotel.

Co. G - 387 Infantry, Fort Leonard Wood, Missouri

Wrote about 5 letters this morning after a good tub bath. So far it has been a swell weekend and will no doubt be our last fling for some time. I inquired about flying home from California if and when I get a furlough. I think III save my dough and do it. I can get priorities which will fly me all the way through to Chicago. The damage is $100. If I happen to strike gold I'll come home that way for sure if and when. That would be a real trip - something I've always wanted to do. Got another letter from George Baumgartner yesterday written in a foxhole. Obviously, he came in on one of the early amphibious landings. He seems to be doing okey so far. Hope his luck continues to hold out. No more news for now. Hope you are both fine. Love. Jack

July 7, 1944

Dear Mom and Dad:

Received the papers today, Dad, but had already handed the others in. I should go before the board in a week or so. Have not heard anything from Lt. Colonel Henderson. I rather doubt if he looks me up. About all I can do is go before the Board and give them the best impression I can and then keep my fingers crossed. It is ridiculous but worth trying.

One kid in the company has a personal letter of recommendation from "Hap" Arnold and also a general in the 9th Corps. His dad is on the Board of Directors of International Harvester Company. I think he's got it cinched already. He was called in again today.

The company is out in the field on an all day and half night problem. I got out of it because of snipers' school - thank the lord. Everything is all packed and it looks like it won't be too long until we move. We move out of the barracks and live between the barracks starting in a couple of days. That is so they can G.I. and fumigate them.

Gotta close - love to you both...JACK.

Dear Mom and Dad

July 8, 1944

Dear Mom and Dad:

Just a note to let you know that all is well. I slept about 8 hours today. We had a sniper's school and since I had fired I just found myself a comfortable spot and slept. Great life!! By the way I am now armed with an 03A3 rifle with telescopic sights and also a brand new pair of Westinghouse field glasses. Looks like I may be a sniper.

Hang on to your hats - when I got in tonight the first sergeant said that I was supposed to have gone before the OCS Screening Board tonight, but since I got in late from detail I would have to appear in a few nights. Just keep your fingers crossed - this may be the break that I am looking for and if it is I am going to grab it. We'll just have to wait and hope. Don't be disappointed if nothing happens - I won't since it was such a gamble. Think we're leaving about Tuesday for California. No more news. Love……JACK.

July 10, 1944

Dear Mom and Dad:

Here it is Sunday night and I am back in camp after a swell weekend. Bob Smith, Stuart Eubank and I headed for St. Louis but landed up in Jefferson City. We really had quite a time. Today, after a good night sleep we ate and then saw "White Cliffs". It was a good movie.

Well, I went before the OCS Board and I now have one less worry on my hands. The board, composed of three majors, was definitely prejudiced against anyone trying for anything but infantry OCS. Of course, I applied for Chemical Warfare. With all the rest, I came out and told them exactly what part I wanted, which was research, and then they neatly figured out that I was merely attempting to get out of the infantry. This may have been true, but.....

Anyway, one of the majors and me definitely didn't like each other's looks - so since he held the cards I had no chance. It was all very simple with me taking the part of the fool. I now have my telescopic sights lined up on two birds when we hit the islands. As it stands now we are going to get three months of amphibian training and that's all she wrote. -If they don't get this outfit on the move soon they'll start a war between themselves. This is the poorest run Regiment I've ever seen, and the criticism by the boys is getting worse. I hope it hits home soon and they have a real shake up and do some "canning" We're shipping with full field packs, steel helmets, sun tans, etc. I don't know why we don't carry two barracks bags and the mess hall too, while we're at it. I now have some field glasses which are great. Friday there was a big bond rally and SUSAN HAYWARD was here. It was quite a show and she was really okey. Some "4-F" accompanied her and he made a fool of himself. Tomorrow, I'll send some stuff that I've got to get rid of. Am going to try and get a field jacket or two and other stuff when we get ready for overseas duty. Time to hit the hay so I'll close. Hope you are both fine. Love....JACK.

July 11, 1944

Dear Mom and Dad:

Just a note to let you know that we haven't left as yet but will very shortly. We moved out of the barracks yesterday and are now living in tents until we ship out. Don't know what we'll be doing today, but I suppose it will be drill. Say, I got some inside information that the outfit that Milt (Kapp) is in will follow us into San Luis Obispo about two or three weeks after we arrive for amphibious training. That may be wrong but it came from good sources. Sent my change of address card yesterday. You can put that in my scrapbook. Don't worry it means nothing except a change of address. No more news for now. Hope that you are both fine...I'll keep you posted. Love....JACK.

Author's note: On July 13 we boarded a troop train and headed west for Camp San Luis Obispo, California. A group of us went out the night before for a final fling and we were all pretty well hung over by

Dear Mom and Dad

the time we finally rolled out and boarded the train which had been pulled right into the base.

Our trip by train was slow, hot and dusty. Troop trains were never given any priority and so we frequently were pulled off on sidings to permit freight trains and priority passenger trains to move ahead of us. Most of the time was spent reading, talking, sleeping and playing poker or shooting dice. Since we took the southern route there wasn't too much scenery - mostly desert. It was pretty refreshing to finally arrive in California and see some greenery.

We arrived in San Luis Obispo and immediately began processing and getting assigned to our pre-designated areas. Thus, began a whole new experience in the military and one which would bring most of us one step closer to overseas shipment and ultimately the combat for which we were being trained. San Luis Obispo was a nice community which was located midway between Los Angeles and San Francisco. It was approximately 13 miles from Pismo Beach - a popular ocean resort community where military personnel spent quite a bit of their spare time. The cab fare from the base to Pismo Beach was a flat $13 each way so we usually got three or four fellows together who wanted to split the expense.

EASTER MORNING WORSHIP
387th Infantry Chapel, Fort Leonard Wood, Mo.
1000 Sunday, 9 April 1944

CHRIST OF THE ANDES
PROTESTANT WORSHIP SERVICE
307th Infantry Chapel
1000 Sunday 4 June 1944

Chapter 9

Co. G - 387 Infantry - 97th Division - A.P.O #445 Camp San Luis Obispo, California

(July 17, 1944 - August 28, 1944)

July 17, 1944

Dear Mom and Dad:

Here it is two o'clock and we are having a very peaceful afternoon. Played cribbage all morning and found that I had lost none of my old skills. It's a beautiful day outside. Guess that California is okey after all. No doubt when I start climbing up the mountain side I may change my mind.

By the way, Dad, will you try and get me a good hunting knife. Make sure you get one with a very good blade - especially high-quality steel. Also, send me a few air mail stamps in case you can get them for me. Had an excellent dinner today. The food is really good out here and we're getting grade "A" milk. We have also had some very good beef, and the fresh vegetables are plentiful.

Had a slight case of dysentery last night and this morning. Almost the whole company was sick in one form or another from some concentrated food we were fed. Am okey now. No particular news so I'll close. Hope you are both fine. Love....JACK.

Dear Mom and Dad

July 18, 1944

Dear Mom and Dad:

This has been quite a day. Aside from such things as almost laying the butt of my 03A3 into a corporal's skull, we had an hour of bayonet drill; an hour of straight drill; and then the obstacle course which is really a tough one.

Wrote four letters tonight. I was hut guard so it gave me a chance to get caught up. Heard from George Baumgartner today. The letter was written on July Ist and sent the fourth. He is still okey. Also heard from Don Heitzman and he thinks that he'll soon be moved out here to the west coast. Tomorrow, we are taking a 10-mile jaunt in the mountains. Believe me - "there ain't no gold in them thar hills". Have seen some of our equipment to be used in our training. They have both "ducks" and "buffaloes". You have no doubt seen them in the news. They run on land and water. Quite a pair of contraptions.

Your letter written on July 13th got here today. That is better time than it was from Ft. Wood sometimes. Hope the good service continues. No more news and time for lights. Hope that everything is fine in Dubuque and on the home front. Love...JACK

July 20, 1944

Dear Mom and Dad:

Here it is Thursday and the week is well under way. We are really beginning to train. Our regiment gets its amphibious training last so now we are just toughening up with Plenty of bayonet, hand to hand combat drill and obstacle courses. Yesterday, we took a 13-mile march out into the mountains. It wasn't bad at all. I'm getting a good tan already. We work an hour in the morning and an hour in the afternoon without our shirts and will gradually increase the time. Really, I think this is going to be okey.

No official word has been spoken yet, but it has seeped out that furloughs are to begin the 26th of July and run until the 26th of August

Co. G - 387 Infantry, San Luis Obispo, California

for the 387th Regiment. So, get somewhat prepared in case you get a wire for cash. Which reminds me, I'm flat busted! And....I didn't lose it playing cards. The reason for the latter was that I didn't have any to lose. I've been breaking since we got back from that last weekend that we spent in Jefferson City before we left Ft. Leonard Wood. Those five straight passes I had over the weekends kind of knocked my wad for a loop. I'm only getting $22 now since I'm taking out a bond a month. Anyway, you might send me $5 to keep me going.

Got a letter from George Baumgartner both yesterday and today. He is still okey. A buddy of his was wounded the other day when the two of them were together getting some stuff off of a dead German. They opened up with some machine gun fire and hit the kid with him. Moral: lay-off of souvenir hunting.

By the way, Dad, will you please check on train connections home from both San Francisco and Los Angeles and send them immediately. I don't know when I'll get a chance to get this kind of information. Looks like flying is pretty expensive, but I haven't completely checked all the angles. There is always the possibility of hitching a ride on a bomber if I could get through all of the red tape without wasting too much time.

Well, it's time for lights off and I'm getting powerfully tired so I reckon I'll say good night. Hope you two are fine. I am!! All my love... JACK.

July 21, 1944

Dear Mom and Dad:

Just call me G.I. Jack!! We GI'ed the hut tonight after dinner and then since I was hungry we set off and I had myself two pork chops, fried potatoes, tomatoes; a piece of cake and 3 cups of coffee. That was on top of dinner that I had eaten at the company mess Send some junk out, please - you know..like boxes of cookies, a small box of crackers and rations and a jar of Kraft cheese, or something. Anything would be okey! Our food is alright but our rations are a little short now.

Dear Mom and Dad

Bob Smith got $10 from home so we're going to Pismo Beach for the weekend. Somehow, we missed both KP and guard duty. I can't understand it. Guess we'll do some swimming and absorb some of this good old California sun out there. Don't know where we'll sleep since we won't be able to afford a room if we expect to eat so it probably be out on the beach. Maybe if I bury my head in the sand I'll get the allusion that I'm covered all over and be nice and warm. Oh well, that's a minor detail - eating is much more important.

Tomorrow we take a two hour climb up one of the mountains. That ought to be great. Then down for an inspection; orientation, and after that we can go on leave. No doubt my rifle will get gigged or something. Got a nice letter from Mrs. Howe today. Must write her soon and will try to take care of that this weekend. She certainly thinks the world of all of us fellows. Almost time for lights off so I'd better close. Love...JACK.

July 24, 1944

Dear Mom and Dad:

Here it is Tuesday and the rumors are really flying thick and fast. I'm sure of one thing, though. I won't get a furlough until after August 5th. That is for sure now! Of course, I may be on this shipment coming up, but I am sure that I'll get a furlough before I leave for a POE (Port of Embarkation).

Just got in from the drill field and the wire was waiting for me. Tonight, I'll have to go up to the telegraph office and claim the check. Had an easy morning. We practiced for a regimental review. No doubt this afternoon (later) we'll have it plenty rough. Tomorrow comes the dreaded 25-mile march. Maybe I'll hit KP or something to get me out of it.

Twenty-five miles is a long way to walk. As usual it is a beautiful day and there is a nice cool breeze blowing. Haven't much more time or room so I guess I'll close. Love...JACK

Co. G - 387 Infantry, San Luis Obispo, California

July 17, 1944 (later in the day)

Dear Mom and Dad:

Just finished sweating out a terrific line at the telegraph office. Pulled a fancy deal and managed to get way ahead of everyone else. Well, things don't look as promising. Of course, it is best I have the money for anything is apt to break at a minute's notice - but it is beginning to look as if I'll make this shipment. Jim Costakis is on it for sure. It is a shipment to POR (Port of Replacement). Guess we'll have to wait and see what happens.

I'm going to either bank the money on the post or get traveler's cheques immediately so that money will be okey. Don't worry! We have a 25-mile hike tomorrow so I've got to close and hit the sack. Love to you both.... JACK.

July 26, 1944

Dear Mom and Dad:

Took the 25 miles yesterday and it was really rough. In fact, the hike was a total of 26.8 miles. Only had one blister but I was dead tired. Took a shower and then a gang of us went over and saw Bette Davis in "Mr. Sheffington". It is quite different and she does some marvelous acting.

The letter with the $5 arrived and thanks a lot. I get paid a week from last Monday. Guess the POE list comes out today and I'm a dead cinch to be on it so I'll probably be moving again soon. I'll let you know whatever happens. Guess there is going to be 50 of us from this company leave on the next shipment and since I am the best man of the bunch how could they not help but take me? Gotta close and fall out - oh, my tired aching feet!

Love to you both...JACK

Dear Mom and Dad

July 28, 1944

Dear Mom and Dad:

Well, things are moving plenty fast. Today the big news came out and Bob Smith and I are on the list. We took our POE physical and I am fit for combat duty. Have no idea when we'll leave for POE, but the rumor is - next week. This was really sudden. There are about 40 of us from the Company. The rumor has it that we're heading for Fort Meade, Maryland. I still think I'll get a furlough before I go over, but of course everything is in such an uproar that I hardly know. All I can do is just wait and let you know as time goes by what is happening.

I hardly know what else I can tell you. Pretty soon all I'll be able to do is make inferences and you'll have to put 2 and 2 together. This whole deal may fall through but I think we'll soon make up a new combat team for the 95th Division. That too is a rumor. Lost my dog tag so I really got a nice barking out. I think they are lying around somewhere but I couldn't take the time looking for them so I reported the loss. There isn't too much more news. I'll let you know what's going on as soon as possible. Love… JACK.

July 30, 1944

Dear Mom and Dad:

Here it is another weekend and I had all good intentions of spending a very pleasant one. Took out a pass to San Francisco and left camp at noon on Saturday. Got into San Luis Obispo and found that there were no seats on the streamliner and that meant a nine-hour ride by bus. We just spent the evening in San Luis Obispo and then came back to camp at about eleven. Now I've got to stay out of the camp until tonight.

The cookies and knife arrived on Saturday. They were delicious and the knife is a beauty. Thanks a lot, Dad. That is the best one I've ever seen. It is perfect and I like it an awful lot. It's just the right length and is well balanced. I'll have to do a little work on the sheath since my ammunition belt is much wider than the ordinary belt. What I am going to do is have two holes punched then dismantle my canteen cover and use the special hooks on it so at I can hook the knife on to my belt. Then I'll salvage my canteen cover and everything will be in good shape.

The rumors are thick and fast. Looks like we'll leave around the 14th or 15th. I passed the POE physical like a breeze. They looked me over with a quick glance and said "you're okey". Am sure I'll get a furlough at POE if I don't get it here and it looks like I won't be getting any here. Everything is in a mess. As you can plainly see even I don't know what's going on so how could General Haney? By the way, I suppose you saw where General McNair got bumped off. As you remember he was at Fort Leonard Wood when I was there - in fact, he walked through with us when we ran a squad problem. I was about five feet away from him. It has also been rumored that Colonel Bender, who was our Regimental Commander when we arrived here, was killed in Normandy. Not much more news. Hope you are both fine. I'm getting tanner everyday with this California sun. Love...JACK.

August 1, 1944

Dear Mom and Dad:

Monday is gone and Tuesday is here already. Yesterday for no good reason at all I was called before the OCS Board again and I waited all afternoon to get in but didn't!! So, we had to come back last night. They had me down for Infantry OCS and I told them very frankly that wasn't what I applied for. I can't seem to talk to those birds anymore. I was really under pressure and I am not kidding. And...my answers were not exactly on the ball, either. So, I don't have to worry any more about that matter again.

Haven't heard any more about shipping or furloughs. Every night, guys leave on furlough but none of us who are shipping have been on the list. Got paid yesterday and I only got $17. They shorted me $6.75 and it looks like I can't do much about it. I was robbed!! Boy, $17 isn't even a drop in the bucket. The $100 is still intact, but I've got exactly $2 for the month after paying some guys I owed cash to. Hope my shipping orders or furlough comes soon. No more news for now. Love....JACK

August 4, 1944

Dear Mom and Dad:

Well, here I am sitting in the guard house. Yep, they finally caught up with me, again. You guessed it!... Guard duty!! I have a 24-hour post and have already walked six of my eight hours. I am slightly tired - I haven't been getting much sleep during my hours off since everyone is walking in and out.

Last Wednesday night, Bob Smith and some of the other guys who applied for OCS were called in by the CO and told that they should withdraw their application. He said they wouldn't have a chance before the division board, and if they didn't get through that board, it would go on their service record as such with no reasons stated. So, I went and asked what had happened to mine and they said I would either have to appear for a physical or go before the division board. I'm completely reamed royally because if you haven't been with this division for at least a year they just look and laugh. So, I'll appear before the Board and let them smirk, and then take a nice black mark on my form 20 (army decora) as not being able to make the grade for OCS. I frankly don't care. If I make it okey - if I don't, okey. I'm disgusted with the whole lousy set up!!! If I only could do a better job on the oral presentation I might stand a 10% chance, but I was jittery as the devil during the last one.

The whole division is restricted this weekend. From what we can gather, The Old Man (that's the head honcho on the base) got a little disgusted with us. Oh well, I wasn't going any place anyway. Furthermore, I'm due for KP. It has been nine weeks since the last time I had that assignment. Almost time for me to eat and then go on duty so I'd better close. By the way if you want to see a good movie I'd suggest that you see: "Mr. Winkle Goes to War". It is really good. Gotta close. Love...JACK.

Co. G - 387 Infantry, San Luis Obispo, California

August 9, 1944

Dear Mom and Dad:

I take my pen in hand and here goes. This life is beginning to relieve me of my good humor! We are doing things which have absolutely no rhyme or reason. Most of us are going crazy. If we don't ship out of here soon they'll have maniacs on their hands. Right now, about five of us are sitting here playing a combination of a tonette, ocarina, and three harmonicas. That's quite a combination. It shows how our mentality is weakening.

Got your letter with the buck enclosed. Thanks, Mom. I've had to use some of the dollar because I only got paid $17 and I was a few bucks in debt from last month. I've still got plenty in case of a furlough. Rumors are still hot about shipping but nothing specific. I hope we get out of here by August 20th. No kidding this same stuff over and over is terribly monotonous.

The mail situation has really been good the last few days. Have gotten anywhere from four to six letters each day. I pulled a sly one today. Instead of carrying my own rifle I borrowed some guy's who was on KP and used it. We were late getting in tonight and we didn't have time to clean our rifles too well. But as for me -the smooth critter that I was - I picked up my own rifle which hadn't been used and was clean, and therefore got commended on a good inspection. Wait until the other guy sees his rifle!!! I'm really getting to be a shrewd character without a doubt. Another 18 months and I'll probably make Pic or General of the Guard House.

Two of the guys from our hut are now taking training as M.P.'s for beach patrol and will not rejoin our outfit until we establish our so-called beachhead when and if we ever start amphibious training. If this stuff ever gets underway it will mean a cruise (10 days) and we'll establish our beachhead down near San Diego. Not much else in the way of news. Send me a few airmails when you can. I can use them. All my love... JACK

Dear Mom and Dad

August 23, 1944

Dear Mom and Dad:

Half the week gone already and seven of the boys shipped yesterday to join a new outfit down in Arkansas. The rumor is that there is another shipment on Friday so maybe I'll be on that one. Have heard absolutely nothing new, however. Yesterday, we had the same old stuff. We've been doing a lot of work with mines and booby traps. In fact, that's about all we have been doing. I got an easy detail yesterday afternoon cleaning up a theater on the post. Saw three movies and then worked 15 minutes straightening the place up.

Had an inspection of our field equipment last night so we are either going to ship or start the amphibious training. I was on fire guard last night - naturally - so I got plenty of letters written. I am rather glad I did get restricted - now I can catch up on my correspondence. Rumor has it that there's a 25 mile march on Friday so I am keeping my fingers crossed that I'll get out of it. They are purely a waste of time and effort.

There's just no news at all and I am not yet quite awake since its only 6:45 A.M. Guess I had better close for now. Will try and pick up some news during the day. Love. JACK.

August 24, 1944

Dear Mom and Dad:

Here I am sitting in the room "on call" in case the high and mighty decides to see if I skipped out of fire guard detail. I am going to catch up on my letters again, if possible. Well, tomorrow I go before the Divisional OCS Board again. This is really it!! It's all a big joke anyway because even if I do get recommended I'll probably ship before I get called and when you're at POE that takes preference over anything including OCS. However, I'll make a good appearance just for the record if nothing else.

I should ship out of here VERY soon. Jim Costakis, who is in E Company had already had his laundry pulled out and he thinks we'll

Co. G - 387 Infantry, San Luis Obispo, California

leave late this week. You see, he was on that same list that I was on for POE physicals. So, we should by all rights ship at the same time. My guess is that it will be Fort George Meade, Maryland. I'll try and call you before I leave if at all possible. When and if I do ship out and get to my POE you'll have to start reading between the lines because I'll have to watch what I write just in case they start censoring.

Today we worked on mines and booby traps all day and ran the obstacle course. The Chemistry Warfare Dept. also put on a good demonstration. Haven't seen George Cassat for ages so I don't know whether he is on shipment or not. The last I heard was that we had been placed on a list. Guess I'd better drop him a note one of these nights.

As you can plainly see everything in general around here is in a daze. We know we'll ship out soon but don't know when. I hope something breaks soon. Just no news – good or bad. All I can say is that I am spending a very sane and sober week in the company area, thanks to Capt. Cuddeback. Will let you know how I made out with the OCS Board. Love...JACK

August 25, 1944

Dear Mom and Dad:

Here I am waiting to go out on a night problem. General Ben (Yoo - Hoo) dear is on catp and everyone is looking sharp. Tomorrow, he'll be nosing around and then on Saturday there will be a huge divisional review. Well, I went before the OCS Board and it was a total joke. Everything was fine - Major Warren from chemical Warfare; Capt. Jack Bosell from the Calvary; and another swell Major made up the Board. I was the last to go in and they treated me just very kindly. I really was on the ball and did okey. I missed some of their questions, but on the whole, I did alright. In fact, I think I would almost get approval to go on but I'll probably be at POE before I could ship out for OCS.

I signed my pay book and I'm definitely on shipping. We should leave in about four days and I think it will be to Fort Meade. I should know for sure soon. Smitty (Bob Smith) isn't on the list unfortunately,

Dear Mom and Dad

but a lot of my other buddies are. I just hope we won't get split up when we arrive wherever we go. I guess I should have started sooner on the OCS deal as I might have had it materialize. I did make a good appearance before this last Board so it should go down on my records as an asset rather than a liability.

(Next morning). Had the night problem and it was a farce. Old "Yoo Hoo" Lear, the general who was inspecting was around nosing into everything, but he didn't get to our company. Brig. General Partridge of the 97th came around, though, and stumbled on some of the prone bodies of those still sleeping. Probably will call you on Sunday if at all possible. No more news and I'd better get this mailed. All my love...JACK

August 26, 1944

Dear Mom and Dad:

Took a quick physical today and got some new dog tags. Looks like we'll be heading for Fort Meade, Maryland, about Monday or Tuesday (2-3 days). Will send a box of stuff home that you can put in storage. There are some letters, field manuals, and my other set of dog tags. Also, one of those new language manuals - this one on Japanese. I even included my swimming trunks which I probably won't need for quite a while.

Sure, seems funny to think that I'll soon be heading overseas. We've been kidding about it so long and working for it for so many months. Now it seems unbelievable that the time has finally come. Have a divisional review this morning which will no doubt be a mess as usual. I've never seen one that hasn't been a mess. I guess General "Yoo Hoo" Lear has gone now. I don't see the officers shaking in their shoes anymore.

Looks like I'll spend the last weekend here in camp. I think I could get a pass but I might as well stay in and get my equipment in order. Will try and call this Sunday if at all possible. I should know about everything by then. No more news at all that I can think of. Am feeling great and I am already for a nice long train ride and then the seven seas. Will write tomorrow and also will call if possible. Love to you both......JACK

Chapter 10

Co. B - 3rd Bn - 1st Repl. Regt. AGF Repl. Depot No. 1 Ft. George G. Meade, Maryland

(September 5, 1944 - September 15, 1944)

At long last the day of reckoning arrived. Most of us were able to leave the base on the weekend prior to boarding the troop train for our trip across the United States and I can still remember "the morning after" although the night becomes a little hazy. Apparently, a group of us decided to celebrate and celebrate we did with a fantastic mixture of drinks. Somewhere along the line one of our group suggested that we have a couple of rounds of Singapore Slings (a beautiful drink made with sloe gin and grenadine) and then top them off with Boiler Makers. That did the job - particularly after a variety of other drinks.

    I can recall that on the way back to the base a couple of us were pretty sick - we should have been nearly dead. The next morning, we not only hoped we were dead, but looked like death warmed over. Our clothes gave the appearance that we had slept in them. The truth of the matter was that we had. However, after several cups of black coffee and some breakfast we were able to saddle up our duffle bags and board the troop train for a six-day trip across the country.

    Unfortunately, troop trains were not given the highest priority, and hence we had a long and hot ride the first couple of days. One of the biggest thrills came when we pulled into Denver. We had a couple of

Dear Mom and Dad

hours to get off the train and roam around the station. This was an interesting coincidence since I had traveled in and out of Denver a few times while stationed at Ft. Collins and Colorado State College. However, the big thrill came when they hooked three of the cars from our troop train on to the back of the Burlington Zephyr - the high-speed streamliner which ran between Denver and Chicago.

This was one of the wildest rides I believe I had ever had on the surface. The Zephyr in those days hit speeds of up to 100 miles per hour on the flat surface that ran from Northern Colarado and on through Nebraska. You can't imagine the amount of sway in those old troop cars we are riding in. To top it off, we were either shooting craps (dice) or trying to play poker during most of the trip. Frequently, the dice and cards would either shift which created many arguments on who won with what cards or on what roll of the dice.

From Chicago to Ft. Meade, Maryland, the train ride was much saner and more sensible. In fact, going from coast to coast aboard a troop train was an experience which as I look back was worth the price of admission. As it turned out it was the only time I made a trip from one coast to the other by train.

September 3, 1944

Dear Mom and Dad:

Just got through calling and I am sorry you couldn't hear me very well. I could hear you both fine. Guess the phone I was talking was a little dead. We pulled in at 3.00 AM and slept till about 5 AM before getting the train. We sat for the whole morning and we took a physical test in the afternoon. Then we went to the joint where you settle all your money affairs and allotments, etc. I now have a bond allotment of $ 18.75 and a class E allotment which will come in Dad's name also for $20.75 and it will come in the form of a check monthly. Just stick that in my bank account and I'll try and build up a little savings till this war is finally over. This will build up about $20x9 a year and $300 worth of

Co. B - 3rd Bn - 1st Repl. Regt., Ft. George G. Meade, Maryland

bonds which ain't to be okay. I get 20% increase for overseas pay which gives me $60.

We were split up quite a bit when we got assigned. Jim Castelis and a buddy of mine from G Company are with me. The funniest thing is it is the same company who shipped from Madison with me and who just caught back up with me again. The Army is really quite a meeting place.

Anyway, we are heading for a new and really great and exciting adventure and all we need is a little luck and a dead – eye which your Jacknny has!!!

Bye for now, my love to Mom and Dad… Jack.

September 4, 1944

Dear Mom and Dad:

We have just entered the south eastern tip of Colorado and we are now heading straight into the old Rockies. Believe it or not, we have three engines on our train. Two in front and one on the rear so it must be quite a climb. I imagine we will see some very beautiful scenery. So far, the trip has been okay. There are no card games and so most of the day is spent reading and writing.

We lost a guy back the way yesterday, so now we have train guards. Before, we could get off the train to buy stuff, but now there are designated men in the cars and the only ones to get off the train to get stuff. Just before we left camp we got a word that a brother of one of the buddies here was killed in Normandy. The worst thing was that he had to call home that night to tell his folks. Seems like some people are certainly hit hard. Guess, we have been mightily lucky so far and so far, as I'm concerned that's the way we're going to stay. I'm positive we'll go to France and by the time we get there everything should be fairly well cleaned up so I'm not worried much. Just they don't ship us to Burma.

This old train is really working hard to get up the mountain. We seem to be hardly moving. The scenery is getting much nicer too and this is a sign we're touching Colorado. Yep, here's the state line and we are now in Colorado. I am really getting hungry. Not much news so I guess I'll close this for now. Everything is okay and don't worry. I'll write soon. All my love to you guys… Jack.

September 5, 1944

Dear Mom and Dad:

Just came out of a period of military censorship so I guess I might as well start watching what I say for it is much better doing it that way then having these letters all cut up. I still have a touch of a cold or hay fever. I can't decide which it is.

Last night Harold Dobbins and I had tickets for the Washington Redskins vs. Green Bay Packers football game, but we got a late start and didn't get to see too much of it. We looked over downtown Baltimore and then came back to camp about eleven. That is the dirtiest town I think I've ever seen. It is filthy and some of the bars on the strip were plenty wild. Nothing like that in quiet old Dubuque, Iowa.

The food has only been fair - however, the PX's have been open at noon so I usually drink a pint of milk and eat some cupcakes and then come back for chow. As yet I haven't gotten any mail but probably will very shortly. I'll be having mail chasing me all over the world very shortly I imagine. I want to get into Washington so I can send some money home after I get paid. I'll get it off as soon as possible. Think I'll call between eight and nine my time either Thursday or Friday night. If it doesn't come through on Thursday by 8:30 P.M. then you'll know something came up and I'll call Friday.

Saw all the boys today. We are all together but in different companies. If I get a weekend pass this week I am going to get to New York. Anyway, I'll have to wait and see what happens. Can't think of anything else right now. Will write when I get some news. All my love…JACK

Co. B - 3rd Bn - 1st Repl. Regt., Ft. George G. Meade, Maryland

September 13, 1944

Dear Mom and Dad:

Got your two letters this noon. The one from Washington and the one from Harrisburg. Sure, am glad you got a roomette. That will make the trip so much easier and this much nicer. Well, today, I woke up and I could hardly see. I have had headaches but this one took the cake. Now I know what you mean, Dad, when you say you have a headache. This one was strictly sinus and it felt like the walls of my sinus were about ready to explode. I went to chow and all I could down was a cup of black coffee so I went back and slept for two hours. Took two aspirins and pulled out of it. By noon I was starved and feeling like a million dollars.

Sat down in a small nickel-dime poker game to kill some time and picked up a cool seven bucks before I cashed in and left. So now I will have a few more bucks to spend if and when I need it. Have played about two straight hours of ping pong. No one had beaten me until just a few minutes ago. Now I am catching up on my letters. It rained all day so far - really dismal outside - the music is good here in the day room so I don't mind.

Have an AGF clothing inspection tomorrow and I have a hunch, we'll leave late tomorrow night. Don't know a thing definite, of course. Last night, I had nothing to do so I went down and saw "Atlantic City." It was a musical and was really pretty good. You might enjoy it. It revives some of the good old songs - "Bye the Sea - By the Sea" - "In the Merry Month of June" and others. Tonight, I may go down and see the movie of "Arsenic and Old Lace". I hear it is a riot.

Got a letter from Dick Bodine yesterday. He has a delay in route and then goes on to California. I feel sure that he'll soon be at Ft. Meade, but he'll go over as a radio operator which is an okey assignment. I forgot to leave this picture for the scrapbook so it is enclosed. The guy is Stuart Eubank. Also, there is a picture, I believe in the field manual of five of my old pals taken in the "Hollywood Jail". If it isn't there I'll see if it is around some place. There's just no more news for now so I'll close. Will write tomorrow if possible. Love...JACK.

Chapter 11

Camp Miles Standish, Mass., Port of Embarkation

(September 16, 1944 - September 23, 1944)

From Fort Meade, Maryland, a large contingent of us was transported to Camp Miles Standish, Massachusetts, which was designated as our official staging area for our POE (Port of Embarkation). From this camp we were to be transported to Boston Harbor and boarded on whatever ship would take us across the Atlantic Ocean. Each night most of us were able to secure passes into Boston for our last fling in the United States. It was about an hour and a half bus ride from the camp into the South Station where we made our connections to return to camp.

Needless to say, we had several enjoyable nights hitting various clubs and bars in the Boston area. Of course, the Old Opera House on Sculley Square was one of the popular places as well as the "combat zone where you could see Gypsy Rose Lee, Belle Starr and many of the other outstanding "strippers" of the day. Also, each night at approximately midnight I would call the folks from the Boston South Station to let them know that I was still in the States. Our parting comment was that if I didn't call the next evening they would know I was on my way.

One of my last letters written from the United States before shipping overseas is featured below. It provides some indication of the difficulty in communicating under the restrictions of censorship.

Camp Miles Standish, Mass., Port of Embarkation

September 18, 1944

Dear Mom and Dad:

Just a note to tell you I am okey. We were given passes last night so Dick Kline and I went into town together. We spent a very sober evening - just in case you were wondering. We had a great time. The extent of passes here is (Censored). Got some mail today - your letter from Chicago; also, a letter from Grandpa and from Fred Sackas. I guess that Grandma and Grandpa will learn sooner or later that I am going overseas.

I should write them, but when they see that APO and censor seal they'll probably really start worrying. Maybe, they won't realize what it means. Anyway, I'll write them and just avoid saying anything about foreign duty. Fred Sackas says that they've broken up all the gang at San Luis Obispo, and he thinks that he will be making sergeant. Not much else. It is hard to figure out what to say. Will write soon. Love...
JACK

Author's note: Finally, the day arrived and we were trucked to Boston Harbor where we boarded the famous south Pacific luxury liner the Mariposa (A 1 son Line ship). This was one of the faster liners of the day with the result that we were established to run the gauntlet from Boston to Liverpool without naval escort. We made the trip in 5 days without incident although on several occasions we saw a few US destroyers and other ships which were checking on us because they have received an alert of German submarine activity. In addition, we also saw some bombers and other aircraft which all proved to be friendly. Needless to say, security at night was very tight on lights and smoking on the deck.

Probably, one of the most unusual events that happened during the crossing occurred on the second day when I ran into Tom E. Nacos, a high school friend, who was a member of the Merchant Marine crew. From that point on, I spent a great deal of my time down in crew quarters where I ate like a king and enjoyed the company of those who were

Dear Mom and Dad

responsible for running the Mariposa. Tom would leave a complete change of clothes for me in a ship's closet on my deck. I would change into these clothes and go on down stairs to crew quarters. Then I'd come on back to my deck, change back into my OD's and meet my obligations at bed and other troop checks. This added so much to the whole trip and was an experience long to be remembered. Also, I was the envy of my army buddies.

On the morning of the fifth day we landed in Liverpool, England, and spent the next several hours getting unloaded and boarding a train for the purpose of transporting us to a holding camp somewhere in southern England near the city of Bath. We arrived early in the evening and marched from the train through a small town and out to the camp area where we were told we would spend anywhere from three to six days. Fortunately, we arrived in time for dinner and then bedded down in large tents. It was damp and very quickly we all began to understand what they meant by typical weather conditions in England. Needless to say, we were all pretty tired after a strenuous day of loading and unloading, traveling and trying to get settled in a new camp.

The next day was cloudy with intermittent showers and was spent checking our gear and in general inquiring around camp as to the procedures and what we might expect for the next few days. We were permitted to go into town but time was severely limited. On the second night, we were all bedded down by about eleven o'clock. A couple of hours later several tents were called out and told to get everything packed and to get ready to move out within an hour. Of course, in the army everything means "hurry up and wait" and so instead of one hour it was closer to two hours. In any event, we marched over to a group of waiting trucks and were taken to another station where we eventually boarded a train and headed for Southampton, England.

Upon arrival at Southampton we were then moved into a staging area near one of the piers and from there loaded on a ship to be transported across the English Channel to France. Our particularly ship brought us within 500 yards of Omaha Beach. Each of us had to go

Camp Miles Standish, Mass., Port of Embarkation

over the side of the ship on rope ladders to board an LST (Landing craft used for combat to get the troops on to the beach heads) which would then take us into shore. On this particular day the English Channel was extremely rough which made boarding the LST very hazardous. In the process one of the men slipped and fell while going down the rope ladder and was crushed between the ship and the LST which I was boarding. Not a very pleasant way to end one's life and military career!

Climbing up the hill at Omaha Beach was an experience in itself since all around us we could still see signs of the initial invasion. Knocked out tanks, LST's, jeeps, and half trucks are all over the place. Everyone was warned about potential land mines if they happened to stray off the road or established trails. We marched inland about five miles until we reached a camp where we re-grouped, got hot food and bedded down for the night. On the next day, we boarded a convoy of trucks and headed out on the famous "Red Ball Express" which was one of the major supply lines in September of 1944. The weather was miserable and most of the day was spent driving in the rain. It was cold and damp and far from a pleasant trip.

We arrived at another camp near the outskirts of Paris where in the mud and rain we stopped and after chow prepared to get some rest. As I recall, we spent three days waiting for further orders. During that period, we were permitted to leave the camp to see some of the sights and participate in local activities. I did not get into Paris during this period but was able to spend a day and evening in Fontainebleau where I saw the beautiful castle and had some fine French cooking. From this camp we faced another new experience and that was riding the infamous "40 and 8 cars" on the French Railway System. The "40 and 8 car" derived its name from the fact that these box cars could transport 40 men and 8 horses. This probably dated back to the World War I days rather than World War II since we were much more mechanized.

By this time, it was beginning to snow and the weather turned very cold. The soldiers in my boxcar found wood and anything else to burn at every stop we made. A constant fire was maintained in a large oil drum. One of these drums, could be found in almost every boxcar. You had to work your way to the heat periodically to try and warm up. Otherwise, you wrapped yourself in your own blankets in a corner hoping to stay as warm as possible. These were the conditions that the infantry had to live under so often during war. Very quickly, you began to realize and appreciate what the infantry has to go through versus many of the other branches of the service.

We finally got to Liege, Belgium, and were placed in a staging area while the powers to be were deciding which units) needed replacements. After a couple of days - during which we were able to get into Liege for the evening - we boarded trucks and were then transported up to the front lines. The following represents some of the letters written after my arrival in England and then on through France. I have no idea where they might have been mailed but they do provide some idea of me on the spot appraisal of the situation recognizing that censorship of mail was in effect. Some of the materials that are covered in these letters probably duplicate my author's note; however, I felt that my uncensored version of the trials and tribulations of moving from the SS Mariposa to a holding area in England and then through France to Belgium to the front lines would be of interest.

Tuesday, October 3, 1944—somewhere in France

Dear Mom and Dad:

As you can plainly see I have again changed location. This is getting to be a joke - is fact, this whole war is seeming more and more like a total gag. The stay in England was good. I wish we could have stuck around long enough to set passes and see some of the sights for it looked like an interesting old country. The people are even quaint.

I caught right on to the money exchange - excuse, please - I mean the monetary system. Some of the money is really funny looking. The pound note and the 10-shilling note are very different from ours. The first night we were there, I went to a PX or a facsimile of one and had a cup of tea and a sandwich. The gal behind the counter mumbled

Camp Miles Standish, Mass., Port of Embarkation

something and I asked her to repeat. She mumbled out the price the second time and I still couldn't understand her, so I gave her a handful of change and told her to take what she wanted. All she took was three pence which is a nickel in our money.

Got my new rifle yesterday and zeroed it in that afternoon. It is a beauty and works like a charm. On my last five rounds for the final zero, I had a beautiful shot group of four right in the bullseye - the fifth was a little low. By the way, in case you've seen some of those movies showing guys boarding ship with those enormous packs - that's no joke!! Everything we own or need is carried on our backs in our full field pack. They weigh close to 90 pounds.

George Morin got separated from us so now Dick Kline and I are the only two guys together. I haven't heard from George Cassat for quite a while. I imagine that he is over here somewhere. The English have many peculiarities. I had an odd thing happened today. We stopped enroute to the post and a girl was selling cakes so I asked her the price. It was three pence and all I had was a shilling and she had no change so I said just give me what you have there and we'll call it square. Whereupon she immediately climbed on my frame with a sharp tongue and said: "I don't take charity from anyone." I about fell over. What a people!! One could learn to like them a great deal. What I've seen of them so far makes me believe that they're okey.

We were paid last night in Francs. So now I have a fistful of French money. By the way, I sent home, last night, the following: 5 Pounds = $20.15; 20 Shillings = $4.03; and 350 Francs = $7.00; for a total of $31.18. I don't know if that is exactly it, but you'll receive about $30. I doubt if I'll get a chance to buy any Christmas gifts so I wish you two would use it for anything you want.

Received some mail today. Most of it was written around September 18-19th. I don't know when the mail will catch up to me again. It is really hard telling. I sure am seeing the world. All I can say is that this is a real experience. Now all I have to do is get back okey and I'm sure I will. I've got the brains. confidence and guts - now all I need is a little luck and I'm

Dear Mom and Dad

all set. I think fate is about ready to see things my way for a change - so I'm far from worried. No more news for now. Love to you……JACK.

P.S. Check my address on the outside in case there might be any changes.

October 9, 1944

Dear Mom and Dad:

Before I forget I want to list some junk you can send me. Try and get me some fur lined gloves - or any kind of lined ones that will give plenty of warmth. I think they are about size 9, but anyway make sure that they are at least one size smaller than dad's and possibly two. Also send some good heavy socks. I think about six pair will be sufficient. Make sure they are ankle socks. I don't want the long boot socks. If you want to send anything in the food line make it candy of any kind and cookies which are boxed rather than trying to send any homemade stuff.

The sun is shining which is really unusual as we are all trying to dry out. Got a chance to go to the PX yesterday. We are rationed to 7 packs of cigarettes a week and 4 candy bars. Tried some German cigars which are not rationed and they weren't bad at all. Now that we are no longer eating "C" rations the chow is okey and you should see the appetite. Man, I could eat any family out of house and home.

Most of the guys that we are with haven't been in the army too long and are ROTC commandoes. So most of us who were with a division are beginning to get disgusted at being referred to as such. Some of these people ought to wise up around here, but then that is the army. Where is Milt Kapp - or do they know at this time? No more news for now. Love to you both...JACK

October 14, 1944

Dear Mom and Dad:

Here is your "sad sack" son once again taking his pen in hand. This is going to be a little hard to read since the V-mail supplies didn't come

Camp Miles Standish, Mass., Port of Embarkation

in today and I am running a little short. It is a great day today...the sun is fine and warm and my stomach is full - at least for the next 30 minutes. Even horse meat hits the spot these days...excuse me, I mean the SPAM. The stuff they call Spam here is slightly different than what we get at home. This stuff is more like a hash and made in such a way that anything - and I mean anything - can be thrown in. Why I even found some wieners in mine last night. Of our last four meals, we have had Spam for three of them. We had eggs for breakfast, and if you ever get a Chance, try some of those dehydrated potatoes. At first, I thought I was getting some of the good old Iowa corn - man was I fooled when it turned out to be potatoes.

Got a couple of gloves and a hard ball this afternoon and played some catch. Sure, did feel mighty good to play that old American game again. Went to see a G.I. movie the other night. The news is on the scarce side so I guess I'll close for now. Love…....JACK.

Jack at Mount Vernon.

Chapter 12

Co. K - 60th Infantry - 9th Division - APO #9
c/o Postmaster - New York, N.Y.

(October 18, 1944 - December 26, 1944)

I can recall the odd feeling when about six of us were dropped off in the woods and told that "the Company Command Post was about 100 yards down that path". We moved out and reported to the Commanding Officer's tent where our orders were reviewed.

In my case there was a great sigh of relief on the part of the CO's right-hand man. When he looked at my records he turned to the Captain (Commanding Officer) and said: "Man, are we lucky! Dauner is expert in firing the BAR. With that he handed me a BAR and said: "Dauner, you better clean that up good. We lost our BAR man this morning because this damn thing wouldn't fire!" With that three of us were led to the first platoon's position on the front lines. As we crawled to our respective fox holes a few rounds were fired in our direction from a German pillbox which sat about 150 yards away.

My foxhole mate was a guy in his early 40's. He was in extremely poor physical condition and a real basket case. Not only that but he had failed to take precautions against trench foot with the result that his feet were so swollen he could hardly get his combat boots off. He was scared to death - married and worried about his wife and kids. At about two o'clock in the afternoon the word was passed to all of us that

Co. K - 60th Infantry - 9th Division - APO #9

in one hour we should begin to start firing at anything that moved over on the German side. The objective was to draw out their small arms fire; then, we would lob in some mortars and ultimately get some of the big guns in action so our planes could spot the location of some of their 88's and other weapons that were giving us a lot of trouble.

Well, it turned out to be quite an experience, and I must admit I thought it was great sport. I picked an opening on the German pillbox which was about 100 yards from our position as my target and just kept firing the old BAR right on the mark. Obviously, someone recognized that an automatic weapon was being used over in our direction because all of a sudden, we began to get some pretty heavy barrages. My poor foxhole mate was fit to be tied and spent most of his time down at the bottom of our hole.

After about a half hour of this type of warfare everything quieted down and we began to survey what had been learned. For me, it was a new experience and I did recognize that a person could be killed in this war. The field kitchen provided hot food and before darkness we would slip back to headquarters to get fed. Our cooks were good ones and did a great job in keeping us with decent food. We would fill our mess kits and coffee cups and then head back to the foxhole so the next group could eat.

Darkness set in early and the password was provided as a precaution against anyone who might try and slip behind our lines. We agreed to stand a three-hour watch in our hole and my foxhole buddy said he would take the first shift. I had just dropped off when he reached down and put his hand over my mouth and whispered that there were four German soldiers crawling toward us about 50 feet from the foxhole. I begrudgingly got up and to my surprise he was right. He was shaking like an aspen leaf in the breeze and wanted to know what to do.

To make a long story short I fumbled around with the only German I could think of and said: "Ein soldats forward!" With that, they all started to come toward us so I repeated myself in a very loud and authoritative voice. In the meantime, I told my foxhole buddy to grab

Dear Mom and Dad

a hand grenade, and be ready to pull the pin if they continued to move toward us. I had already done likewise so I figured we could put them out of commission and at the same time have an opportunity to fire a few rounds at point blank range.

Fortunately, the first soldier came forward and we grabbed him. He was unarmed and wanted to give up. We called for help from neighboring foxholes and one by one we captured all four of the "Supermen". Actually, they were Poles who had been recruited to fight for the German army and were happy to come across the lines to us. The tragic side of the story occurred the next morning when a staff sergeant from one of the other platoons volunteered to take the prisoners back to Company headquarters for interrogation. After marching them back about 200 yards we heard four shots and learned later that because of his hate for German soldiers he had shot them in cold blood.

October 22, 1944

Dear Mom and Dad:

Here it is Sunday already and another week is over. I just had breakfast and let me tell you, your one and only son is right on the ball as a cook. Of course, it all boils down to heating up a can of rations, but Jack R. Dauner does it to perfection.

I am afraid this paper is a little dirty, but no other was available at the present time so that's the reason. Yesterday, was really nice for a change. There's nothing like a nice day to make one feel in "tip top" shape. Last night it was also nice. The nights over here seem slightly damper and chiller than back home.

A couple of Jerry's (German soldiers) walked over this morning and surrendered. It happens frequently. Yet, the war goes on. Most of them would much prefer ending this thing, but the S.S. Troops keep their bayonet too far in the German soldier's backs. One can never tell what will happen. They might give in tomorrow or they might hold out for another year.

Co. K - 60th Infantry - 9th Division - APO #9

Everything is okey over here. I am feeling fine and aside from being hungry right now things are alright. Guess I'll eat a can of vegetable stew which is one of my favorite rations. Give my regards to everyone. All my love......JACK.

October 25, 1944

Dear Mom and Dad:

A new day has dawned and I've just finished what might be called breakfast. Meat and vegetable stew and some hot cocoa. Well, the cocoa was appropriate anyway. Things have been pretty quiet the last day or so. Aside from having a sniper directly across the way taking some pot shots at me every now and then, there has been very little excitement. Last night, it was really beautiful out here "on the Western Front" for a while. The moon was up and very bright and it really illuminated the whole area. That was the first time I've seen the moon in a long time. I hardly knew what it was when it came up.

Dick Kline walked over here to see me a few minutes ago and I set him up with a little breakfast. My other buddy in this company is still in the Aid Station getting treatment on his feet. Does that sound familiar, Dad? By the way, how are your feet these days? All I can say, Dad, is that it is a good thing you were in the navy during the last war and not in the good old infantry.

There is a possibility that we may get back to a rest camp for a few days. Everyone is keeping their fingers crossed and I am sure no exception. Am low on news of any kind so I guess I had better close. Will write soon.

Love to you both.... JACK

October 28, 1944

Dear Mom and Dad:

Well, we're out of the front lines for a few days and are now in a rest area. Sure, feels good not to have to worry about someone taking a pot-shot at you. I have my tent pitched and am sitting in front of a nice warm fire. And have we ever been getting the chow. The food we get here is better than any that I ever got back in any of the camps in the States.

We've had some of the best hot cakes I've ever eaten other than yours, mom. Last night, we even had some steak. Then we went to a movie and saw "Standing Room Only." It was really good. You can't imagine how great it is to get off the front line and away from the "shooting war". The only thing that gets a little disgusting is seeing all of these rear guard "commandoes" wearing combat boots and other equipment that is supposed to be for the guys who are up front fighting the battles. No more news. Just wanted you know I was okey and not in a foxhole. It would be nice if I could spend another week right here in this rest area. Love...JACK.

October 29, 1944

Dear Mom and Dad:

Here is Sunday and Dick Kline and I started the sabbath off I by going to church services. Even attended communion and it really felt good to hear a sermon and sing some of the old familiar hymns. Sunday dinner was good and we got our candy and cigarette rations, even got a big cigar which hit the spot. Last night, they provided us with a real treat – some old good German beer. So, all in all, they're taking good care of us.

Have been working on my rifle all afternoon. Even washed every piece in hot soapy water, if you can imagine your son getting so eager. Frankly, I don't know what got into me. The last time I ever did that was back in the 97th Division when we had a big ordinance inspection. Had a good hot shower and a change of clothes yesterday so I feel like a new man. Almost look like a human being again. It's about time for chow and I've got to get in line so I'll have a chance to go through the line for seconds. I think I am getting a reputation around here as being a "chow hound".

Co. K - 60th Infantry - 9th Division - APO #9

Hope everything is okey at home. I'm fine and in fact I couldn't be better. Even have some money in my pocket - $8 and no way to spend it. Poker games are even nil! Not much else to report so I'll close. Love to you both...JACK

Monday, October 30, 1944

Dear Mom and Dad:

Just had myself a nice big meal with seconds on everything, so I'll take time out and write a quick note to you. It is foggy out today and really pretty chilly. I sure hope that winter hasn't decided to set in so soon. There is a good chance that we may all be issued sleeping bags of some variety or another and so we're all keeping our fingers crossed.

This makes almost 22 months in the army for me - or have you been counting them, too. Went to a show last night. It was "This is the Life". Not too bad - not too good - but it was something from the good old USA, and that's all that really counts. I've been planning on writing every other letter on stationary but I haven't been able to get any air mails so it is no use. Guess you will have to put up with V-mails and like it. These are still in my own handwriting even if they don't look like a letter.

Have been wondering if my bonds and allotment for my bank account have been coming though. Also, if the money I sent you from England ever arrived. There was approximately $32 in various types of currency. No more news nor room on this V-mail so I better quit. Hope you're both fine. Love....JACK.

November 3, 1944

Dear Mom and Dad:

Guess what! Your son was called upon to do some culinary duties today. It was a good deal and I've been doing nothing but eating as usual. KP is somewhat unusual up here, but occasionally they do need people and I got the call. I'm not kicking though since I am missing a rifle inspection. Well, the miracle has happened. Your son has finally

Dear Mom and Dad

been promoted. At the rate I am going I might be a third Lieutenant in the Underground Balloon Corps by the end of the war. Anyway, they tell me that you can start writing Pfc (private First Class) on my mail. I forgot to on this letter so I'll do it on the next one. They say the first stripe always takes the longest - 22 months...hmmm. Cut out the laughing - that doesn't mean I can't make my first million by the time I am 25 providing I ever get out of the army. Hope you are both fine and that the war is over by the time you get this. Love...JACK.

November 7, 1944

Dear Mom and Dad:

Sorry I haven't written for a few days, but I've simply had no opportunity whatsoever. Right now, I am lying on my shelter writing this by a home-made candle. I just found out that it was okey to tell you what division I am in. It's the old good 9th Infantry Division in case you haven't already figured it out from the APO number. The division really has a great record. It started out in Africa in Casablanca; then to Sicily and finally they landed in France on D+4. So, if you see anything about the 9th Division - that's my outfit.

A bunch of us got the combat infantrymen's medal which means an extra $10 per month in pay. Also, I can wear a gold star on our European Theater of Operations (ETO) ribbon. But then those are the least of a guy's worries. The main thing is to get back home. What I wouldn't give to jump into a good steaming tub of hot water and just soak. That's my idea of luxury, now. Everything is fine over here and will remain as such I assume so please don't worry. Will write when I can. All my love...JACK.

November 16, 1944

Dear Mom and Dad:

This is just a note to let you know I am okey. Haven't had a chance to write for a few days - that is the reason you haven't gotten any letters.

Co. K - 60th Infantry - 9th Division - APO #9

This is really tough writing. My hands are on the cold side and I am juggling this on my knee. I hope you can read it okey. The snow is really beautiful around these parts and if I were home I'd say it was perfect. Got paid the other day but believe that I'll hang on to it since it wasn't much. There is no news as I can't write whatever is happening here. Just wanted to let you know everything was okey. I am feeling fine. Love......JACK.

November 17, 1944

Dear Mom and Dad:

Just had myself a good shower and some hot chow so I really feel great. The shower wasn't in a building - just an improvised tent but the water was hot and we got a change of clothes and I'm not kicking. This mail situation has me going. I got that one letter a few days ago and since then nothing. When it all gets here it will probably take me a week to read it. I'm keeping my fingers crossed that some will come in tonight.

No doubt, you are wondering just what your son is doing these days. First, I write about seeing action and next I talk about showers and hot chow and like I'm having the time of my life. I wish I could tell you the story, but I can't. All I can say is that I am absolutely okey and everything is fine so just don't worry. Must close now - hope you two are fine. Love...JACK

November 22, 1944

Dear Mom and Dad:

The day before Thanksgiving and believe me it is really a bad one as far as the weather. The European continent must get more rain than any other part of the world. I finally hit the jack-pot on mail yesterday. I got a bundle of about 25 letters - one as late as November 10th. That was a V-mail and that made it in eleven days. There were letters from just about everyone. One was from Herman Eschen and I learned that

Dear Mom and Dad

his brother, Carl, is in the same division as me but a different regiment so anything he says in his letters might coincide with my activities.

You asked what Army I was in. Well it is the First. Your guess on that was good, but as to position you weren't on the beam. Anyway, that is the $64 question and is definitely classified as a military secret so it is thumbs down on answering. You wouldn't want your roving son to wire you someday to meet me at Leavenworth, would you? Time to fall out and grab some chow. Hope your both okey - I am! Please send me some candy and edibles. All my love...JACK

November 26, 1944

Dear Mom and Dad:

Sunday and after a good breakfast of pancakes I went to church services with Dick Kline and a bunch of the buys. There was really a big group there. Then back for chow and now a little time to knock off a few letters. Mail call should be in a few minutes and 1 am expecting a mess of it since I haven't gotten any for a couple of days. They said that there was really a lot of it that came in for the regiment which sounds plenty good.

The sun finally decided to come out for a few minutes and it really looks good. Haven't seen it for quite some time. Some of the boys have been getting passes now and then back to various large cities. I should be getting along on the list and if and when I do get a leave I'll try and pick up a few little souvenirs and things to send home. Imagine, I could get some very beautiful linen articles, etc. We'll have to wait and see. The news is scarce but what I've heard has been good. No doubt the U.S. newspapers all but have the war over - well I hope they're right. Must close. Love... Always...JACK.

Co. K - 60th Infantry - 9th Division - APO #9

November 27, 1944

Dear Mom and Dad:

We lost our platoon leader, Lt. Bowden. I was under him through France and all the way up until we joined this company and then I was put in his platoon. He was really a swell guy and everyone in the platoon hated to see him leave. Company L got him and he will be executive officer over there. I fell in a mud hole today and went knee deep in water so I have been drying clothes the last couple of hours. Hope everything is okey. I am feeling just fine - the only question is where to next? No more news...Love...JACK.

November 29, 1944

Dear Mom and Dad:

Well, today is really an unusual one. The sun has actually been shining and the sky is blue. Sure, seems good to have a decent day for a change - now if it will only continue. I've been thinking about raising my Class C allotment to $40 instead of the $20.75 which it is now. I am now drawing a total of $79.80. Not too bad, eh!

Have finally learned where Milt Kapp is located. In case you haven't, he is in Holland fighting with the First Canadian Army. They were doing guard duty along the Red Ball Highway. Then the 104th Division went into action. That is why all of his letters indicated that he was close to me. The above information was in the November 27th Stars & Stripes so that is the only reason I happen to know his location.

The news seems to be good, but none of us can get too optimistic as yet. Naturally, the rumors are running wild as to what we're going to do. They've got us going everywhere in the world - from the USA all the way out to the Pacific. Take your pick! No mail today - probably will get a load of it tomorrow. PLEASE SEND CANDY BARS!! I don't need any cigarettes - just candy. Thanks a lot, and love always...JACK.

Dear Mom and Dad

November 30, 1944 (Note: This V-Mail was delivered on Feb. 23, 1945)

Dear Mom and Dad:

Pay day today and I drew about $25. I'm going to hang on to a little extra cash so if and when I ever get my pass I'll be able to buy a few things to send home. It was another nice day - I don't mean actually nice - it just didn't rain, that's all. Any day, when there is no rain is considered nice over here. I've found that out rather quickly.

Got your letter written on November 16th today. No boxes have arrived as yet. The miracle of the century happed the other night when we were given two D-Rations per man. They are the concentrated chocolate bars. Something like 600 calories in each one. Boy they really hit the spot. We're supposed to get candy rations now and but they have to pass through too many hands. I have an idea that originally there were about 5 allotted per man but by the time they get to us there is one per man and then we feel lucky to even get that one bar. So, please send candy when you can.

No news. I wish I can tell but I can't. Am feeling fine so don't worry. If you don't hear from me for a few days I am probably on the move. Love...JACK

December 2, 1944

Dear Mom and Dad:

Well, we're here I guess - at least that's what they say. Have no idea what is scheduled for the next few days. Keep track of the dates on my letters, however. Just don't worry if you don't hear from me for a while because I imagine I will be a really busy character. Am spending the night in luxury. We are even sleeping under cover and Dick Kline and I are fortunate enough to even have a bed. It's down in the basement of a shelled house. Really it is a good deal if we could only stay here for the duration. The last two nights were a little rough for me. I got caught without a shelter half and slept in my sleeping bag under the stars. Well, sometime in the middle of the night the stars must have disappeared because I woke up soaked to the skin. This confounded weather!!

Got your letter of November 21. About the money!! It was sent from the 190th Repl. Co. - APO #129 on December 3, 1944, through the 90th Finance Disbursing Section. I have the receipt with me. It was for five pounds, 20 shillings; and 350 francs - which is a little more than $31. Let me know if it has or has not arrived as yet. I can easily have it traced with the receipt. It is made out to Dad. Also let me know if the $18.75 bond and that $20.75 checks are coming okey. Otherwise, I did not change my allotment.

There's no more news. I'm feeling fine and everything is okey. Looks like I may get in on the biggest show of the war - guess we'll have to wait and see. Hope both of you are feeling fine. Don't worry - I'll be okey. All my love to you both...JACK.

Sunday, December 3, 1944

Dear Mom and Dad:

Have had no opportunity at all to write so I'll try and take time now. This will be mailed with a letter written on November 30th so you should get them together. Thought sure I might get a chance to see Carl Eschen a few days ago, but it looks like there's not a chance now. Have had an opportunity for the first time to actually observe German village life. It is surprising how well dressed the people are.

Nothing much going on. Watched a few German planes shoot off a few rockets from the new attachment on their wings. Got a stack of mail this morning. The dates ranged from Sept. 2nd to Nov. 18th. Mail is never consistent and there is often a long period like that in each group. One V-Mail made it in 10 days - airmails are slowed down these days by the Christmas rush. Am feeling fine and all is well so don't worry. Hope you are both fine. Love...JACK.

Dear Mom and Dad

December 8, 1944

Dear Mom and Dad:

A new day and mail call brought me your letter of October 27th saying you had received two checks - one for $22 and one for $9. That was the cash I sent from England so I guess that is all settled okey.

Had a marvelous sleep last night. Three of us slept in a real honest to goodness bed. It was really great and I'm not kidding. Picked up two pretty little knives. I don't know when I'll ever get a chance to send them, but maybe one of these days I'll get them off to you. Am enclosing a few pieces of paper money - some from Belgium, France and Germany.

One can hardly realize how confounded crazy the American soldier can be. This morning about four GI's were walking down the street in silk top hats and tails. Bicycles were prevalent and even a few guys were buzzing around on motorcycles even on the front lines. Don't worry!! Everything will be okey. Love...JACK.

P.S The Cablegram arrived today!

December 12, 1944 (Evacuation Hospital located in Liege, Belgium)

Dear Mom and Dad:

I am writing this and an airmail immediately so that when you receive a government telegram saying I was wounded in action you'll have no cause to worry. Well, the big push is on and we were right in there. Everything was going beautifully and then the Jerries started throwing mortars on top of us. I can honestly say I've lived through one hell already, but I guess the good Lord decided it wasn't my day. I got through that, but it was in the evening just when we started digging in that they let us have it again.

As you know there are two parts of my anatomy which really protrude - my feet and my seat. It so happened my 10 1/2's were out of the foxhole too far and some shrapnel went neatly and cleanly through my galosh, shoe and three pairs of socks, and into my big toe and leg.

Co. K - 60th Infantry - 9th Division - APO #9

Mom, if I'd have inherited your size 5's instead of Dad's size 11's I'd have been all set, but those are things over which we have little control from what I am told.

They brought me back here and X-rayed the toe and the result was no imbedded shrapnel which is okey by me. I feel great but I don't walk too well. Dick Kline was about 10 yards from me and got a slight scratch in his leg. We'll get the Purple Heart I imagine so in case a medal comes in the future you'll know what it is. Please don't worry - I'm fine and with all the sulfa and tetanus shots I have been given not even rigor mortise could set in. Good night, now, and love to you both...JACK.

December 12, 1944 (Evacuation Hospital located in Liege, Belgium)

Dear Mom and Dad:

Couldn't find any stationary so I'll use this V-Mail and send it in an airmail envelope. I don't know which will arrive first - the V-Mail I just wrote or this letter, but I hope that one or the other or both beats the government telegram saying that I was wounded in action in Konzendorf in the Hurtgen Forest, Germany. My big feet happened to be sticking up a little too high and a piece of shrapnel from a Jerry mortar made a nice journey through my big galosh, size 10 1/ Shoe, three pairs of socks and finally my big toe. I also picked up a couple of slivers in my leg. Fortunately, it went right on through and missed the bone and did not lodge in my foot. Just a clean wound. It is a little sore and quite stiff thus making me walk none to precisely but it will be okey in short order. I was mighty lucky to have not gotten anything worse. We were under terrific mortar fire and all I could do was lay flat on mother earth with a prayer on my lips. I believe I can truthfully say I relived all my past and quite a bit of my future as I lay there.

Checked my head for gray hairs tonight, but all I could find was a little dandruff. Such is life. Just don't worry - and I'll soon be up and at 'em. The food is fine and surroundings great - particularly the American nurses. Love...JACK.

Dear Mom and Dad

Letter written by Jack after he was wounded.

Co. K - 60th Infantry - 9th Division - APO #9

Battle of Huertgen Forest badge.

Dear Mom and Dad

December 17, 1944

Dear Mom and Dad:

Here I am back in Normandy. This is where I started after getting off the LSD on Omaha Beach. I knew that being in Paris was too good to be true. They got us on a train and so here we are not too far from Cherbourg. The beds are soft and the rest is marvelous and I am feeling great. My foot is still a little stiff, but there is no pain and it is healing just fine. Guess maybe it was a lucky hit. I am back where I can spend a nice quiet Christmas. It isn't going to be like being home, but at least I won't be ducking mortar shells and 88's.

Well, I can truthfully say I saw old Paris. It is everything that they say - and even more. Things are generally modern. Some architecture is definitely ultra modern. The streets are wide and one would hardly believe that the war had even touched it. And the clothes... well I can see why Paris leads the fashion parade. The old Eiffel Tower is just as she is pictured and as I watched it from the train window I wished we all could be seeing it together. There's a slight chance that I may get sent to England. You see they push the not too serious cases back as far as possible so that serious cases can get quicker attention as they come off the front lines. That's how they keep hospitals near the front always available. No more news. I'm okey and am feeling in tip-top shape. Just need some long-awaited sleep and I'm really catching up on it. Love... JACK.

December 18, 1944

Dear Mom and Dad:

Don't know just where the day has gone, but here it is evening already and I've accomplished nothing. I had a good old headache late this afternoon. It has cleared up now. You know I was just sitting here thinking. The War Department telegram saying that I got wounded in action will arrive just before or a little after Christmas. In a way that's going to be a lousy Christmas gift, but for me, getting hit when I did was perfect. I'll at least be able to spend a peaceful day back where we don't have to worry about shells.

The weather has been perfect the last few days. Sure, seems good to have that sun out. Have been listening to the news broadcasts with interest. Looks like the Jerries are making their last stand. I have been doing some reading. There's nothing like the Reader's Digest. This is the best magazine on the stands without a doubt. Also, read a pocket book "Science Yearbook of 194h". There's just no news. Sorry this V-mail is so dull. Just wanted to let you know that I was feeling okey and coming along just fine. Love, always...JACK.

December 20, 1944

Dear Dad: (Sent to Morrison Bros. Co., Dubuque. Iowa)

Well, I guess I am already for duty much to my regret. I would have given anything to spend Christmas back here but it looks like I'll spend it in a Replacement Depot and will eat good old K rations instead of turkey.

Dad, I can honestly say I hate like hell to go back up there. Once you get back here and see the life some of these rear echelon commandoes live you wonder just what you're doing up there for there's not a guy that's been up on the front lines and gotten hit that wants to go back up there again. I was mighty damn lucky - all I hope is that my luck will hold. I'd give anything to get another hit - this one right through the shoulder. That would give me the Purple Heart with one oak leaf cluster and in the 9th Infantry Division that gives a guy a good chance for a trip to the states for a furlough. I'm dreaming again, I guess.

When you're holding a position, the front is okey. In fact, I'd rather be there than in a rest area, but when you begin the attack and watch some of your buddies fall it makes you think. Your blood begins to boil and the whole damn German Army in front of you doesn't mean a thing. You just keep moving and throwing lead at the bastards. It is a fascinating situation and one filled with a great deal of emotion. For

Dear Mom and Dad

some reason or another you seem to lose all sense of fear and simply keep forging ahead hoping that you don't get hit by a bullet or shrapnel.

I think that's why I came through the worst part of the barrage. Dick Kline and I had pushed way on ahead mowing everything down and the shells fell mostly behind us. Yes, we were lucky! That night when I was hit we had a BAR, two carbines, two M-1's and an automatic "burp gun" in our foxhole. Too bad we didn't have a counter attack as we could have slaughtered a lot of the damn Jerries.

Am hoping that tomorrow they will come in and give me my Purple Heart. It is one of the most beautiful medals given even though damn near every guy that has been on the front for any length of time owns one. It is for wounds sustained in action against the enemy. You know, Dad, an infantryman is one of the most unique human beings on the earth. He can look at blood and guts strewn all over the place; he can slaughter a bunch of the enemy without flinching an eye; he can live, eat and sleep in lousy, stinking mud holes; and, yet, he'll crawl around through hell to spend the last few minutes with a dying buddy or he'll pick up a befuddled cat or dog in the middle of battle and carry it to safety. It is really amazing. Well, Dad, I guess I had better close and hit the hay. Don't let Mom worry too much. You know me and with the Dauner luck we'll get through. I do have to admit this has been one helluva of an experience......Love, JACK.

December 20, 1944

Dear Mom and Dad:

Well, here I am all ready to go back and let them take a few more pot shots at me. Thought I'd be around for Christmas but the Doctor ordered me back to duty. Don't know just when I'll be leaving, but I imagine it will be in a few days. Then I'll have to go through the replacement depots again - it is just like starting all over. I am hoping they'll send me back to my old outfit. If they don't I'll just have to take off and rejoin them on my own. This I will very readily do!!

Co. K - 60th Infantry - 9th Division - APO #9

Am feeling great! With the rest I have had the last 9 days I am all set to get back into action again. I just hope they have stopped that counter attack and that they've captured Duren (Germany) by now. By the way, I sent some junk from Paris that I got off the front lines. It is worthless, but I wanted it! Sure, wish I hadn't left that P-38 (automatic pistol) laying in my pack. I'll never see it again. Maybe I can get a Luger on the next trip. Will soon be starting my trek through France and Belgium again. Will probably spending Christmas on a 40 & 8 boxcar heading northeast. Hope you are both fine. Love...JACK.

December 21, 1944 (La Haye du Puit, Normandy)

Dear Mom and Dad:

I am still here at this hospital location and hoping that they will forget or lose my records so I can just stay here until after Christmas. Looks like I'll get back on line just in time for someone to paint a new picture entitled "Dauner crossing the Rhine". Only this kid just ain't going to be standing up there waving the Stars & Stripes. Guess, George Washington was just a better man than me - or maybe he never faced any Jerry "burp" guns (a very high-speed automatic hand weapon). They call them "burp" guns because they spit lead so fast that it sounds just like a good healthy burp.

I hit the hay at nine bells last night and slept right on through. Got up for breakfast and then hit the sack once again. This time a nurse dragged me out. I can't say I minded because she is a real doll. Her name is Angel Paul (Lt. Angel Paul from Pennsylvania). This confounded place has more cute nurses than you can ever imagine.

Today my ward got the radio so we'll be listening to all of the good programs and bad news. Oh. I am having a tooth filled sometime soon. Had a cavity between my teeth in the back. Everything else was okey. I picked up my equipment from supply yesterday. It's a waste to give it to this kid because I'll just dispose of it. All I need are the clothes I am wearing, a rifle and a few bandoleers of ammunition. This army is crazy, believe me. No more news so I'll sign off on this V-Mail. Hope you are both fine...Love...JACK.

December 22, 1944

Dear Mom and Dad:

Just ate and now I am ready to write a few letters. Slept all morning. I seem to be dead tired for no reason at all. I ran into one of the fellows from old Co. G - 97th Infantry Division back in California. He informed me where a bunch of the buys were shipped. In fact, he had met a couple of them in the hospital in Paris when he was there. The old gang sure did spread out.

Forgot whether I told you that I got a letter from Jim Costakis saying that he was sent from Ft. Meade back to San Luis Obispo to join the 86th. He was marked as a messenger so they didn't send him over. He sure was pretty lucky. It is sort of dreary today and there is no news. Still hope to spend Christmas here. Will keep you posted. Love...... JACK.

December 23, 1944

Dear Mom and Dad:

Well, here I am still back in this hospital in Normandy and it looks like I am going to be able to stay until Christmas and possibly until about the 30th. At least I hope so. For some reason or another, my stomach has been giving me a rough time. Had a slight case of dysentery and a really rough stomachache. It has cleared up some and by tomorrow I should be okey.

Doesn't seem possible that Christmas is only two days away. I was just thinking about last year, how we planned everything at the last minute and how everything worked out so perfectly. We certainly had a wonderful time. What I wouldn't give to be back there again this year. However, if all goes well with this crazy war maybe things will work out that I'll be home or at least back in the States next year.

Tomorrow is Sunday and I guess I will start the day off right by going to church services. Saw "The Song of Bernadette" today. It was very good. Time to close. Hope that everything is okey. Love to you both...JACK.

December 26, 1944

Dear Mom and Dad:

Here I am still around and enjoying life in the hospital. All I hope is that they hang on to my mail and packages so they won't be chasing me all over Europe. It has been a lovely day. Definitely chilly outside but the sun was shining and after all the rain and mud I've seen, a clear sky is really appreciated. Slept some this morning and then gave a few of the boys some instructions on the finer points of ping-pong. Stood all comers for about two hours and then some guy got lucky so I went over to the movie. This is really a very pleasant hospital operation and 1 am going to hate to leave.

Went over to the Red Cross today. Later I saw Phil Baker in "Take It or Leave It". Had seen it before but it was just as good even the second time. One can hardly be choosy over here in the ETO (European Theatre of Operation) when it comes to movies or anything else for that matter. It is almost time to go to dinner and news is pretty slim. Hope everything is fine. Don't forget to drink a few Tom and Jerry's for me on New Year's Day. All my Love......JACK.

December 27, 1944

Dear Mom and Dad:

Am sitting in the Red Cross listening to a re-broadcast of Charlie McCarthy. He's still as good as ever. It sure is great to be able to hear a radio again and be able to listen to some real American music. I decided that I would play a few hands of poker last night and the results were anything but good. I guess my luck has run out on cards so I better quit.

Dear Mom and Dad

Had hot cakes this morning with honey and they really hit the spot. We were getting a lot better food up on the line then we are back here, but I would be more than willing to eat the food back here if I could stay. Have no idea when I'll be pulling out of this hospital. I imagine it will be about Saturday. Then I will be going back through those darn Replacement Depots.

It is another beautiful day outside. Cold but clear and the sun is shining. Have been wondering if you two maybe decided to go into Chicago during the holidays. Hope you have something on the fire and have a good time. I could sure go for a nice big breakfast at Henrici's in Chicago like the good old days. Love......JACK.

December 28, 1944

Dear Mom and Dad:

Well, it looks like I'll be pulling out of here tomorrow. I got the Purple Heart medal and providing I get the actual medal I'll send it on to you immediately. I'll let you know whether or not it is coming. Ran into my platoon sergeant back here yesterday. He is heading for the UK (United Kingdom). Has a badly fractured arm and a couple of other bad cuts. I was sure surprised to see him.

Saw a good hypnotism act last night up here at the Red Cross. It was put on by a sergeant from around here and he was darn clever. Then I headed back to the ward, read a while and hit the hay. Boy, I am going to miss that nice bed in not too many days. Hate to even think of it.

It is a dreary day outside but the music is good and I am warm and dry at the moment so I can't say I mind. Here it is almost a new year. Don't know just where 1944 went, but one thing 1 do know - 1945 better bring an end to this war. Everything is okey so don't worry. Better close as it is almost lights out. Love...JACK.

Co. K - 60th Infantry - 9th Division - APO #9

December 29, 1944

Dear Mom and Dad:

Well I reckon today will be my last day here and I must say I am going to hate to leave. Will be awarded my Purple Heart this afternoon if all goes as scheduled, and then pull out early tomorrow morning. At least I will get one more good night's sleep in a bed. Saw "Cover Girl" yesterday. That makes the fourth time I've seen it but it was in technicolor and really was good so I didn't mind it at all. Then I educated a few of the couple of letters boys on the art of playing ping-pong. Spent the evening reading and also knocked out a couple of letters.

Last night, it was really beautiful outside. There was a full moon and not a cloud in the sky. I've never seen it so bright. Sure, did make me feel a little home sick. Will drop you a line later in the day when I know more of what's going on. Love for now...JACK.

December 27, 1944 (later in the day)

Dear Mom and Dad:

Just a note to let you know that I'll be leaving here tomorrow so you probably won't hear from me for quite a few days. Got my Purple Heart Medal and am sending it on to you today. I imagine it will take about a month although I really don't know. There's an extra piece of ribbon wrapped in that small piece of tissue paper.

It is a beautiful day outside. I just hope this weather keeps up. I certainly won't argue about that. Enclosed are the Special Orders on my getting the Purple Heart Award. Hang on to them for me. I'd like to keep this document. Must close. Love…...JACK.

December 30, 1944

Dear Mom and Dad:

Was supposed to pull out this morning but there was a change in plans at the last minute with the result that I am still here. We're leaving tomorrow definitely!! This can't keep going on forever even

Dear Mom and Dad

though I'd sure like it too. Went over to the Red Cross and saw "Hail the Conquering Hero". It was pretty good and I can say that I enjoyed it. They finally hit a movie I hadn't seen. Sure, has been good seeing a few movies again.

There's really no news. I just wanted to let you know that I hadn't left as yet, but would be pulling out soon. So, it looks like I'll probably spend New Year's Eve in a boxcar. Hope everything is okey and that you two are having a swell time over the holidays. Also, I am still hoping my letter beat that government telegram. I am waiting to find out. Must close and get on over to chow. Love, always...JACK

Author's note: Shortly after leaving the front lines and while proceeding through the military hospitals to my final destination I initiated a writing program to reconstruct what happened on the fateful day when Co. K., 60th Infantry, and the whole 9th Division, launched its full scale attack out of Konzendorf, Germany, with a military objective of reaching the outskirts of Duren, Germany. I prefaced the story with a brief "Dear Mom and Dad" letter. I wrote it under the dateline of December 11, 1944. While making a business call on the President of Viking Pump Co of Cedar Falls, Iowa, Dad showed him my letter, and the "front line" story that I had written. Permission was requested and granted to publish the story. It appeared in the Winter 1945 – 1946 issue of The Viking Vacuums shown on the next three pages.

THE VIKING VACUUM　　　　　　　　WINTER '45 - '46

God Grant We Won't Forget

Editor's Note . . . While only four months have passed since the end of the war, we are already settling back into an air of complacency. So that we won't forget these horrors and what they mean, we feel we are fortunate to be able to print the following letter written by Jack Dauner to his dad and mother, Mr. and Mrs. W. W. Dauner of Dubuque, Iowa. Mr. Dauner, sales mananger of Morrison Bros. Co., Dubuque, has kindly given us permission to print Jack's letter in this issue of the Viking Vacuum. The letter was written only a year ago this month. It probably will not seem possible to you that this could have been happening only that long ago. We suggest you keep this print and read it again next year. By doing this, we know you will remember what our boys have gone through and do everything in your power to help prevent the necessity of your sons and daughters fighting another war.

Dear Mom and Dad:

Just a note of explanation. The little story enclosed is the story of something which happens every day on that thing they call the front. I sat down and scrawled it out a couple of days after the incident but the facts were still well in mind —I imagine they always will be.

December 11, 1944
................, Germany.

It's five o'clock in the morning. Darkness still blankets the cool December atmosphere. Down in the basement of a bombed building, hurrying figures busily work under the flickering glow of flame boxes giving forth their smoky, heavily carbonated light.

Around the old stove some of the men are heating a quick cup of coffee, others C rations of meat and beans. Here and there men are cleaning ammo and rifles—packs are being carefully made, and everything is discarded except the essential.

Time flies—someone calls down that the hour to move out approches. Belts are donned; then packs; bandoleers of precious ammo are slung and grenades hooked conveniently on loose straps.

Everyone takes a last look at "home"; then at each other. They

Page 5

THE VIKING VACUUM　　　　　　　WINTER '45 - '46

know what that look means. It conveys a wish of good luck, success, of "Thumbs up old man—everything will be okey." And so, on to the street above.

Would the 88's start now? Have we given our movement away? The silence is broken only by a tank occasionally turning over its cold and sluggish motor. Streets are lined with mechanized equipment. We, the infantry, start to move. The familiar "get your five yard interval" is passed down. Dawn is breaking as the column moves down on either side of the street. Through the town and into the country.

There before us is no man's land. Along the road are sights of recent battle. Tanks burned and helplessly knocked out. Dead animals with mutilated bodies. Dead G. I.'s— American boys who had given their all and had paid the supreme price.

A thousand thoughts run through each man's mind. Will this be my day? Will I soon be lying in a pool of my own blood like that Captain lying there in that blood stained ditch? Will I soon have a cavity in my head the size of a fist like that G. I. at the side of the road? Or will God somehow, somewhere forgive me for all my sins and bless me with life throughout this day?

Packs are growing heavy. Sweat —beautiful beads of dirty sweat fill the brows of every man. The mission comes within sight.

The crackle of an MG—artillery, our own whistles overhead in salvos. It is music, sweet music. Then the drove of planes. P-47's and 51's dart over like birds of prey. Sighs of relief can be heard in the column. Everything is clicking—it is up to us now—the infantry move in for the kill.

Somewhere, someone had looked at a map and decided that we should take such a position. Everyone works for the infantry to a certain point and then the G. I. Joe must take over by himself—and as a team with his companions set forth. It is that period after he, the infantry, takes over, that wins or loses a battle in the final analysis. The infantry must do the dirty work. It must do the sweating—its home is mother earth, and its tools are guts, guns, and ground.

We move on. The first phase of the attack is ahead. We start across 800 yards of open ground. Rifles start spitting hot lead. Two hundred; four hundred; six hundred yards we advance without a casualty. An M. G. is heard on the hillside. A platoon sargent drops—dead!! The rifles open up— B A R's chatter and all is quiet. We move on; the hill is taken. Two bewildered **"supermen"** walk out shaking like beaten dogs.

We rest. Some smoke nervously —some chew on a chocolate "D" ration. Then the tanks move up and the inevitable fire begins on them. Its like watching a game of checkers. The 88's are now trying to zero in. A flash of light—an explosion and we see one of our T D's in flames. A prayer goes out from every man that the boys in that sweat box will get out. They do and then we listen to the rhythmic sound of exploding shells within the inferno.

Its time to move. Cautiously we circle the hill—prisoners—wounded, shaking, shocked and speechless pass by. We go into the last phase of our mission. We push on—our fire power breaks loose—rifles barking shrilly in the crisp air. We move again—more prisoners file out. Our mission is taken—we've done it.

But then—as if hell itself had broken, the enemy exposes itself.

Page 6

THE VIKING VACUUM

WINTER '45 - '46

Mortars—shell after shell—more mortars. We are helpless. Bodies now alive now lie flat on mother earth. The shells come. Each one brings a new cry for the medics. One by one brave men roll in anguish. A rifle cracks—a kid of 19 leans over to his buddy, asks for a drink and dies. More mortars—more wounded.

I lay there praying. My eyes closed, teeth clenched, jaws set ready for my time. I can feel myself undergoing the first phase of hell itself. I pray to God Almighty to give me faith, strength and courage. I want to run—to get up and run and let off steam, but I know that is sheer folly. I gather my wits and start reliving the past. Everything good and bad that I'd ever done flashes before me. It is as if this was the time when the Lord above was tallying my good and bad deeds in an effort to see if I deserved to wear a halo or burn in the caverns of a living hell. I broke into a cold sweat. A shell bursts near me. I figure this is it. I hear the singing fragments but feel no sting of pain. I look at my pack. It bears the jagged tears of shrapnel and I am amazed to find my pack lying about three feet away from me.

Between bursts my buddy and I check to see if either of us has been hit. We build each others morale up as much as possible—and then the barrage is over. We count heads and discover too many missing faces. We find a trench and eleven well shaken men jump in to take a smoke.

Communications are nil. Here are eleven men—the remains of a platoon of forty seven. The shells again—but we are safe this time. Then an M. G. and we realize we are cut off. Eleven men against God only knows how many. This is it and we all swear we'll never be taken alive. Suddenly we spot G. I.'s. They are moving over. Contact is made —we are spared again.

It is evening — reorganization is complete and we start the inevitable "digging in" for the night. Then come the mortars. We lay there motionless hoping and praying no one would feel that sting and numbness of being hit. A shell bursts—I feel a peculiar sensation in my foot and realize I'm hit. The enemy finally turns off his mortar fire—our artillery is now singing **his** song of death.

The medic administers sulfa to me and bandages the wound. Darkness sets in and the password comes down. Night and the moan of a wounded enemy comes from the woods to haunt us. It is pitiful to hear, but it is one of those things of war. Too many of our own men to care for so he must lie there and suffer. He is delirious now, but his groans of pain give us an eerie feeling.

Hour after hour of silence passes by. It begins to rain—an air of musing sets over our hearts. Silence!! Rain!! Mud!! Oh God, when will this thing ever come to an end? When will men cease killing each other so ruthlessly? Why must there be this needless suffering. They say those men back there died for a cause—but think of what they could have lived for. Grant us most merciful Father that Thou will watch over those boys who have passed into your supreme realm this day and give us who remain faith and strength and courage to someday, somehow— make this world a world of peace and unity where a true spirit of brotherhood will henceforth rule. Silence!! Mud!! Rain!! All is quiet on the western front!!

Chapter 13

GFRS - APO 545
c/o Postmaster - New York, N.Y.

(January 2, 1945 - January 12, 1945)

January 2, 1945

Enroute by train - Somewhere in France

Dear Mom and Dad:

    Just a note to let you know that I am on my way. By the way, don't use the above address. Just forget it and use the one you have been using all along. Well, we had a very enjoyable ride here. Much to our surprise we got coaches instead of 40 & 8 cars and ours was in excellent condition. Had numerous stops. In fact, I almost missed the train once. So, all in all the ride was okey.

    Even celebrated the New Year in style. Three of us had a bottle of champagne and it was excellent. It was an old vintage and very delicious. Naturally, there was one thing wrong - there wasn't enough of it!! Arrived here and led things off with a good hot shower so I am starting with a clean slate once again. Don't know how long I'll be here, but I rather imagine the stay will be short. They need good men back on the front lines.

    Am okey, but am keeping my fingers crossed that I might slip and break a leg. That would send me back to the good old USA. Must close for now. Love to you both…...JACK.

GFRS - APO 545c/o Postmaster - New York, N.Y.

January 4, 1945

Somewhere in France

Dear Mom and Dad:

Here I sit next to a nice warm stove trying to warm my bones after sweating out a classification line. It was the same old nonsense and I should be heading back to my old outfit soon. Finally. got myself some combat boots. Maybe I should say river barges. They are size 10 1/2 B's. Wonder if I'll ever be able to wear "civvy" shoes again.

Last night, I bought myself a cigarette lighter. Prices are terribly high on everything. The French are really making money hand over fist off of the GI's. It is a pure case of highway robbery. Linen handkerchiefs that are about a dollar a piece in the States are 150 francs ($3.00) over here - see what I mean?

Enclosed in this note you'll find a money order for $20. Just add it to my bank account. Thought I might be needing it, but I don't imagine I will. It is a miserable day and so I hope that we just spend the day here inside. Man, this is a lousy letter, but there is absolutely no news so you'll have to excuse it. Maybe, I can dig up some red hot news by tomorrow. Everything here is fine, but do hope my mail catches up to me soon. Haven't had any since December 10th. Love to you both...
JACK.

January 7, 1945

Dear Mom and Dad:

Sunday - and for once it has actually seemed like such. Slept late and then went over to church services. the Protestant Chaplin here is a real Southerner with a wonderful old Southern drawl. Last night, a few of us went up to the Red Cross for coffee and donuts and then played a few rounds of bingo. My luck just wasn't with me. I signed up for a pass tonight so maybe I'll go into town for the evening.

It really turned chilly today. Hope it warms up again before I pull out of here. Hate to think of starting to live in a foxhole again after

Dear Mom and Dad

being under a roof for such long period of time. Don't know why but I really feel lazy today. There is just no news at all - maybe I shouldn't have even started this letter. Wrote Herman Eschen last night so I am pretty well caught up. Now if I would only get some of my mail everything would be okey. Hope both of you are feeling fine. I'm great. Love...JACK

January 9, 1945
Still somewhere in France

Dear Mom and Dad:

Just call me "lucky" - that's all!! Nope, I'm not getting a 90-day furlough - just hit the right numbers on my bingo card last night and won the best prize in the house. It was a GI flashlight. Didn't get a pass so a few of us went up to the GI Club and after having our coffee and donuts we went in to try our luck with good results.

Went out on the range this morning and fired a few rounds on the new rifle I drew from supply. My shooting was sad. All I can do is blame the rifle and say it is no good. Rather imagine I'll be leaving here soon but naturally don't know when. No more news. Will write soon.

All my love...JACK

January 12, 1945
Somewhere in France

Dear Mom and Dad:

Well, I am still here but I'll probably be leaving soon. If you don't hear from me you'll know that I've pulled out for places unknown. Went in town last night but there wasn't much going on so we came back here to the barracks and went over to see a GI show. Everything is okey and I am feeling fine. Will write soon. Love...JACK.

GFRS - APO 545 c/o Postmaster - New York, N.Y.

January 16, 1945

Somewhere in Belgium

Dear Mom and Dad:

Haven't been able to drop you a line the last few days due to the fact I was seeing the scenery between here and my last stop. We had about a five minute notice that we were leaving so all we could do was throw our stuff into our duffle bags and pull out. The ride up was pretty air conditioned. These 40 & 8 (40 men and 8 mules) boxcars are anything but comfortable - not like the Burlington Zephyr. We all but burned the car down trying to keep warm.

However, last night was almost like home. We stayed with a Belgium family, and after sitting around a nice warm stove all evening we were shown to a room with two large double beds. Two of the boys slept in one and I took the other alone. Man it was like home...almost. I'll be going on up to the front soon so if you don't hear from me as frequently you'll understand. Everything is okey so don't worry. All my love...JACK

Author's note: We were trucked to the 9th Division Headquarters where those of us who had been previously wounded in action were scheduled for a thorough physical examination. When I went in to see the doctor he gave me a very thorough examination, looked me in the eye and said: "What the hell are those silly bastards sending you back here for? - You're in no shape to go back on line!"

Then with a smile as he was looking over my military records, he said: "Hell, soldier, you don't really want to go back up there again, do you? Haven't you found out that you might go back home feet first rather than having a chance to finish your college education?" With that he tagged me as suffering from hypertension and tachycardia as a result of wounds not properly healed. His final words to me as I left his office were: "Good luck, Jack, I hope this will get you ZI'ed (back to the States) or at least on limited assignment in England".

Dear Mom and Dad

    I have to admit that was probably one of the nicest things that ever happened to me in the military - and probably saved my life since the 9th Division really caught hell during the ensuing days on the front lines. It also showed me that every now and then in the military you found a few officers who had some compassion for their fellow man - particularly those of us who for some reason or another had the right credentials but were in the wrong place when it came time for OCS and/or getting a commission.

Chapter 14

Co. K - 60th Infantry - APO #9 c/o Postmaster - New York, N.Y.

(January 16, 1945 - January 20, 1945)

January 18, 1945

Dear Mom and Dad:

Well, I got a letter here yesterday. Don't know how, but a Christmas card from Milt Sutherland arrived. That probable explains it. Anyway, it was quite a surprise. Maybe, if I am lucky a couple of packages will get to me here since most of them had my first APO on them.

Went up to the GI Club last night for coffee and donuts and then tried my luck at bingo. All I could win was a comb. By the way, if you can get a hold of any please send me two flashlight batteries. I have a good flashlight but batteries are tough to come by. Also, enclose a few candy bars, etc. while you're at it. Don't know when I'll be leaving here but I imagine it will be soon. I think our group has darn near a record for staying here. No more news for now so I'd better close. Hope everything is okey at home. Love...JACK.

January 21, 1945

Somewhere in Belgium (Liege)

Dear Mom and Dad:

Just ate and so I thought I'd sit down and drop you a line. Don't know just how long I'll be here but I imagine I'll leave either today or

Dear Mom and Dad

early tomorrow morning for a general hospital. This is just one of the stops on the way back you might say.

Am feeling okey - just don't worry!! Have picked up a few Time magazines and read articles concerning the Western Front. It seems odd to read about military things that you've participated in. The news facts are there but the "behind the story" just can't be found and maybe it is a lot better that way. Went to church this morning and it was a very enjoyable service. Lots of singing and among the songs were some of my favorite hymns.

Please don't worry about me. Meantime give my regards to the Karbergs, Kapps and everyone else who asks how I'm doing. Love... JACK.

January 22, 1945
Somewhere in Belgium (Liege)

Dear Mom and Dad:

Just had breakfast so I'll sit down and drop you a line. Well, I am still here with no idea when I'll pull out. It definitely should be today sometime. However, I guess we'll have to wait and see. Wrote some letters last night and then shot the breeze with one of the boys in the ward. Dropped Dick Kline a line and told him that in case any packages arrived for me to go ahead and open them and make use of the stuff. I let him know that I could get anything that wasn't food when I got back to the company. There's just no news at all. Nothing else to report. Love...JACK

January 24, 1945 (Paris)

Dear Mom and Dad:

Well, another day and I went in and got a pretty thorough physical check-up by the Major. He didn't say anything - just asked me questions and looked me over. Guess I'll have to wait and see if anything is going to be done or not. Dropped the Kapps a note last night and wrote the Karbergs, too. Am past the point of knowing who I owe and who I don't so I just drop them all a line every now and then.

The food here is marvelous. In fact, this whole hospital really tops. I believe it could compare quite favorably with some of the good ones in the States. Fitzsimmons Hospital in Denver still is the most perfect and most beautiful one I've ever seen.

Got my PX rations today and think that I will take in a movie downstairs tonight. Don't know what is on but it will be good to see one regardless. No more so I guess I'll close for now. Will keep you posted on what is going on. Love...JACK

January 25, 1945 (Paris)

Dear Mom and Dad:

My pen is writing terribly light. I don't know what is the matter with it. Hope you can read this okey. Found out today that I am tagged for the UK so in case you don't hear from me you'll know that I am on my way to Jolly England. From all indications the news looks good and the Russians seem to be pushing right on through. There's just not much else to report. Will keep you posted on my developments. Love...JACK.

January 26, 1945
Paris (in the hospital)

Dear Mom and Dad:

It's really a beautiful day here. The first nice sunny one since I arrived and the view from my window is perfect. I can see the old Eiffel Tower, The Arch de Triumph and Napoleon's Tomb quite plainly in the distance. It is really quite a sight. It is a great view of Paris and I feel fortunate to have such a nice hospital room.

I received a partial pay and so I am once again carrying a little cash on my person. The news continues to look very promising. Hope the Russians can keep on pushing in there and maybe facilitate ending the war. Nothing more so I'll close. Love...JACK

Dear Mom and Dad

January 29, 1945
Aboard U.S. Hospital Ship *St. Olaf*
Enroute from Cherbourg, France to Southampton, England

Dear Mom and Dad:

Am writing this as we are pulling into dock. When I left Paris, I thought we might possibly fly over to the UK in a C-47 but the weather put the clamps to that. So, we came by train to Cherbourg and then boarded this hospital ship. It is just like paradise on board. The beds are a dream - nice white sheets and the food is marvelous. Had some real milk today and an orange. My enthusiasm over these items may seem odd, but when you think back it has been quite a while since I have seen either of them.

The nurse that I got to know quite well had a new camera and naturally didn't know a thing about it so I explained the general working features, etc. The next day she was going into Paris and she asked what she could bring me. Not being supplied with too many francs, I told her to just pick up some nice views of Paris.

Am enclosing a picture out of Yank. It was taken the day I was hit - December 11, 1944, and no doubt right behind our positions. I remember seeing that same amphibious half-track and crew the day before we jumped off. Won't be able to mail this letter until I hit a hospital so Ill be able to add a little more at that time... Read three books so far since I've been back: "The Secret of Dr. Kildare"; "Horse and Buggy Doctor" and "Jeeves". They were all pretty good. I had no idea that Hertzler was synonymous to the Halsted Clinic and the book itself.

The music is marvelous on-board ship. The radio is going almost constantly. It is really delightful on board this hospital ship. Hope I run into some of the old gang from back in the 97th Division over here. I am afraid a lot of them were sent to Italy, however. It would certainly be nice to shoot the breeze with some of them. Not much more for now.

I'll write more a little later. Love....JACK.

Co. K - 60th Infantry - APO #9

January 30, 1945

Enroute from Southampton by train to a hospital outside of Mansfield, England.

Dear Mom and Dad:

Arrived here early this morning. I was so sleepy that I practically fell in bed. The train ride from where we docked was on the rough side. I did not think that we'd ever get here. It is snowing outside and from all outward appearances you'd almost think this was home. It got plenty chilly last night - particularly when we came from the train out here. There is no news in particular. Don't worry - everything is okey. By the way, I imagine I'll be here a while so you might write me at the address listed below. All my love ……JACK.

Chapter 15

Det. of Patients- 184th Gen Hospital 4200 U.S. Hosp. Plant - APO 514 c/o Postmaster - New York, N.Y.

(January 30, 1945 - February 20, 1945)

January 31, 1945

Dear Mom and Dad:

    A new day and the end of another month. It is a beautiful day here and everything in general seems to be fine. I even had enough ambition to wash my field jacket. It was a terrible mess, but I wouldn't trade the darn thing off for anything. Was checking it over and found about three spots where shrapnel had gone through it, but had missed me. Now you can see my reason for being a little superstitious.

    Read a couple of more books, but have been more interested in the news. I'd almost lay my remaining four shillings and three pence that the war will be over by the time you get this. Guess I am getting optimistic, but after all that is a little more cheerful viewpoint. Everything is fine in this hospital so don't worry. In fact, I almost wired home for some money but I was afraid the shock might be too much. No more for now. Love...JACK.

Det. of Patients- 184th Gen Hospital, 4200 U.S. Hosp. Plant - APO 514

February 2, 1945

Dear Mom and Dad:

It is evening and I've really been terribly slow at getting a letter off to you today. The main reason is that I've been reading "The Robe" by Lloyd Douglas and I absolutely can't lay it down. by all means read it if possible. I think my interest is probably encouraged through my "excellent" knowledge of Latin - thanks to "Maggie" Rue (Dubuque Senior High School Latin teacher). I can readily see why the novel has been praised by some circles and damned by others. Regardless, I am quite taken by it.

After reading this far, you two will probably think I am in the Section 8 Ward (Psycho Ward, thank you). Also, I am feeling great because I have done nothing but rest since I hit the UK and there's nothing like it. When I left the division to come back my heart was pretty fast and I was tiring way too easily. I just wasn't quite like I always had been when it came to holding up physically. Result: They diagnosed me as having tachycardia and hypertension. With all of the rest I have been getting, both problems seem to be improving very rapidly. I guess that I needed this rest, and I am certainly getting a good one.

Haven't sent those cards from Paris as yet, but will try to do so soon. Today the Stars and Stripes said that the 9th Division jumped off on an attack. I sure hope the resistance was light, but I know better through experience. They'll crack through the Jerries soon for good and the American armies may even be shaking hands with the Russians -How's that for a well calculated prediction? Time to close. Love to you both...JACK.

February 3, 1945

Dear Mom and Dad:

It is a beautiful day here and I'd give anything to just get out and walk. Maybe next weekend I'll be doing just that since the pass

Dear Mom and Dad

privileges here are very good. So, I am actually going to get to see a little of the country this time.

Went over and had an X-ray of my chest and also a Fluoroscope check. Had to take some of that barium sulfate mixture and now I know how you felt, Dad, when you had to take it. That stuff tastes worse than Limey beer. This place and particularly my ward is tip-top when it comes to treatment. The Captain in my ward amazes me as to how conscience he is about the people in the ward. In comparison to most of the army doctors this one is really A-1. Really it is an experience to go through the various hospitals from the front lines back to the UK. I'll relate the whole story sometime.

There is little more in the way of news. Everything is fine and I am really enjoying life in this hospital. Only hope I can stay here for a while. Say hello to everyone. Meantime love to you both...JACK.

February 4, 1945

Dear Mom and Dad:

Well I guess that I am okey and everything is all right because I was marked for duty. Probably won't leave here for a while due to the slow movement of orders. Am getting a 48-hour pass before I go, which I am looking forward to, provided that I get paid. I really feel great. Never felt better and believe it or not I tipped the scales yesterday at 158 pounds. Doubt if you'd recognize me the way I am falling into flesh. Think I'll go in town tonight and look the situation over and maybe have myself a few short beers - rather, I should say bitters. Who knows, I might even run into some of your English ancestors, mother.

Got my clothes and was even issued a battle jacket. So, it looks like 1 may be a sharp looking character for the next few days. By the way - after receiving this letter, start addressing my mail to the company - you know - my old address because I'll be heading back in the near future. Love...JACK

Det. of Patients- 184th Gen Hospital, 4200 U.S. Hosp. Plant - APO 514

February 7, 1945

Dear Mom and Dad:

It is a beautiful day here for a change. It rained a lot yesterday and was pretty damp so the sun is much appreciated. Well, last night I went into town. The one closest to us is pretty good sized (Mansfield). One good thing about being in England is that they at least speak the same language though at times you wonder. Ale is one shilling a pint which is about 22 cents in good old US currency.

Ran into a young kid in the New Zealand navy who happened to be around these parts and it proved to be an interesting acquaintance. Am hoping that we get paid soon. At least soon enough so that I can go on that 48 hour pass. Doubt if I'll try to go into London. There's really a lot to do down there but it would use up a considerable amount of my time to make the trip. Time to eat and I can't miss that. Hope you are fine. Love...JACK

February 8, 1945

Dear Mom and Dad:

Just finished by daily duties as head latrine orderly so I guess I'll sit down and let you in on the latest. Went in town yesterday afternoon and walked all over the place just seeing the shops and sights. Thought it best to go in by myself so I could do just as I pleased. That's that independent nature of mine, I guess. Along the numerous streets I passed two very old churches, so remembering how George (Baumgartner) used to speak of their beauty I went in. His words were really those of truth. It is something you read about and then finally - - like a dream come true - - you actually see these magnificent buildings. The huge stone pillars and arches are fantastic.

Also, the exceedingly high ceilings - the beautiful rose windows are something to behold. In this one church the caretaker happened to be there when I came in and he told me many interesting facts about the place. The organist has been there for over 50 years and the bench on which he sits is actually visibly worn. Guess it ought to be after that long. I wondered how his pants must have looked.

All kidding aside I really had a very enjoyable time. Then I came back to the hospital for dinner and on out to another town. Went to an early movie "Home in Indiana". It was a very modern theater and here I must say the English really excel the Americans in one respect. The seats are made to comfortably squeeze in two people. I guess you know what I mean. My luck was not so good or the little usherette didn't like my looks for she anchored a little kid next to me. Things are getting tough all over these days.

So, then I went on over to ye old Pub and had a couple of pints of ale. I guess the Limey's in there thought that "that bloody Yank was a bit of a hog the way he drank his ale." Those blokes sit and drink one glass of ale all night. Guess it's cheaper that way!!

I can now write carbon copies and there is no chance of getting caught up with either. That is what you call being right on the ball. The only trouble is that I've got no carbon paper. Guess I will blitz into town this afternoon and look around the stores. Haven't been paid yet but should be in about two days. No more news or anything else so I'll close. Regards to the Kapps, Karbergs and everyone. Love...JACK.

P.S. Next time you're in Washington, Dad, you might remind King Franklin (Roosevelt) IV that this war has gone on long enough and let's get it over soon. The troops are getting tired of his "fireside" chats.

February 9, 1945

Dear Mom and Dad:

Finished up my culinary duties here in the ward so here goes a quick note. Am going on a 48 hour pass starting Monday and then I suppose I'll be heading back to duty. Last night I went in town and saw a stage show. From there I ducked out of the rain and into a Pub which was lacking GI's thank the Lord. There were a couple of young Englishmen sitting at a table so I joined them. One had been in the Marines in the Pacific and had just recently come from New Zealand.

Det. of Patients- 184th Gen Hospital, 4200 U.S. Hosp. Plant - APO 514

I was practically penceless (didn't even have a shilling to my name) but they graciously bought the ale.

The English Pub is really an institution. If you can find one not frequented by Yanks you can observe the English at their best. There is always a fireplace with a dart board hanging above it. And let me tell you these guys are sharks at the game. My only regret is that I won't be able to stay here much longer. I really enjoy the place. Not much else to report so I had better close. Love...JACK

February 10, 1945

Dear Mom and Dad:

Well, guess what? I got a letter yesterday. It was written December 31st and was sent back to the company. The church program was certainly good to see. Looks like I don't rate much - just one line! Pretty sad! Guess I'll have to get married like Johnny Graves or come back to the States and be a USO Commando.

Went into town last night with some of the boys. Left them about eight and joined my two English friends down at another Pub. Then we went on to a dance. This afternoon I am meeting the boys to spend the afternoon. As you can plainly realize I finally got paid, but it was only a drop in the bucket (6 pounds or about $24). Am going on my 48 hour pass on Monday and am looking forward to it. Hope some more mail arrives today. Love...JACK.

February 13, 1945

Dear Mom and Dad:

The doctor called me in last night and after talking for a while he told me that he would put me on limited duty for a while and see how everything went. That means no combat until it is changed so I have no idea what will be done. I'll go to a Replacement Depot and then get another assignment. So, I imagine one of these days I'll have a new address and APO. It is funny how everything works out. You know when I was at Division that last time I wasn't even going to bother to see the surgeon - then something told me I ought to - and with these results. Am going to leave in just a little while so I think I'll close for now.

Hope everything is okey at home. I'm feeling fine. Say hello to everyone. Love, always...JACK.

February 14, 1945

Dear Mom and Dad:

Here I am back once again. Had a marvelous time, but unfortunately didn't have enough money and ran short. Should have cabled home for money the first day I was here. It's water over the dam, now. Visited Nottingham among my numerous travels.

Thought I might go to London but my definite lack of funds helped me to change my mind. Got a swell bed at the Red Cross Club where I even got a REAL cup of coffee and there was no charge. Spent the next morning looking around town and trying to see some of the famous sights. Don't know when I will be leaving here but I am sure going to hate to leave. I wish they would just lose my records and let me stay at this location. I have some folders and pamphlets that I picked up and will send them when I can get a chance. Everything is fine here so don't worry. Hope both of you are okey. All my love, always......JACK.

February 18, 1945

Dear Mom and Dad:

Sunday has already rolled around, and it has really been a perfect day. Went to church this morning but was so confounded sleepy that I could hardly keep my eyes open. Came on back for dinner and then headed out for the wide-open spaces. Took a long walk and then I came back just in time for chow this evening.

Had a perfect day yesterday. Movie and then dinner out. All I can say is it is a good thing that Steve has been winning at poker. I am dead

Det. of Patients- 184th Gen Hospital, 4200 U.S. Hosp. Plant - APO 514

broke!! No mail again today. Am about ready to give it up as a lost cause. I am getting plenty anxious to get a letter from the University of Michigan. Am afraid it won't be too long until I am heading out of here. Really, this place is tops in every respect. Must close. Love…… JACK.

February 20, 1945

Dear Mom and Dad:

Got a bunch of mail yesterday and among the letters was the one giving Milt Kapp's address here in the UK. If the letter could have reached me sooner I could have seen him for sure. He is only about 30 miles from me and I could have gone almost anytime. Planned to go up today, but I can't get a 24 hour pass because I am shipping out. So once again he and I are practically in the same place and can't get together. I was terribly tempted to take off and head up there but the AWOL gamble wasn't worth it. Not much else to report. Hope all is well in Dubuque. Tell the Kapps how sorry I am that I haven't been able to get together with Milt. Love, JACK.

Chapter 16

G.F.R.P - APO 874
c/o Postmaster - New York, N.Y.

(February 22, 1945 - February 25, 1945)

February 23, 1945

Dear Mom and Dad:

 Sorry, I haven't written for a while, but they are definitely overworking and underfeeding me. Arrived here at this "repple-depot" and immediately drew a detail calling for a carpenter. Today I had KP so I performed the duties of a fireman. Just call me a jack-of-all-trades. Went in town both nights so there wasn't much time for letters.

 By the way - I've been given an L.D. (Limited Duty). My new specialist number is Chem. Lab. Assistant but don't get your hopes up. I don't think it means much. However, I will be getting reassigned so you might as well write to me at the address on the envelope and not to good old K Company. Have no idea what, when, or where I am going. It could even be the air corps. Again, we must wait and see; and, in the meantime "sweat it out". Everything is okey so don't worry. Will keep you posted on developments. Hope that both of you are fine. Love...JACK.

February 24, 1945

Dear Mom and Dad:

 Just a note to let you know everything is okey - in fact, it appears to be tops. Hang on to your hats now while I tell you the latest. I am

G.F.R.P - APO 874 c/o Postmaster - New York, N.Y.

going back into the air corps and will be stationed here in the UK. Will send you my new address and APO as soon as I get there. Went in town tonight - I mean really into a city for it is one of the largest in this general district. Looked the place over and then came on back.

I guess I might as well give up on my packages as lost causes with this never ending moving around that I am doing. Hope to get a couple of them. No more news for now. Don't worry if you don't hear from me for a couple of days. Love...JACK.

Chapter 17

161st Reinforcement Co. 131st Reinforcement Bn. (AAF) - APO 652 - c/o Postmaster - New York, N.Y.

(February 26, 1945 - March 10, 1945)

February 26, 1945

Dear Mom and Dad:

Just a note to let you know that I have arrived here in the Air Corps Replacement Depot. Am now awaiting further assignment to some organization. I may go to France, Holland, Belgium or even stay here in the UK. Frankly, I hope I stay in England. If I do stay here I will be in the 8th Air Force. On the other hand, if I am assigned to the continent I will be in the 9th Air Force - not that it makes a heck of a lot of difference.

This depot is darn near like heaven in comparison to those serving the infantry. I am in a room with three other fellows - actually steam heated - and the food so far is excellent. Why I ever busted out of Cadets the way I did back in the States I'll never know. I should have had my head examined at the time.

Have no idea how long I'll be here but I don't imagine it will be too many days. I am anxious to get assigned and see what my new deal will be. I'll get you my new address as soon as possible. Use this one until

161st Reinforcement Co. - 131st Reinforcement Bn. (AAF) - APO 652

you get it! It will all catch up to me some day. I sure wish some mail would roll in from the University of Michigan one of these days!

No news in particular. Everything is tops as you can plainly see. Gotta run. Love…… JACK.

February 27, 1945

Dear Dad:

Just went through a classification board and it looks like I am going to get in with that Chem. Lab. Specialist assignment number. It is very possible that I'll end up somewhere here in the UK which is absolutely to my liking. Dad, I actually think I must be the luckiest guy in the world - that is, in everything but cards at the present. Yep, I'm broke - but, I've been that way ever since I got over here, so what the hell!! Someday I'll have to give you the whole story - it is really a good one!!

Haven't had any mail for ages. I guess it is all over on the continent. everything is okey at home. Couldn't help but be, Dad, with you running the show. Gotta close. Love…JACK.

February 28, 1945

Dear Mom and Dad:

Just a quick note before I go eat and then take off on a pass. Don't know which of the neighboring cities I'll head for as yet since the pass is only good for 6 hours or I'd be on my way to Sutton-in-Ashfield. My main worry is my lack of money. I only have one pound which doesn't exactly put me up in the Big Leagues!! Tomorrow I am on detail - probably will be testing my arm out on a mop and broom. Saw a good USO show this afternoon, in fact, in comparison to a lot of them I have seen - this was actually okey. Lots of laughs and good music. It is really amazing the difference you find in these USO shows after you have had an opportunity to see so many both here and in the States.

No more news for now - everything is okey. Will keep you posted on what's going on. Love…JACK.

Dear Mom and Dad

March 6, 1945

Dear Mom and Dad:

 Well my mail rolled in yesterday and it took me two full hours to read it. A grand total of 70 letters. The first one that met my eye really set me spinning. It was one I had written to Karl Eschen and on the front was written in bold letters the untimely words "Deceased". I was afraid all along that he had been killed because of various reports I had gotten from some of the guys in Karl's battalion, but naturally I didn't mention it. The next letter was a V-Mail from Herman (Eschen) giving what details they knew and also telling of his being reclassified. I hope that he is rejected somehow. I told Herm if there was anything that I could do or that the two of you might do to let us know.

 I had many letters. Most were dated back in December and January. Nothing at all that was written in February. I hope it keeps coming in. Oh well...Gotta close. Love...JACK.

Chapter 18

2nd Station Compl. Squadron A.P.O. 557 - New York, N.Y.

(March 12, 1945 - April 17, 1945)

March 12, 1945

Dear Mom and Dad:

 Today starts another week and frankly I can't quite figure out just what happened to the last one. Spent all day Sunday trying to get in tune with some more of the routine that I have to learn. The guys around here informed me that censorship at this place is slightly on the rough side. This is something that I haven't been used to for quite some time so in case my letters look like something that the cat drug in you'll know the reason why. I frankly can't imagine anyone going to the bother of reading all of these darn things word for word but I guess it is possible.

 As far as my work, I can sum that up in a few short words. It is something entirely different and I like it a tremendous amount. For once, I am doing something that I actually enjoy and that is half the battle in my opinion. By the way you can start sending me some packages now and I'll actually be receiving them. Please send me my sun tan shirts and also my little dark green overseas cap. As far as food and stuff, you can send some cookies, candy, crackers, or anything along that line. Also, you might include some tea. You see, even that is rationed over here.

Dear Mom and Dad

I finally managed to get a little cash today. In fact, I received three months' pay with deductions – believe me! So, don't be surprised Dad if you see a cablegram roll in asking for some dough PDQ. Your son is strictly a garrison soldier from now on and let me tell you it feels great. Will be needing a watch and can buy a good one through the PX so I'm going to throw what cash I have into one. Also, am going to pick up a second hand bike if I can find one. Not much more room on this V-mall so I'd better close. Love to you both......JACK.

March 14, 1945

Dear Mom and Dad:

Am working into my new job in good order. Every day, I learn something new and really, I enjoy the whole set up. I have all the confidence in the world in myself - even think the brain cells are getting back to their old standard. Everybody is really tops, and regardless of the numerous questions I ask, someone takes time to give me the answers. Gotta close. Love...JACK.

P.S. Send cookies...please!!

March 18, 1945

Dear Mom and Dad:

Sunday and one would hardly guess it. Around here Sunday is just like any other day of the week, and there is just as much work to be done and sometimes even a little more. I slept late this morning and then came on over and put in a full day. So far everything is going along in good shape and I still like my work as much as ever. One has to be slightly insane to work up here and that is the reason I am getting along so well. I really have a terrific set up and the men I am working with have all been great.

Tonight's paper gave out some information on the old 9th Division and from what it said the boys must be right up in the thick of it as usual. They are across the Rhine and somewhere in that bridgehead area.

2nd Station Compl. Squadron A.P.O. 557 - New York, N.Y.

Frankly, I am glad I am where I am right now, because I can well imagine the beating they are getting regardless of what the papers say about losses. Sure, hope that Dick Kline and that old gang of buddies of mine are resting leisurely in various hospitals with nothing but fresh wounds.

Have been debating whether to have you send my camera to me. I can have it over here okey and it is even possible to get some 35mm film, but what worries me is whether they'll insure it. Take a look into it, Dad, and if you can get it insured please go ahead and send it to me as I could really take some very beautiful pictures over here. Also, please send the exposure meter. The latter will have to be wrapped very, very carefully - cotton would be the best bet I believe. Insure the stuff for about a hundred dollars if you can send everything. Let me know what the deal is as soon as you can.

By the way in case you get a wire from me one of these fine days asking you to wire me about $50.00 just take it out of my account. It will probably be put to use on a 7-day furlough which I'll be able to get in the near future. I'm looking forward to seeing Scotland. Much love. JACK.

March 24, 1945

Dear Mom and Dad:

Haven't written for the past couple of days and I imagine you can guess the reason. I decided to go out on a 48-hour pass, and I really did have a wonderful time. Went back to see all the old gang at the hospital and had a great visit. Well, I walked in the front door of the Red Cross and who do I run into but Russ Garden, an old buddy of mine from the 97th Division. He, Dick Kline and I used to run around a lot together at San Luis Obispo. He had made Staff Sergeant about the third week he was on line and had seen quite a few of our mutual buddies. We took off and really made an evening of it. He had been wounded in the leg and has been put on "limited assignment" so we are both hoping that he will get assigned to the Air Corps and land somewhere near me.

Dear Mom and Dad

By the way he was at the same convalescent center as Milt Kapp, but had not run across him. I'm almost certain that Milt is still around but we just can't get together. I'll bet we do eventually though. Friday, I went back up to Mansfield to see Steve. Missed my bus back to Nottingham. I guess that I was a little too preoccupied with the result that my only alternative was to go spend the night in the local calaboose which I did -- believe it or not. There was no Red Cross in town and I had to go to some place where somebody would wake me at 5:00 A.M. so I could catch my train. What a night! I got back to my base on time, and that was what really mattered.

As far as Russ Garden and I could figure from all the guys we've run into none of the old gang that we were within Co. G, 97th Division, have been killed in action. Almost everyone has been wounded and a couple of the guys were shipped back to the States. I hope that all of us continue to have such good luck. Had quite a few letters come in today. One was as late as March 6th and considering that it wasn't addressed to my new address it certainly made very good time. Got a letter from Milt Kapp that had been written on the eleventh of February. I feel quite confident that if he has as bad a case of trench foot as indicated that he won't have to go back to the front lines. Most of these hospitals are really giving the infantry boys a break these days when it comes to handing out limited assignments - and in all reality that is the only fair way to handle returning combat soldiers.

By the way, I forgot to tell you that while I was loafing around Nottingham I visited the Robin Hood caves. That city is literally built on one huge cave. Practically nothing but a maze of passages. The news continues to look very encouraging and I just can't see how the Jerries can last much longer. It looks as if this might be IT!!! Running low on room on this V-Mail so I had better close and get it sent off to you. Love...JACK.

2nd Station Compl. Squadron A.P.O. 557 - New York, N.Y.

March 30, 1945

Hi, Folks:

Didn't get a chance to write yesterday so here goes a quick one for today. Believe it or not I got my first and only package. It was the one from the Serups so I'll have to drop them a line. Also, I received word about the death of Ben Pickard and Chuck Doran. How about sending me the newspaper story. Also, is there anything more on Karl Eschen? My mail is making better time! Got a V-Mail from the Kapps in 9 days. That is pretty good!

Went up "in the blue" yesterday for about 5 hours and it was terribly rough. In fact, a gunner, the radio operator and I practically took turns on the bucket. I'm still looking for my stomach!!! Everything is okey and hope you have a Happy Easter. Love, JACK.

April 2, 1945

Dear Mom and Dad:

Was up at four o'clock this morning and now that I have some time on my hands so I'll drop you a line. Things are really quiet this morning in comparison to yesterday. I was on in the afternoon and it was practically a mad house at all times. Got another letter from Milt Kapp written on March 9th. I still have hopes that he and I can somehow get together. Also got a letter from Russ Garden whom I met up at Nottingham on pass. He had heard from Dick Kline's mother saying that Dick had been wounded again - nothing serious however. Sure, hope he doesn't have to go back up to the front again.

There's no news. Hope you are both fine. Love...JACK.

April 10, 1945

Dear Mom and Dad:

There's not much news so I'll just knock out a quick V-Mail. I got another batch of letters today - some of them ranging as far back as November. Only a couple of them had been written as late as March.

Dear Mom and Dad

Some air mails made good time; and others don't. It is just a toss-up as to the fastest means of getting letters over here. I was off yesterday afternoon so i decided to catch a ride and go flying for a while. We went on an air speed calibration course and I rode in the bombardier position which is really great as far as the view. You can really see everything from that vantage point.

The news continues to look excellent. Glad to hear that Don Head is a prisoner and no longer listed as missing in action. That is some consolation to the Head family even though there might still be cause for worry. That is one of the problems with combat. It so hard to determine what the situation is with MIA's. No more news. Love...JACK.

April 11, 1945

Dear Mom and Dad:

All of my records rolled in yesterday. I learned to my great amazement, etc. (and at the same time almost rolled out of my chair laughing) that I had been awarded the Good Conduct Medal three times now. The last time was January 20th. Man, this is getting to be a joke. I went thru all of my forms and they are generally a mess. My pay was also off and I owe Uncle Sam a few bucks which he will no doubt deduct from my already diminished pay. In fact, all of my May pay has already been taken over and now they've got a foothold on June. Fortunately, I still have enough to tide me over for a while.

By the way - referring back to those records of mine - I received some darn good recommendations from back at the Meteorology Cadet program at the University of Wisconsin. Considering my dislike for the work I was surprised in some respects, but considering my actual conduct I think I rated them.

There's no news - I'm just rambling on as you can see so maybe I'd better close and call it a day. Am okey and hope both of you are the same. Love...... JACK.

2nd Station Compl. Squadron A.P.O. 557 - New York, N.Y.

April 13, 1945, morning

Dear Mom and Dad:

Friday the 13th and I am wondering what sort of ill fashioned fortune will befall me. I was off yesterday and am off again today. I'll be going on duty again tomorrow morning.

Well, Roosevelt finally died!! Certainly, was sudden. I'm wondering how Truman will make out. They elected him so now they can put up with him! I hope he turns out better than the type of person he appears to be. He certainly should be an improvement over good old Franklin D. Roosevelt. At least there won't be any more of those famous "fireside chats". No more news. Will drop you a long air mail in a day or so. In the meantime, keep the home fires burning. Love…JACK.

April 13, 1945 (after being court martial for going to Cambridge and missed the bus)

Dear Dad:

Got a hold of a few "blue envelopes" so I'll sit down and write you the whole story on this place and whatever else which enters this feeble mind of mine.

Here's about the Summary Court Martial. Don't get any gray hair over it as it means little if anything. Any sensible man who ever happens to look at the records can see the offence was anything but serious. It is not fair to judge a man who has an excellent record throughout by a small mistake- missing the bus on the way back from Cambridge. The joke comes when on my official record I've been awarded the good conduct medal three times and here I am being punished with 30 days restriction to base, rank reduction and pay cut. This particular major who is at the head of this 2nd Station Coml. Sqd. You see, Dad, what a guy he is up against. He throws a court martial for the smallest fraction. If it weren't for the beautiful set up I have here I'd volunteer for infantry OCS and go back up. I've never told you just how this deal works.

Dear Mom and Dad

We live on the field near the control tower and don't have to stand any formations whatsoever. When you're off duty you're off and that's it, your time your own. I'd give anything to get that commission, Dad, but it seems like the Dauner's just "ain't" Army men. That's the only thing which would cause me to volunteer back into the infantry, to get a commission. To every one, it must look like Jack Dauner certainly hasn't done anything in the Army. I'm not making any excuses, Dad, there aren't any. Will and I and thousands of other guys with good heads on their shoulders and strong bodies are leading this lousy life. All I do I say that someday every dog has his day and mine is coming. There's only one thing I wanted to do in the army and that was Fly. That didn't happen but I'm doing plenty of it around here, though it is only at the controls, but that's the only way to travel. These B-17's really cruise beautifully.

Have been wondering what business trends look like back in the States, Dad. Does it look like there's much hope for a private enterprise in the days to come? I still have ideas that you & I might start a Dauner & Dauner. If a guy could only get out of this army right now he'd be in great shape. I don't know what will happen, guess we'll have to wait until this war is over. That too, with Roosevelt gone, I'm wondering how condition will be with Truman as President. That, too, is something we'll have to wait and see how it works out.

Well, Dad, here's not much more. Hope everything is okay and take good care of our little mom and also of yourself. Love always… Jack.

April 16, 1945

Dear Mom and Dad:

Haven't written for a few days as I've really been on the go. So, I'll try and catch up on the events of the past couple of days. First on the list - I really had a great ride yesterday. Took an 8-hour trip across the English Channel over on the Continent. It was a beautiful day and you could see for miles. Went over Paris and on this trip, I picked out all of

2nd Station Compl. Squadron A.P.O. 557 - New York, N.Y.

the main spots easily. Even saw the old 108th Hospital where I spent one week.

Passed over many other spots where I had been. When we went over Rheims I recognized it right off the bat by a cafe right across from the railroad depot. This flight was much better than the other one I took about a month ago. The old Eiffel Tower certainly stands out as a dominate feature of Paris. As far as beauty it doesn't appear to have too much from the air, but it is quite an interesting structure.

Other than that, there is little to add. I may have a new address in a few days, but it won't necessarily mean a change in location - just an absorption of the 2nd Station by a larger outfit. Guess I'll close and get this mailed. Everything is fine here and hope both of you are feeling okey. Give my regards to everyone. Love...JACK.

Author's note: Early in April, I decided to get a 24-hour pass which, along with my normal daytime pass would cover me for 36 hours. I headed for Cambridge to see the famous university. Lost track of time and missed my first bus. At the same time, I found that I had inadvertently left my short-term pass in the barracks which meant I was now AWOL (Away Without Leave). Everything ran smoothly until I got to a small town a few miles from the base. I saw a jeep in the distance - hailed it - and unfortunately it was an M.P. jeep from a unit which hated our guts. They hauled me in - worked me over with several body punches in a holding cell, and then called the orderly room of my outfit on the base.

The first sergeant personally came to pick me up and immediately announced: "Soldier I'm going to Court Martial for screwing up and getting yourself in trouble with this lousy bunch of local M.P.'S". He wasn't kidding! I got a Summary Court Martial (even though I explained that I had a pass to cover the situation which was inadvertently left in the barracks). My sentence was 30-days, reduction in rank, and most of my pay for the month. After telling my story to my Commanding Officer in the Control Tower he called Colonel

Dear Mom and Dad

MacDonald, Base Commander, and advised him how badly he needed me in the tower. Fortunately, Col. MacDonald agreed and my sentence was reduced from 30 days in the brig to a 30-day restriction to base. However, I did lose my rank and pay!

Chapter 19

413 Air Serv. Grp - Hdqs. & Base Hdqs. Sqd. - APO 557 - c/o Postmaster, New York, N.Y.

(April 18, 1945 - May 6, 1945)

April 18, 1945

Dear Mom and Dad:

Great news - another box rolled in today and I think it must have been one of the first ones that you sent, which reminds me - starting about the first of May don't send anything of any particular value or too much extra clothing as one can never tell when he might have to pack a barracks bag - and extra equipment takes up just that much more room and means that much more to carry. Don't let that worry you - but this thing over here in Europe can't possibly last too much longer, and it is only reasonable to figure that sometime after VE-Day I'll get moved - maybe to the Pacific or maybe to the States. Toss a coin and you'll have the answers. If it lands on end I'll probably stay right here!

Went up on about a two- and one-half-hour flight this afternoon out over the Channel. It got a little rough, but it was a good ride. Nothing exciting was seen or happened. Hit one air pocket and dropped 400 feet - just like that! What a feeling. I happened to be watching the altimeter at the time and I thought my eyes were playing tricks on me. There's not much more news. Haven't heard from Milt Kapp for

Dear Mom and Dad

a couple of weeks. Is he still in England? Will keep you posted on the latest. Love, always.... JACK.

April 27, 1945, England

Dear Mom and Dad:

Thought I'd sit down and drop you an airmail on this Momentous Day. Hell, the Russians and the Americans linked up. After checking up, I came to the conclusion that the old month division must have almost made the linked- up, but some reports said it was the sixty – month. I'll bet that must have been quite a sight. Then, too, the San Francisco Conference finished its big day and reports have been coming in on it. So, the 27th of April seems to be quite a day.

I sent a wire today for $50 and told you to telegraph it back to me. I am going on furlough the tenth of May and will be gone for seven days and eight with my day of grace. As I told you before, I'm going up to Aberdeen and then Dundee; Edinburg; Glasgow and where ever else I have time for. I've saved as much money as possible the last month and will draw my regular pay the 30th of April so with the $50 I should have about $100 which should just about take care of the trip. I'm going to pick up some things here and there for Jeanne and Mom and maybe a bright plaid tie for you Dad. Am looking forward to the whole thing with a great deal of pleasure and particularly after being restricted for 30 days.

Rumors continue to run wild. Just hope one of these days I'll be climbing on a transport heading home again. That will be the day!!! Being in flying control as I am, there is a stormy chance I'll be left here at the bush even though the bomber group moves. But then that can be changes with the flick of a pen. There's no more news, everything is fine, Nite and love…Jack.

413 Air Serv. Grp - Hdqs. & Base Hdqs. Sqd. - APO 557

April 30, 1945

Dear Mom and Dad:

Mail call today and I received letters from you, mom; Dick Kline, and Jinny Shannon (Dick Bodine's gal). Jinny's letter was really newsy. Along with the good news came some of the bad. A clipping enclosed from the Evanston paper said that my old buddy, Bob Smith, from the 97th Division was killed on January 8th in Luxembourg. Bob, Dick Bodine and I were at Colorado State College at Ft. Collins together and at Ft. Leonard Wood. Funny thing, Bob always had the feeling that he would be killed in action. Guess I'll drop his folks a note as I met them in St. Louis one weekend.

Was paid today and have accumulated about $60. Another $50 now and I'll be ready for furlough and that should be on the way if my wire reached you okey. Everything is fine. Dick Kline is back with the 9th Division. It is really hard to believe that Dick has been sent back into combat after being wounded twice. No more news! Love...JACK.

May 1, 1945

Dear Mom and Dad:

Good news - another box came through. I haven't picked it up as yet, but I saw it and it looked like it had been through everything including a Cologne bombing. Everything was still there, I believe. Also, Dad, your letter arrived with the $20 money order. Good thing you sent that in case your wire for the money I asked for doesn't arrive. I'll be able to manage if I watch the budget.

Word just came in over the radio that Hitler died. The war goes on, however. Guess that shot up a lot of people's theories. Looks as though we'll just have to conquer every inch of ground over there. News is pretty scarce and this surely is a terrible letter. Hope this finds you both okey and everything in Dubuque shipshape. All my love.... JACK.

Dear Mom and Dad

May 3, 1945

Dear Mom and Dad:

 Didn't get a chance to write the last day or so. Hence, I'll take pen in hand. Well, I all but got myself behind the eight ball once again. Was trying so hard to get a hold of Ralph Dewey that I slipped up and accidentally wrote him to call me at my number here which naturally is listed as SECRET. I forgot all about it and wrote it down - so naturally it was kicked back and I was informed that it was a court martial offense, etc. - which I knew after I realized my mistake. It appears that all I can do around here is get into trouble. From here on, I believe that I'll stop all conversation, letter writing and other actions since I'll probably pull another smart one like that. What a life!!

 I am fine and am doing my best to keep out of the Guard House now that the restriction is over. Gotta close. Love…JACK.

May 5, 1945

Dear Mom and Dad:

 Well, tomorrow night I'll again have a new address - so be prepared. Am being transferred into the 305th Bomb Group, and therefore will be in one of those squadrons. That is somewhat of a record - three different addresses in eight weeks. That's the army; though! Am still hoping that I'll still be able to take my furlough though it may be delayed a little now

 The European situation seems to be fast coming to an end. Hope by the time this letter is in your hands that all hostilities will have ceased. There just isn't any other news at all.

 Everything is okey over here. Hope you are both okey. Love…JACK.

May 6, 1945

Dear Dad:

 This has been one of those days - you know the kind, Dad. The only trouble is that there have been too many of them lately. So - today

413 Air Serv. Grp - Hdqs. & Base Hdqs. Sqd. - APO 557

- like a Morrison pressure tank with a weak seam - I blew my top. I know what your opinion on that is - but just remember, son like father. I'll be damned if I'll let someone walk all over me after I've been knocked down. One of these "fly boys" without wings up at the control tower thinks there is a Tech/Sgt. rating open; thus, he is shooting many brown flares and is really bucking. So, when he phoned over and left word he wanted me to work half of his shift, I blew my top and left him slightly speechless.

The past two weeks I have finally struck light on one subject. Dad, the only time I was every really happy in the army - aside from my brief stay in Madison - was the other extreme - up in a foxhole in Germany. I wish I was there now!! It is there that you learn team work. No man is bucking for stripes - they're too easy to get. The attitude is altogether different. Yes, and men are men, and not just a bunch of words. That's one place where actions speak louder than words! I get so tired of hearing these guys complain about what a tough life they lead. Next thing they'll try to put a bill through Parliament in an effort to get padded gutters and lamp posts for use when they get too inebriated. They might catch cold on the ones in present use.

Oh, it has been great being back here tasting life again, but if this is life I don't want it that way. After you've seen so many good guys go down - this sort of stuff doesn't hold at all. Frankly, if I knew where old Dick Kline was and could get up there with him I'd damn near go back. There's no branch like the good old infantry. It's the toughest - the guys in it bitch the most - but, there's something there that other branches lack.

It may sound funny, but I actually miss that old M-1 rifle and even that confounded BAR. I almost went down and tried to draw one out just so I could take it apart and clean it. Then it struck me how crazy I'd appear. Well, maybe I could get a Section 8. (that is the Psycho ward). I miss firing the damn weapons - heaving grenades - cussing out that old BAR when she jammed, etc. I even miss those torn up towns - there's somewhat of a grewsome beauty to them as I remember. The

Dear Mom and Dad

whole trouble is I ought to be up there rather than back here and I know it. It's no hero stuff or anything like that. I just like that life better than I ever realized.

Most of these guys are sweating out the Pacific. If we go; we go - maybe it wouldn't hurt them. The way I look at it - I've seen this much of the world, why not see the rest of it! Sure, I'd give anything to get home for 21-30 days, but what's "gotta" be has "gotta" be. With a little luck though I might be seeing you before the end of 1945, and that's said without a smile. Seems like a long time, but Tempus Fugit as we know.

Still hope to go on furlough though there may be a mix up with this transfer of outfits that a bunch of us are getting. My status is still up in Flying Control, but now I'll be in one of the Bomb Squadrons which is to my general liking. Guess I'd better get that furlough or take a 48-hour pass. I think this life as an inmate is driving me slightly nuts. By the way the restriction is over! I am a free man once again!

I am okey - hope you and mom are too. don't worry - everything will be okey. When I get out of this blasted life of regimentation and prevarication. No more news. the war still isn't won. Personally, I think they need me up there again with the old BAR. Must close, Dad. Love... JACK.

Chapter 20

8th Air Force - 365 Bomb Sqd. – 305th Bomb Grp. - APO 557 - c/o Postmaster, New York, N.Y.

(May 7, 1945 - July 25, 1945)

May 19, 1945

Dear Mom and Dad:

    Well here I am back on base, and believe it or not I got back on time for a change. The furlough was really great and I had a bang-up time. My papers were lost here on the base and I was delayed a day getting off. Spent the first night up in Nottingham and then made the 10-hour trip on to Edinburgh. It was a somewhat tiring ride though we did pass through some very beautiful country. Stopped at Sheffield and Carlisle for a few minutes, but other than that the train went straight through. Got a bed at the Red Cross and then took off. After a good dinner I hit the first Pub and met a Pilot Officer from Canada who had his commission for only about a week. We had a great time together for the next three days. He was one swell person and knew his way around Edinburgh extremely well so that I was able to have some personally conducted tours of the best spots to visit.

    Saw many, many points of interest. One of the most beautiful sights I got to see was my last night in the city. Edinburgh Castle was flood lighted for the first time since the war had ended. The castle sits on a rock foundation almost in the heart of Edinburgh and looks over the

Dear Mom and Dad

main business district. I hope someday I can bring you too guys over here and we can all walk down old Princess Street together and duck into a couple of my hang outs for a short beer. The Red Cross was the old Royal Hotel. Officers, enlisted men, Wacs and nurses all stay there and it is always packed. By the way that was almost the first group of Wacs I had seen over here, and many of them had on their new uniforms which looked plenty smart.

All my intentions of going to Glasgow fell through. Edinburgh was just too good a spot and I didn't feel like leaving. There were so many famous spots I saw that I can hardly begin to name them. Only one disappointing feature: I couldn't buy any plaids (tartans) to send back. Material is all rationed and I needed coupons. And, by the way, that stuff runs into a lot of "dough". It's about $5.00 a yard for the real good material and the very best quality is even higher. I did pick up a few things to send back if I ever get the chance. Bought quite an interesting book on the Scotch Clans which had full page color reproductions of the various plaids conforming to each clan. Also, I picked up quite a few good views of the city and surrounding countryside.

My mail really collected this past week. Surprises never cease to happen. Also, about four more of your packages arrived. Thanks a lot - everything was great. It is almost like raiding the icebox to open one of them. Well, best we give up the hope of me getting home. I will make a rough estimate for you. It should be between six months and five years before I see the good old USA. We have a big job to do over here and until it's done the thoughts of going home are quite dim. I hope we stay in England, but there is also a possibility of going to France according to all of the rumors.

I've got a million and one letters to write so best I close for now and write another tomorrow. Everything is fine here - hope you two are okey. The food on base isn't too bad but I certainly could go for dinner at Leisers. Love to you both...JACK.

8th Air Force - 365 Bomb Sqd. – 305th Bomb Grp. - APO 557

May 21, 1945

Dear Mom and Dad:

Wrote a long letter yesterday and since I didn't have any airmail stamps on hand I just sent it "FREE". So, it will probably be a little slow in getting through. Anyway, it gives all the details on my furlough so I won't do any repeating in this note.

Yesterday I took a physical and was still classified limited assignment and put in Class IV. I'm not sure the exact meaning of that, but someone said that Class V was eligible for discharge. At least, the class is down close enough to be interesting. I also took two shots. They really caught me hard. They gave me a typhoid and typhus. I suppose I'll get a tetanus shot in a few weeks and then I should be all set for a few more months. I have had so many shots since I have been in the army that I am beginning to feel like a sieve.

Got a letter from Ralph Dewey a couple of days ago and he said we was leaving the hospital and heading for a replacement depot. It seems like one can be so close and yet so far away from seeing your friends over here. The main difficulty lies in getting off duty at the same time, and then overcoming the travel conditions. Sure, would like to see him - maybe there is still a chance yet. Also heard from Don Heitzman. He is still here in England. Hope he can get a hold of a ship and fly down one of these days.

Got my watch from the PX and frankly I am disappointed in it. Keeps time okey, but they just haven't been getting in any good American watches. This one is a Swiss. Anyway, it will tide me over until I get back to the States where I can get a good one. It sure seems good to have a watch again, though. I was really lost without one.

Hope you are both fine. Love....JACK.

May 24, 1945

Dear Mom and Dad:

Spent most of the afternoon putting out a man-sized washing including a sun tan shirt which I turned around and ironed so now all

Dear Mom and Dad

I need is another pass. Then tonight I packed a big box of stuff which I'll try and get off. The little round metal emblem with imposed horse head came off a dead horse up near Duren, Germany. The cute little cap came off some sweet little ATS gal. The red, white and blue button from a little number I met in Nottingham, and the broach with emeralds from the little French girl I met in Edinburgh. The cards were actually purchased - believe it or not! I enclosed some of those letters just for keepsakes. No more news - everything is okey as usual. Love... JACK.

May 28, 1945

Dear Mom and Dad:

Just got back from a 48-hour pass down to Bedford and have just enough time to knock out a quick note before going to work. Before I left I got a letter from Dick Kline and he said that they were living the life of Riley up on the front lines right now. There are two or three guys living with each German family and these families all treat them like they were their own sons. Some of the old platoon members have returned, and I guess it's already like old times. I wouldn't mind being with them again!

There's no news at all. Just though I'd drop you a quick V-Mail and let you know that all is well. Love to you both...JACK

May 31, 1945

Dear Mom and Dad:

You know I was just sitting here thinking - I'll bet we could compile a book about the size of "Gone with the Wind" from my letters home. We could call it "Dear Mom and Dad"- who knows, we might have a best seller. Another brainstorm - that's all. And so on to more pleasant things.

Have to work this noon and then tomorrow morning. Then I think that I will take a little "sortie" down to Bedford and have Marion

8th Air Force - 365 Bomb Sqd. – 305th Bomb Grp. - APO 557

(Cameron) meet me there. Sent a big box of stuff home yesterday so you can be expecting it in about three weeks. Hope you enjoy looking at all that junk - some of it is very interesting. Have to run - Love... JACK.

May 31, 1945 (later)

Dear Mom and Dad:

Another day and it was definitely on the quiet side. Ewing "Bo" Bodine, one of my room mates, won a bottle of champagne at a big raffle. I don't know whether I got one or not - hope so. One of the combat officers brought quite a few cases back from Germany so they drew for them. The last time that I got loaded on champagne was back at old Fountainbleau, France. By the way, I read in the Stars & Stripes where the Jerries had killed some high French official in Fountainbleau woods while they still occupied that area. I was in those woods and it is very beautiful around there. Of course, some of the trees were cut and a lot of foxholes and trenches dug throughout - but there wasn't much actual fighting in that particular area. That is quite a historic place.

Now for the laugh of the day. Went down to draw my pay and did I get a setback. I reported, and then I heard the Major say three shillings six pence. I almost burst out in hysterical laughter. Three shillings six pence is exactly 70 cents in cold hard American cash. I felt like telling them to donate it to the poor officers in the Courts and Boards office to add to their $400-$600 per month pay. So, I took it and laughed with everyone else. Under the circumstances I hereby send a plea for some money. Had ideas of taking a 3-day pass to London and seeing the sights down there just in case the Group was scheduled to be moved, but it looks like that plan will fall through.

I'd give anything to have my camera over here. Listen, I think I'll give you the green light on that. Go ahead and send camera and exposure meter; also, a few rolls of film. Eastman Plus X is preferable with a card giving the speed factors on the film just in case there have been some changes. It's a pretty safe bet that everything will get over to me

Dear Mom and Dad

okey now. Just pack it all pretty well and also send one roll of color film. Take the expenses out of my bank account. Wish now I would have had you send it a while back.

Have a bunch of good pictures we took on that trip to Germany. One is a picture of the cathedral in Cologne with that famous bridge in the background. It is excellent. Also, some of the Ramagen Bridge and many others. I'll send them when we get the official okey. I know you'll find them interesting. Also, don't forget to look in that book on Bedford in that box I sent. You'll find some good shots in there. In fact, go through everything with a find tooth comb - no telling what all is in there.

Gotta work tomorrow morning and then I guess I'd better put out a little washing. I am really getting to be quite the guy at these domestic doings. Taking after you, Dad, - guess. Everything is okey except for my financial condition and that of the world in general. Hope you two are fine and dandy. Best I hit the sack for the night. Love...JACK.

June 1, 1945

Dear Mom and Dad:

This is going to be quick since I am going to make a local run tomorrow; then, 1 am going to meet Bunny (Cameron) at three bells down at Bedford, and spend a 48-hour pass with him. So, it looks like I've got a big weekend coming up. Worked this morning and have it all arranged so that I won't have to go back on duty until Monday afternoon.

We went out today and had an hour of close order drill, and believe it or not I put the boys through their paces for a while. I was a little out of practice, but I gave them a pretty good workout. It seemed good to get out there and drill a few guys again for a change. As a steady diet it would be the death of me. I am getting more and more allergic to anything which resembles work. Must close for now...Love...JACK.

8th Air Force - 365 Bomb Sqd. – 305th Bomb Grp. - APO 557

June 4, 1945

Dear Mom and Dad:

I forgot when I wrote last. I believe it was about Friday night. Well, since then I have been having one wonderful time as per usual when I am out on the loose howling in the local communities. Took off from base on Saturday morning at ten o'clock - ate down at Bedford after hitching a ride in a gas truck. I hitched hiked half way on a GI truck - caught a Limey coal truck for a few more miles and then a jeep for another few blocks (not the MP's, thank you) and on into base in another coal truck. I did make it on time, believe it or not!! Now my only problem is that I am so broke that a man with one quid ($4.00) looks to me like John D. Rockefeller. The pitiful thing is that it is still the first of the month.

To continue - I bring thee tidings of evil. I am afraid that I am going to get released from flying control. Now don't draw any wrong conclusions. It seems as though there is a lot of work coming up in the Meteorology Department and since I have it on the records that i was canned from the miserable stuff once, they think I am the proper man...naturally. That is the Army for you. Don't know when I'll have to make the switch - hope not for a while. The Meteorology Department is almost one-half Jewish so you can see what a great time I'll be having. Happy days never cease to roll around.

Enclosed is a clipping from the Evanston paper. It shows old Smitty (Bob Smith) with his most common expression - always laughing. Put it in the scrap book for safe keeping. Also enclosed is a little article from the Stars & Stripes. I guess you can see who has done all of the fighting in the tough spots. That is almost two complete divisions of replacement for the 9th Infantry Division. It is really amazing the combat reputation that the 9th Division has developed since the beginning of the war.

It was a nightmare up at the tower this afternoon. In fact, I usually had a telephone in each hand and was carrying on a conversation with both at the same time. Seems like it is a lot busier than it was when we

Dear Mom and Dad

were on operational. Met a guy down at Bedford who had been with me in the 97th Division in the states. He recognized me and called me by name.

He came over with Smitty (Bob Smith) one time and that group had landed up in the 106th Division. He spent 5 months in a POW camp. He was looking okey and we had a good session about all the gang. Guess quite a few of the boys ended up as POW's in that outfit. There's not much more news. Everything is okey here and hope it is the same back home. Will keep you posted on what is going on.

All my love……JACK.

June 7, 1945

Dear Mom and Dad:

Here, I am back at base once again after a really marvelous trip. We left at about nine o'clock yesterday morning and went over by truck. It was about a two-hour ride. When we arrived, I took off on my own and hopped on a special tour. Went out to Anne Hathaway's cottage first. Everything was so crude in comparison to present day luxuries. There was much beautiful woodwork and carvings throughout. The main floor was of stone and the upstairs, of course, wood planks. I'd sure hate to go barefoot on that stone on a winter morn. If you look at the little snapshots of the cottage you can get an excellent idea of the whole place. The one on top shows the "family" room with the hearth and oven for baking bread. Everything is original and none is imitation.

The second view which shows the parlor gives you an idea of THE room of the house in those times. It was here that guests were entertained, etc. Notice the paneling on the walls - a sign of wealth during that period. The next two views also show scenes in the parlor. Personally, I wouldn't want to do any courting on the "courting settee" shown there. It looks pretty uncomfortable.

From there we went on to the Nash home which is now a museum. The gardens here were magnificent as were those at the Anne Hathaway cottage. There were a lot of ancient relics in this museum, and

8th Air Force - 365 Bomb Sqd. – 305th Bomb Grp. - APO 557

many beautiful oil portraits of various famous people of that time. I left this group and then took off on my own once again. Went up the street and ran across the home of John Harvard which was quaint in every respect. The significance of Harvard can easily be accounted for since he founded Harvard University in the USA.

By this time, I was starved so I went down to the Red Cross (the old White Swan Hotel) and had dinner. Then I went on to look at Shakespeare's birthplace. As you can see by the pictures it is a very nice home. However, inside you find the same crude floors, furniture, etc. Many treasures of his or pertaining to him are displayed throughout. The gardens were also a thing of great beauty.

Time was passing swiftly so I hurried on down to the beautiful new Shakespeare Memorial Theatre to see the matinee. The place was packed and I couldn't get a seat so I had to stand throughout the performance. Some Lieutenant from the base and I grabbed a post right behind the last row of seats so we could have something to lean on. It was well worth the effort and time. "Anthony and Cleopatra" was being shown and it was a marvelous spectacle. "Much Ado About Nothing" was scheduled for the evening, but the house was sold out so I couldn't see it. From what I heard, they pack them in there night after night without a let-up in attendance. It is really amazing.

After the performance was over I had tea and then decided to whip around and see some of the old pubs. I ended up in one of the most famous Pubs in Stratford-on-Avon. It was called "The Dirty Duck". The first time I saw the sign I thought I was seeing things, but that was it. They even had a jukebox. It was here that I met a little WAAF so we promptly proceeded to visit a few more of the more renowned pubs where no doubt old Bill Shakespeare himself probably had spent a few hours shedding a tear in his beer when he couldn't find a word to rhyme with "hullabalioza" or something. Since the trucks were leaving at ten o'clock I had to watch the time to a certain extent.

I was afraid for a minute that I had it when I looked at my watch and it said ten after ten. So, I took off on the double, catching the last truck on the run just as it was pulling out. It certainly was a great day and I enjoyed every minute of it. Went through the State register and found Milt Kapp's name in there. Sure, do wish it could have been him there in person so we could have had a good visit. I picked up quite a few postcards, etc., and would have picked up some other things had finances permitted. It is just too bad that my resources are so limited!

Mom, you would have gone crazy in that place. The antique shops there were really excellent. The china and other stuff are terribly old and quite beautiful. Dad, it would be a good idea not to bring mother over to these parts. She might spend us right off the map. You just can't imagine all of the china and items like that until you see them in person. It's really quite a sight. Will try and send these post cards one of these days. I'll enclose a few things in this letter for now. Everything is Okey so don't worry. Hope you two are feeling fine. Love...JACK.

June 8, 1945

Dear Mom and Dad:

It is pretty quiet up here at the tower right now so I'll take time and knock out a quick note. This afternoon we had an hour of close order drill as per usual once a week, and I drilled the guys for a while. Have three letters over at the barracks waiting for me and I don't know who they're from. One of the guys picked up my mail for me so now I'm sweating them out.

It is so dead around here that it is pitiful. Am just hoping that I can scrape up enough funds to go down to Bedford on Monday and Tuesday. I put out a big washing yesterday so I am all set to go again. There's absolutely no news whatsoever. Just thought I'd drop you a line and let you know that your "traveling son" was still of jail and going strong.

Will write when I dig up some news. Love...JACK.

8th Air Force - 365 Bomb Sqd. – 305th Bomb Grp. - APO 557

June 13, 1945

Dear Mom and Dad:

Just got back into camp after a grand and glorious two days. Borrowed a few quid from one of the boys and took off for Bedford. It is now evening. I have just eaten or a reasonable facsimile. Aside from that it was a busy afternoon and I got in difficulties as per usual. This Major walked in from a B-26 and wanted to get a certain phone number off the base. I took it for granted that he knew what he was doing so I had the call put through. Well, the call was to a restricted place so I got my tail in a sling for being a good guy!

It looks like I'll be leaving Merry England in the not too distant future. I must admit that this has been a fantastic assignment! When and if we make a move Lord only knows where we will go. I really will hate to leave England. It has been great over here - every minute of it.

The guys are going down to the ARC for a few sandwiches and cokes so best I close this epistle and run down with them. If I keep on with this letter I'll have you believing your only son has gone completely wacky - and he's not - not completely. Gotta close - will keep you posted and don't worry in case you don't hear from me for an extended period one of these days. You'll know that I have been captured by either a French Mademoiselle, German Fraulein, or Dainty Danish Damsel!! Love...JACK.

June 14, 1945

Dear Mom and Dad:

Another day and all I am doing is sweating it out. There is a chance I might get "ZI'ed" so went the rumors today. That, in case you don't know, means going back to the colonies- otherwise known as the USA. Then there is an even, a better chance I'll go over on the continent. One thing for sure is that I won't be in England too much longer.

Hold on - just got a long-distance call from my old buddy, Russ Garden, and he is going to meet me in Bedford on the 20th. He's got 8

Dear Mom and Dad

months' pay due as Staff Sgt. and is drawing it tomorrow so we'll probably raise the dead. Last time I saw Russ was when we ran into each other down in Nottingham. Sure, hope I can get down there. We're under a half way restriction already.

No more for now. Love...JACK.

June 16, 1945

Dear Mom and Dad:

Am on duty this afternoon and since it is pretty quiet I'll take time and drop you a line. Your letter saying that financial aid was on the way arrived and I hope it gets here real soon. Am meeting Russ Garden on Wednesday. as Staff Sgt. so he'll be flush - and 1 do mean flush. Almost 250 quids worth or in other words, in the neighborhood of $1,000. So, you can imagine what kind of time we'll have. The pass situation is what is worrying me. Hope they have pulled the pass restriction off of us for a few more days.

Jack manning the control tower.

One of the guys here in the tower is really sweating it out. He was supposed to get married in a few days and all they would give him was an overnight pass. We've all tried to convince him he's nuts to marry over here but he is reconciled. Don't know how much longer we'll be around here. It is hard telling. Nothing new has been said about my chances of going back to "the colonies" so I am just forgetting that idea. Must close. Hope everything is okey back home. Love...JACK.

8th Air Force - 365 Bomb Sqd. – 305th Bomb Grp. - APO 557

June 19, 1945

Dear Mom and Dad:

Just got back in from a trip to Bedford and a 24-hour pass. Right now, I am sitting here sweating out Russ Garden. He is supposed to arrive pretty soon unless, of course, he is restricted at the last minute

It is a beautiful day here - the weather has been surprisingly nice. By the way you were asking what insignia I wear. Right now, I wear the 8th Air Force patch. Also, for ribbons I have a spread of three with the ETO ribbon, good conduct and purple heart - above which is my combat infantry badge. I've gotten two battle stars but should have four. That is the way they are working it now. Two of them from the infantry and two from the air corps. At present I have about 50 points and if I get these other two stars I'll have 60 points. That would go a long way in getting me headed toward the States.

Hope all is well. LOVE...JACK.

June 21, 1945

Dear Mom and Dad:

It is pretty quiet around these parts today so I'll knock out a little quick note. 1 am working in the morning and then tomorrow afternoon I am going to Bedford. Then I have to get back Saturday noon to work again. Don't know how much longer we'll be here or what the deal is. I drew a sleeping bag, gas mask, and carbine yesterday, but I don't think it means a thing. What I am sweating out now is payday and I do mean I am sweating it out!

Had a long letter from Lucille (Dauner) yesterday and she seems to really be covering a lot of territory and all of the sights. I sure do hope that all of you can get together to celebrate the grandparents 55th wedding anniversary. Looks like I'll be the missing face. Well, who knows, one of these days I might barge in unexpectedly and give everyone the shock of their lives. I think that if and when I ever get orders to go home I won't say a thing until I get to the Burlington Station in

Dear Mom and Dad

Dubuque. Then I'll give you a buzz to pick me up! Boy. there's just no news! Am trying to squeeze out 62 points. I wrote the old 9th Division to try and get a couple of more battle stars. Will write more later. Love...JACK.

June 23, 1945

Dear Mom and Dad:

The mail is all screwed up again. Seems like it is taking ever and a day to get over here. I imagine it is this redeployment of troops that is doing it. Our trip to Denmark has fallen through so now we're just sweating it out once again. Sure, wish we knew where we were going to go. If we move to the Continent there is an excellent chance of my getting back to the states - I think! Don't get your hopes too high, however, because one never knows what might come up since this army of ours does some mighty funny things.

If it weren't for the above reason I'd take a shot at OCS and just stay in the army if I got a commission. But, I'll sweat it out as an enlisted man if there is a chance of getting home. I suppose that you read that I can call Radio Telephone (R/T) now. May go down to London one of these days and do it. If I do, however, I'll wire about a week in advance and tell you the exact day to expect it. Let me know if you want me to do it. I think the cost is between three and four quid - roughly $9 to $12 for three minutes.

Just heard a program from one of Smitty (Bob Smith) and my old hang outs - the Starlight Roof of the Chase Hotel in St. Louis. It was about a year ago that he and I made our last trip there for a final spree. Too bad he isn't around anymore to make one next June. He sure was a good Joe - a great little guy! Got a letter from my old buddy Dick Kline. They're down at Ingolstadt, Germany, and I guess they will be doing occupation duty. Sure, hope that Dick can get over here to the UK one of these days. Also, wish that Milt Kapp could get over here and meet me in London or elsewhere.

8th Air Force - 365 Bomb Sqd. – 305th Bomb Grp. - APO 557

It is getting late and I have a rough day tomorrow so I had better close. With a full day tomorrow, I hope that it is good and busy. I'll really give those "little" WAC's up at division a hard time if it is. I am getting known for that! Hope you are both okey. No more news for now so I'll close. Please say hello to everyone and give my very best to Karbergs. All my love...JACK.

June 25, 1945

Dear Mom and Dad:

Just thought you would like to see what it is like in Gay Parie'. I couldn't put it in better words. An average evening is pictured and you can see how the guys are getting hosed. Over in England that same evening would run you about one third of that. that might give you a slight idea for the reason I have been putting out an SOS for money of late. 1 Franc = 2 cents (supposedly). A thousand francs is $20 - but 1,000 francs is a drop in the bucket with the prices in Paris. Oh, well, read the article - it's strictly for the book and one more reason I don't want to go back there - as a buck private! Love...JACK.

June 27, 1945

Dear Mom and Dad:

It has been a beautiful day and I've really accomplished a lot. Worked this morning and then this afternoon I put out a tremendous washing. Washed and ironed two sun tan shirts - an OD shirt and a pair of OD pants plus a lot of other smaller stuff. Needless to say, I have a beautiful pair of wash woman's hands tonight. No mail whatsoever so tomorrow should bring in a few letters. Hope the camera and filter hurries up and gets here. 1 am getting mighty anxious to take some pictures so you can see what your son looks like.

After dinner, a few of us went out on the grass and shot a little golf. I've still got my old hook, but I got some nice iron shots. Should be able to shoot about an 88 if I played a round by myself, so I could use the

Dear Mom and Dad

old "hand mashie" for tough approach shots. Everything is fine over here. Love...JACK.

June 30, 1945

Dear Mom and Dad:

Pay day and my morale is exactly eight quid higher. In fact, it is so high that 1 am going to pour on a blitz to London and see all of the sights this coming Monday. And so, to continue...last night we went to Northampton and saw a mighty different movie: "The Picture of Dorian Grey".

Went to work at noon and there were only three ships up all afternoon so it was mighty quiet. Hardly a thing to do but sit and read - which I did. Well, it looks like we will pull stakes from here about October 1st, and the destination will be somewhere near Frankfort, I imagine. If I don't get sent to a hospital or back to the States before we leave I've had it. We'll probably rot over there as we'll stay as long as the infantry. In other words, the Army of Forgotten Men. I look to anywhere from 3-5 years by which time I'll be good for two things: nothing and no good! I'll be strictly a European and that's no lie. About all, we'll do if and when we get there will be to look forward to passes and then it will be Brussels, Paris, the Riviera, Sweden (maybe), or Switzerland. That's one thing we have been promised - liberty runs via planes to all points such as these.

Frankly, I don't care anymore. I do wish they would give out some stripes, but as I said before there is no hope. This outfit has been over here for 33 months. One of the boys up at the tower - and a good man - has been with them all the time and still is Pfc. It's morbid as the devil having just so much dough and not being able to work up to any higher level. What a bloody life!!

I've made up my mind that if I do get shipped to Germany I am going to throw this physical classification and everything else to the four winds and try and get a crack at OCS. I might as well spend the rest of my life in the army if I've got 3-5 years to stick out. With a commission I could almost see it.

8th Air Force - 365 Bomb Sqd. – 305th Bomb Grp. - APO 557

Took a few pictures today. It was actually sunny for three hours. However, rain has once again set in. Sure, does rain a lot over here. There's quite a poem that you frequently hear over here - it goes on verse after verse and ends up to the effect –

"Same old place...same old time,
Same old Yank... with the same old line!"

Well, I have to write a couple of more letters so maybe I had better close. Hope everything is okey - I am fine and am looking forward to my trip to London. Love...JACK.

July 4, 1945 (London)

Dear Mom and Dad:

Well, here I am almost ready to get started back to base after a grand and glorious trip to London. II came down by train on Monday afternoon and got in about 4:00 P.M. Checked in at the Washington Red Cross and then proceeded to start doing the town. Saw Loren Bacall and Humphrey Bogart in "To Have and Not Have" and then to Piccadilly Circus to watch the "Piccadilly Commandoes" peddle their wares. All bars close at about 10:30 P.M. except at hotels and then you have to be a resident.

Started out early in the morning to see all the points of interest and I'll bet we walked 10 miles; and if you don't believe me I'll gladly trade feet with you. First on the list was Buckingham Palace where we watched the new guard get posted. The Palace is a dismal looking thing. It looks more like a huge hotel. There is absolutely nothing beautiful about the exterior at all. When I think of a palace I always think of towers and spacious grounds surrounding it so I was a little dissolution. From there we went down to see Parliament and also No. 10 Downing Street. Heard old Big Ben strike 12. That is one of the most beautiful structures I have ever seen. Westminster Abbey held many wonderful sights; and, naturally all of the famous people buried there. It is a magnificent piece of architecture with high ceilings and beautiful

Dear Mom and Dad

rose windows. Saw the graves of Dickens, Livingstone, Isaac Newton, and many others.

We hopped on to the subway then and went out to see the famous Tower Bridge and Castle. It was in this Castle that they held Rudolph Hess when he came over from Germany. The Tower Bridge looked exactly like the pictures which I had seen.

St. Paul's Cathedral proved another magnificent shrine. The area around it had been redid to rubble, yet the Cathedral had just barely been nicked. It is really amazing that after 2 years of bombardment, only a few of the famous points had even been touched.

(Continued - July 5th). Back at base once again and everything is okey. I'll continue where I left off. After leaving St. Paul's we walked on down Fleet Street where all of the newspapers and journalistic materials are published. It was around here that we stopped to eat at Ye Olde Cock Tavern. The bill came to exactly 15 Shillings - the equivalent of $3.00 in cold hard American cash. Passed by the Old Bailey and also the Civil Courts building out in the district along with many other sights.

Then on to the River Thames where we saw the oldest thing in England. It is known as Cleopatra's Needle. It was moved from Egypt to London many centuries ago. I had "Thako" take a picture of me reclining in the arms of one of the high sphinx characters. Needless to say, the people surrounding us got quite a kick out of the whole procedure including some old character who had spent the morning picking up cigarette butts and who at the time was drying all the tobacco under the monument.

After that we boarded the famous old ship - "The Discovery". It was one of the first boats to go to the Antarctic and it held a lot of interesting features. Saw Bob Hope in "The Prince and the Pirate". By the way, Hope was in London and was going to put on a big show yesterday evening, but we couldn't stay as we were due back at base by 4:00 P.M. We felt badly that we couldn't see the "Master of Mirth" demonstrate his talents. Ran into a couple of generals along the way. One of them was a major general - division commander of the 44th Division. The

8th Air Force - 365 Bomb Sqd. – 305th Bomb Grp. - APO 557

brass was really plentiful. I never even threw one highball - not even to the general. I did get a kick out of one second looey when he saw this division commander. He was really squirming.

I got a good night's sleep then caught the eleven o'clock train for Kettering. I decided we ought to get off at Bedford so we did and I finished my roll of films. Now listen to this one. I took the films in and to have the roll fine grain developed and an enlargement of each picture it cost me 19 shillings 9 pence which was $3.95 and I can't get them for three weeks. From now on I am going to send them all home to be done. It costs too much and you have to wait for long over here. Caught a lift into base - had dinner and grabbed the liberty run to Northampton where we finished off whole trip with a real blitz. After pub time we hit some dances and then caught the trucks for base at eleven o'clock.

The author with London Bridge in the background - July 4, 1945

So now I am already to go to work this noon. Sure, was great to get in a real city again. So now Bond Street, Fleet Street, Leicester Square, Piccadilly Circus, and all the many other places just become names on the passing parade of events and things that I have seen. Brussels is still the one place I would like to get to now - prices there are terrific, however - even worse than in Paris from all reports.

There's not much else to report. Will try and send a few of these things I picked up in London back to you. Just a few folders, etc., that I thought you would like to see. Everything is okey. Sure, wish you two guys could have been with me. Who knows maybe one of these days we'll all come over again and I can really show you around. Love, always...JACK.

The author at the wheel of "The Discovery" in London - July 1945

Dear Mom and Dad

July 8, 1945

Dear Mom and Dad:

    Just a quick note before I go down for chow and then work. Went to Bedford last night and "Thako" and I had quite a time. They started a new liberty run down there so it's really convenient. The trucks leave Bedford for the base at eleven o'clock. Played baseball yesterday afternoon. All of us fellows up at flying control formed a team and our first game is this afternoon. No doubt we will lose, but it will be a good experience and exercise.

    In case you haven't done so, please send my check for $20 as I'll be needing it before the end of the month. It is a beautiful day today and I sure wish I wasn't working. Invariably when I go on pass it decides to cloud up. I was lucky one day down in London when the sun came out. They tell me it is unusual down there to see the sun for a whole day. Not much going on - it has been busy up here at the tower the past week or so and probably will continue. In the meantime, I have to put out a man-sized washing tonight, believe it or not. Hope you two are.
    Love... JACK.

July 9, 1945

Dear Mom and Dad:

    Another day and I was really busy. This morning I was up at 4:30 A.M. for an early take-off so I am a little on the tired side. Your V-Mail of June 28th came in and I think I must have sounded a little too optimistic on this idea of getting home. Best you just forget about it so there will be no disappointment. The chance is about 100 - 1 and I am not that lucky. This Class D Physical I am monkeying with is a total gag. I am in absolutely A-1 physical shape - never was in better health except when I was up on line. Of course, if I can get home on it I'll pull it, but I don't think I can. Aside from that I only have 48 points with fifteen more on the way if nothing fouls up. But 60 points is a drop in the bucket. So, I am planning to stick around. I have been reamed both

8th Air Force - 365 Bomb Sqd. – 305th Bomb Grp. - APO 557

ways – the 9th Division is definitely occupational so no matter where I might have been I would have had to remain over here for the occupation. However, it's much better here in England and as long as I can take a furlough every 3 months and plenty of passes while maintaining the set-up we have - why I am living the life of Riley. Woe be the day when Riley comes home! That's all of the news for now. Love……JACK.

July 10, 1945

Dear Mom and Dad:

Mail call brought in your V-mails of the fourth and fifth of July, Mom, and it seems like you two guys have been really stepping out on your son. Glad to hear my "gambling mom" hit the jack-pot. How about a loan? By the way, I am planning on going on furlough about the eleventh of the month (August) so please send me about $50 from my bank account. I think the way the mails are coming through on letters you had better send it about the last week of July and then when my check comes for the first of August you can deposit it in my account. I've decided to go down to Bournemouth unless I can get a plane going to Ireland. Bournemouth is down in southern England, and it is beautiful from all of the reports I have read.

In the meantime, I have been taking it easy. Am going to save a little cash this month if I can. By the way, I got quite a letter from that little number (mom). She was worrying that I had left - really touching, you know. Lt. Rodgers, one of our officers in the control tower, went over to Germany and brought back a B-17 load of beer. So, we've got a case of it here. Only 8% and it is delicious. In fact, it is such good stuff that he "blew his top" down at the officers' club and was in the hospital last night and this morning. He was on duty at noon though. What a character - but a mighty good guy to all of us in the control tower. We are very fortunate to have a team of control tower officers who are great to work for and with!

Nothing in particular new. Same old story and I am catching up on my beauty sleep. Got up at 11:30 A.M. this morning so you see what I mean. I never get up earlier than ten o'clock except on mornings when I work. What a beautiful racket... and they pay a guy for it. Good old Uncle Sam!!

Gotta close. I am hungry and think I best fry a couple of eggs that I picked up at the mess hall. Everything is okey - so don't worry. Love, always.... JACK.

July 14, 1945

Dear Mom and Dad:

Sorry I haven't written the last couple of days, but I have been on pass and didn't have the opportunity. Picked up my mail - an accumulation of about three days and found your good letters - particularly the one with the money order. It couldn't have come at a more needed time. I was down to my last 10 shillings.

Well, it looks like we are definitely going to pull stakes one of these days. An advance party is going the 18th of July and I don't imagine the rest of the outfit will before September. From all appearances we have a field near Brussels which wouldn't be too bad. In the meantime, yours truly is sweating it out. Will I go or won't is the question? So here I sit with the galloping dandruff and smelly feet. Everything is fine - except that I am hungry. I've got to head out for food. Love...JACK.

July 17, 1945

Dear Mom and Dad:

Just in case my V-Mail might have gotten lost - the money order got here okey: And just in the nick of time. Now for the big news. We're actually moving and it will only be a matter of a few days I think before the field is dead as the famous door mouse. Some of the guys have already flown over, but no doubt those of us in flying control will be last. We are going to a little place that lies between Brussels and Liege and is about 30 miles from each. So, it looks like I will now get to see that famous city.

8th Air Force - 365 Bomb Sqd. – 305th Bomb Grp. - APO 557

Last night I really had a time. Took the liberty run into Bedford and met this Captain that I was with a few nights ago and we immediately headed for the Swan Hotel where he knew the barmaid. So, she naturally kept bringing all the good stuff out from underneath the counter. At ten o'clock they put the towel up, but we kept on getting served until ten thirty. We decided that we were hungry so we went down to the officer's club and had waffles and tea. It was then that I realized that I had missed the liberty run.

So, he and I hopped into a jeep and rode out to his detachment where it so happens he is one of the "wheels". All he did was get on the phone and call the Officer of the Day and ask him to give him permission to use a staff car. About ten minutes later a car and driver arrived and we piled into the back seat and drove off in style. They took me right up to the gate where I bid them a fond farewell. What a guy! A really damn nice officer.

Have to go down for an X-Ray of my chest today. Everyone on the base has to do it. Don't know exactly what it's for as they will probably just throw them away. Such is the army. I am now in the 9th Air Force so you can add that to the mounting number of outfits and patches that I have been in and worn. Who knows, my next outfit might be "Civvy Street" but that's talking in fantastic terms now.

Next, I'll be writing to you about some demure little Belgian mademoiselle - or more probably a Belgian horse. You know one of those huge furry beasts of burden. One of the boys in the barracks came in last night with two little kittens and a dog. He is about 6'2" tall and weighs well over 200 pounds. So, he put the whole menagerie on his bed and slept on the floor. One of the kittens is in our room now and it is really cute - just a little ball of fur.

It looks like an awfully busy afternoon coming up. Almost every plane on the field is flying or else being checked. This just doesn't make my disposition too good. Oh well, a guy has to do a little work once in a while. Tours from the continent to Switzerland have been instituted and I am hoping to get one someday. The charge is $35 for the tour

Dear Mom and Dad

itself; then your food and lodging are extra. So, all in all I imagine it would run about $75. It would be well worth it I am sure. It is handled through the Red Cross, but the tours are directed by native Swiss guides. Just something to look forward to.

Enclosed is a picture of yours truly at the stick of a A-26 attack bomber. That's where I should have been all of the time. I guess I wasn't quite that lucky though. Anyway, that is how I might have looked and someday I can show my grandchildren (if I have any) that photo and tell them how I fought the battle of Britain in a B-26 as a 4-star General. Not much more to report. Hope you are both fine. Love...JACK.

Chapter 21

9th Air Force - 365 Bomb Sqd. – 305th Bomb Grp. - APO 140 - c/o Postmaster, New York, N.Y.

(St. Trond, Belgium, July 24, 1945 - November 24, 1945)

July 26, 1945
St. Trond, Belgium

Dear Mom and Dad:

    I'm sitting up here in a tower that looks like one of those forest preserve observation look outs. We're right out here almost at the cross section of the runways with a full view of everything. Yesterday afternoon at 3:30 P.M. we took off from Chelveston - landed at Thurleigh for some gas - got stuck in some soft gravel and it took two half-tracks to get us out. Finally, we left at about 5:30 P.M. and three of us were up in the nose navigating all the way over. I took a few shots here and there along the way.

    We landed at about 6:30 P.M. and they hauled our stuff out to the Chateau - a huge place about two miles from the air field. It once was the Belgium "West Point", but the tides of war have definitely left their marks. All of the troops are living in the building right now - however, we are going to get a home of our own near the base. This flying control is "in like Flynn" and we get everything we want and do almost the same.

Dear Mom and Dad

Guess that I was lucky to get into this outfit. The food at the Chateau is prepared by civilians and we have a bunch of gals dishing it out. Civilians also clean the place and sweep the floors and keep the place looking good. Between the air base and the Chateau are plenty of beer parlors so all is well. Which reminds me - do you know what I tip the scales at these days? Believe it or not I am a flat 165 pounds the last time that I weighed in

St. Trond is only a few miles from here and there is a pub at every corner, and at least fifteen in between. Shops are also prevalent between the base and town. No doubt, I'll be going in to check them out but prices seem high. Liege is only 20 miles away and a trolley that goes directly to downtown Liege runs right by the base and Chateau. It is a great set-up. We slip out of the Chateau and hop on a street car FREE. It picks us up right at the base. Personally, I would prefer being in England, but I know that I'll be able to see a lot of things over here so I am not complaining. Also, it is easy to get back to the UK. Just grab a plane and take off when the clearance comes through.

Just came back from marshalling a plane into a revetment. We lost our radio contact for about an hour and had to give this guy a green flare to land. So, I went after him in a jeep - no shirt or anything and led him to a revetment. After he cut his engines I started wise cracking with him - asking him where he learned to make such a lousy landing. He kidded right back and then I asked him for his name and status. It was then he said - Colonel Quinn - so out of the kindness of my heart I drove him to Headquarters.

I imagine that I have some mail down at the squadron but don't know when I'll be able to pick it up. Haven't gotten any for a few days so there should be quite a stack of it. Also, maybe my pictures will be included. Sure, hope they turned out good. Not much more news for now. Everything is okey as far as I am concerned. Hope you two are fine. All my love...JACK.

9th Air Force - 365 Bomb Sqd. – 305th Bomb Grp. - APO 140

July 30, 1945

Dear Mom and Dad:

It is a beautiful day and I hope the flying is at a minimum. That's a foolish hope! I go off duty at noon for 48 hours, but at present I have absolutely NO francs. I am dead broke - flat busted! Good thing that tomorrow is pay day. Then I think that I'll head for Brussels and do a little fraternization. The staff around here is really sad. Went into St. Trond night before last and it is a second East Dubuque. No matter where you go in the town it is "Slumming" with a capital "S". What a place!!

In the meantime, things haven't changed much except for the fact that we now have 12 guys in the room instead of four. Also, there are "skateeen" million MP "Off Limit" signs all over the base, and besides that some dumb jerk just started driving a jeep down the live runway. That is an invitation to suicide! Well, that's one way of getting out of the Army, but it sure would be messy as the devil. Some of these guys can't figure out that these are live runways that are designed for aircraft to take off and land. If this keeps up, we'll probably add one more plane or jeep to the wrecked aircraft at the end of the runway.

I should get a good stack of mail about today. The last I received was Saturday and it was about a month old. Mail has slowed up considerably. I guess it is due to crowded shipping conditions. Looks like we'll be over here for a couple of years, I would kind of like to stay around here for about three months and then get sent out to the Pacific. By that time, I would have seen everything of any major importance or interest. Also, there are no points to be accumulated in this Theatre of Operation except through service. I guess that I better get into an active Theatre where I can pick up some battle stars. However, I am not too sure that is possible at this stage of the game.

I would sure like to get down and see Australia and New Zealand; then stop in Hawaii enroute to San Francisco. Since I have a few more years of this army life ahead I might as well see everything I can. This idea of being an international traveler suits me okay. I love it - in fact, I think I ought to find a racket in civilian life that would keep me going to all corners of the earth. In some respects, I hope that they move us out to the Pacific Theatre instead of over into Germany. This is just a temporary stop here in Belgium until the other airfield is serviceable.

Looks like the Japs are really taking a beating over there. This life of leisure is okay for a rest, but there is still nothing like being in combat. Will probably go to Liege tonight. No dough, but I would like to look around. Brussels will be the next target and I'll hit it this weekend if all goes well. Must close - hope everything is okay. Give my regards to everyone Love…...JACK.

August 4, 1945

Dear Mom and Dad:

It is a beautiful warm day here and naturally I am on duty. However, I have been sitting out in the sun most of the afternoon. Last night, four of us "bloody yanks" went out to terrorize the neighboring villagers. After a steak dinner with french fries, tomatoes, and beer we hit one of the hangouts - a Cafe ala "beacoup de music" - "beaucoup de fem" and "beaucoup de cognac".

Every letter I get mentions that everyone is playing bridge here and there. I am suspicious - when that bunch of gals can sit down and concentrate on bridge, then I know it is time for me to go out and see a psychiatrist. Frankly, I don't think any one of them can sit still that long. No more news for now. Everything is okay so don't worry. Love……JACK.

August 5, 1945

Dear Mom and Dad:

Just came in from a 15-mile bike ride. Three of us started out after dinner and headed for the wide-open spaces. We leisurely pedaled on and on - having a beer now and then - and taking a few pictures. We enjoyed some lovely scenery on a very pleasant evening.

9th Air Force - 365 Bomb Sqd. – 305th Bomb Grp. - APO 140

The country side is very pretty - lots of orchards and little gardens. People were very friendly and waved and spoke. Our first stop was at the little village of Cartenhbosch where we batted the breeze. From there we went on down some back roads, wound around and finally started back toward St. Trond. About a mile from town I had a flat tire so I had to walk as my means of locomotion home. Will probably take a three-day pass to Liege - I mean Brussels - in a week or so. I think the pass situation will clear up by then. Frankly, I just want to get in there and shoot a lot of pictures and see the city. I was able to buy a roll of film over here. There seems to be plenty of 35 mm., but I don't know how good it is. It costs 65 francs for 36 exposures which is about a dollar and a half a roll. In the meantime, I am still waiting for my London pictures to arrive. Hope nothing happened to them!

Last night, I didn't get off work until 1:30 AM and then we were up at five o'clock for an early take off. I slept a couple of hours this afternoon so I feel great now. I didn't think noon would ever roll around again. A bunch of the boys are going up to Iceland for a while and some more are going straight to the Pacific. It looks like I am not in the group to leave. Almost took a trip down to Austria, but got kicked off the plane at the last minute. Some "Hot-shot Charlie" Captain was flying who "wanted to be alone" Usually our guys are more than happy to have you sign on board.

Tomorrow I have to fix a bike tire and then maybe I will buzz into Liege and shoot some pictures. Frankly, I never make plans any more - I just take off and go when and where the spirit moves me. I may try and get to Henri Chapelle Cemetery and shoot some pictures of Karl Eschen's grave. I guarantee you I'll get there some time.

Not much more for right now so I guess I'll close and hit the sack. Love to you both from Jacques (Flemish for Jack).

August 5, 1945

Dear Mom and Dad:

Came off duty and learned that we guys in flying control are moving. So, I packed once again and brought my stuff down to our new

Dear Mom and Dad

home. We are living in a large one-story house just outside the city limits and about a mile from the field. We're all by ourselves and no one bothers us whatsoever. Have things all cleaned up and it is beginning to look like the move is going to be okey.

Everything is okey and I am having a great time as usual. Hope to take that trip to the Riviera soon. The restrictions on Brussels haven't eased at all. No more for now - I'll keep you posted. Please say hello to everyone for me. Love...JACK.

August 7, 1945

Dear Mom and Dad:

Your two letters came in yesterday just before I took off for Liege. Went in about one o'clock and had a great time shooting pictures and looking around. Prices are terrific. They don't seem so high. It's just that our pay doesn't last too long! The value of the franc is just too low in comparison to the dollar. As a result, I am cold flat broke and I am determined not to crack that $50 money order. Just start sending my $20 check on over as soon as you get them.

Well, to continue - I've gotten some maps, postcards, and other things to send home. Last evening, we went down and had a tub bath in very lovely public bath - then to a beautiful night club on the top floor overlooking an equally magnificent indoor swimming pool. Had a few short ones for an appetizer and then headed for a little spot I was familiar with and had a beautiful sirloin steak. It was about half to three quarters of an inch thick and it covered the plate. It had all the entrees with it - the bill was 165 francs or about $3.50. See what I mean about prices. You can get anything you want in Belgium, but you pay for it. No more news for now. Love...JACK.

9th Air Force - 365 Bomb Sqd. – 305th Bomb Grp. - APO 140

August 9, 1945

Dear Mom and Dad:

No mail yesterday so maybe today some will come in. Worked yesterday morning - Slept in the afternoon and then walked into St. Trond last night and had a whole cherry pie with a mere three scoops of ice cream on it. Started back to the barracks at about eight thirty o'clock when a "recon" drove up and asked if we wanted a ride with the result that we went all the way into Liege. Ducked down to the G.I. Club, had a few short ones and danced a little before taking off for the "liberty run" trucks. Got caught in a deluge of rain on the way and was absolutely soaked. When we got back to base it hadn't even rained so we looked mighty odd walking in soaking wet.

Not much flying today - weather was none too good so things were plenty quiet. Rumor has it that Russia declared war. Maybe they will move this outfit to Vladivostok or elsewhere. Frankly, I am all for getting into combat again - more battle stars - and more points for getting out of the army. Cheers for now. Love...JACK.

August 10, 1945

Dear Mom and Dad:

It has been raining all day and not a single aircraft has taken off or landed so you can imagine just how quiet it has been up here at the control tower. And, what's more, it looks like it will continue to stay this way. News has just come over that the Japs are willing to capitulate. So, what - why don't they bomb them into oblivion. Now that they've made all of those atomic bombs let's use them up rather than just sink them in the ocean. In the meantime, forget all hopes of me getting home even after the Pacific war is over. I've bloody well had it on this point system - I have a total of 50 points and five more on the way.

Next week I am going to begin getting things lined up for this Switzerland trip if I can arrange it. My PX watch is Kaput so I am going to buy another watch once I get down there. I was going to Brussels for the day tomorrow, but if this rain continues, I am going to forget about it. There is simply no use to get a pass and head for Brussels or any other place if you have to travel in the rain! No more news. Love... JACK.

August 12, 1945

Dear Mom and Dad:

Everything is pretty quiet up here at the tower today so I'll take time and give you the latest. At eight o'clock yesterday morning another guy and I got the wild brainstorm that we ought to go into Brussels - so we dressed, picked up a twelve-hour pass, and started hitch hiking. Caught a ride after about five minutes of waiting. We were in the heart of the city within one hour. It is really quite a place!

Started out by seeing the unknown soldiers' monument which is a 300-foot tower. There is a staircase going up to the top so we climbed it and shot a few panoramic views of the city. Then down to the Civil Courts building; numerous famous churches; some other well-known buildings and statues, etc. I shot about a dozen pictures here and there. There are some beautiful stores all over the city. I looked around for some things to buy but nothing doing with the money that I had with me. Prices are terrific in comparison with our pay. We American soldiers are stabilizing these people's currency and it is a lousy deal.

Well, let me go on with my numerous travels. Street cafes lined every avenue. Night clubs are wide open and the floor shows are red hot!! Some more of the Follies Bergere of gay Parie. We had to get out of town by seven o'clock since we weren't on leave. Result: we didn't get to stick around when things were good and lively

Had dinner at the beautiful old Hotel Metropole. It is now under the Allied Expeditionary Forces control, but much has remained unchanged. The string ensemble still plays and the waiters are all very formal. The Red Cross has set up some very good places to spend leaves or furloughs. There is the Ardennes Club - G.I. Joes - and many others where all the facilities of necessity for a good leave are available.

9th Air Force - 365 Bomb Sqd. – 305th Bomb Grp. - APO 140

Frankly, I can't afford a three-day pass in Brussels. A hundred bucks would be like water through a sieve. However, with some future planning I might give it a whirl.

As it is, 1 had to cash my $50 money order already and only half the month is gone. I still have around $40 of it left, however, and I am going as easy as possible. Please send that money order immediately when it comes as I am definitely going to Switzerland about the 6th of September, and I'll want all of the cash I can get. That ought to do it. I am going to buy a watch down there and also get some knick knacks to send home. Also, don't be surprised if you get a long-distance call - the rates are much lower down there and it is much easier to put through the calls. Don't plan on this but don't be surprised if the operator calls and says that Switzerland is on the line.

To continue - once again - the Black Market in Brussels is terrific. I got stopped numerous times and went into several back rooms on some deals. However, I didn't do any business. I had an offer of 5000 Guilders (Dutch) for my camera. The guy had all the Dutch cash - so I told him if he would change it to 100-franc Belgium notes I'd work the deal. 5000 Guilder is $210 in American dollars. Other offers for the camera were 4000 Belgium Francs or about $100. These guys will buy anything, and that is no kidding. Have no fear - I'm not taking any chances on any of this stuff.

After taking a last look around we hopped a street car for the outskirts and then started hitch hiking. Caught a truck going all of the way to Aachen. He was supposed to go via Maastricht, but I talked him into going via St. Trond, Liege, Henri Chapelle and Aachen. Result: we got a ride right back to base.

Think that I'll hitch hike up to Henri Chapelle Cemetery early next week and shoot some pictures for the Eschens. It will probably be another spur of the moment trip like this last one, but after all, those are more interesting. Everything is okay - hope you two are fine.

Love...JACK.

Dear Mom and Dad

Jack Dauner, Don Williams (Mendovi, Wis.), Carl Camp (Conyers, Georgia), Liege, Belgium - August 15, 1945.

Belgium War Monument.
(l to r) Eric Heinz, the Burgemeister of Hergenroth with his driver.

Locks and dam near Maastricht, Holland on the Albert Canal

Pete Scatura along one of the canals in Maastricht, Holland

A bridge that was blown up at the edge of Maastricht, Holland

9th Air Force - 365 Bomb Sqd. – 305th Bomb Grp. - APO 140

August 15, 1945

Dear Mom and Dad:

Well the war is over - so what! Last night or I should say at one o'clock in the morning we heard the joyous news. Personally, I am against it! We ought to rain that whole island with all the remaining atomic bombs we have in storage. I claim the German case was different - the Japs are totally and racially no good to mankind. So, the world is at Peace!

Really, I am in excellent spirits this morning though you'd never guess it. No hangover! Also, ten hours of sleep - sunshine - life is wonderful. Alas, it has been two whole days since my last stab at letter writing. Since then my travels have been hither and yon. Spent one day in Liege. Sold my no-good watch for 1,000 Francs (about $22), and then spent a quiet evening in the G.I. Club drowning my sorrows (there were four of us) at the terrific price of 3 Francs (about 6 cents) a glass for beer. They have the best and strongest beer at the Club than in the whole city. Anyway, we had a mighty good time. I only lost an OD cap and spent 100 Francs so the evening was quite reasonable. By the way the Liege G.I. Night Club is outstanding and I'll probably spend quite a bit of time there.

The next morning, I woke up at noon - had dinner - took a refreshing shower and grabbed a plane to Bordeaux. Yes, I said Bordeaux!! It was about a two- and one-half-hour flight. Landed and got a good look at the situation. Personally, I am sorry that I sold the place - it would have made my fifth wife a nice wedding present - that is, if I ever have the fifth wife.

The airdrome had the living hell bombed out of it. One could see it had once been very beautiful. On the whole, the city had hardly been touched and it is a very lovely place. One thing that was very noticeable was a magnificent stadium - also, some beautiful churches and buildings. Shipping had once been a major industry there, and the docks were really quite a sight. So, were the huge concrete and steel submarine pens that the Jerries had built. There had been many direct hits on those little babies, but down below the damage was little, if any. The once busy harbor is filled with sunken ships of all types and varieties. Quite a morbid sight - just like the scrap pile of Jerry planes out at the airport or like the two huge scrap piles of crashed B-17's, B-24's, and B-26's here on this field. It is certainly representative of what one of these aircraft looks like after it crashes.

As you can see I am fast becoming a new "1st". My theory is Daunerism and I am the self-made leader of this powerful Daunerist Movement. I'm all for myself and to the devil with everything else. The Movement is definitely on the uphill trend. In fact, there is only one trouble and that is that every other guy has the same theory. There is Jacksonism,. Morganism, Smithism, etc. - and they are all working on the same theory. My question now, Mr. Anthony, is how to get them all working for Dauner and Daunerism.

Today is VJ-Day and I am no longer in the Control Tower. Canned? Not yet - but I am working on it!! I am now in the front office - I'm literally and figuratively a "WHEEL." So I sit behind a desk with a telephone in each hand and tell everyone below the rank of major to go to hell, and that if he doesn't like it to try the Antarctic. In a way, it's a better deal, but I like the control tower where we got some sun and where a bunch of dumb yaps couldn't walk in and ask a thousand ignorant questions. So as a lowly private (excuse me. Pfc), I can't make a mistake. You see as a private first class I don't have any brains, education or intellect so I can't SNAFU. If I make a mistake I simply tell them that as long as I get paid as a private I use that corresponding amount of grey matter. I'll save the remaining 9/10ths for future duties.

I put in for a furlough to Switzerland today and was informed it should come in around the first of the month. You are allowed to take in $65. Thirty-five dollars are immediately donated to the Swiss government for food and lodging. That leaves $30 to splurge on. So, I'll buy a good watch with $20 of it and hand the other ten in for some silk stockings for you, Mom. I think your size is 8 1/2 - best you let me know immediately!

9th Air Force - 365 Bomb Sqd. – 305th Bomb Grp. - APO 140

I think I'll go to work this afternoon since I am up and at 'am. That is if I get the ambition. The sack still looks mighty good. As you can see I am well on the way as a psycho case, so best you get the straight jacket ready. Must go to hear the Colonel tell us that the war is over. Meantime; all my love...JACK.

Jack Dauner and Eric Heinz
August 18, 1945 - Liege, Belgium

Jack Dauner and John Poole at
the Rockdale Club in Dubuque

Jack Dauner, Roscoe Wells and Carl Camp
August 31, 1945 - Liege, Belgium

Dear Mom and Dad

August 19, 1945

Dear Mom and Dad:

Haven't written for a couple of days due to the fact that I have been traveling again. I haven't been to work for so long it is pitiful. So yesterday, Eric Heinz and I grabbed a pass for Henri Chapelle (where the American Military Cemetery is located) and started hitch hiking. We were in Liege about noon so we ate and then caught a street car to the edge of town. It was only about 10 minutes until a civilian car drove up and I hailed it. We piled in and it turned out to be the Burgemeister of Hergenroth, Belgium, which was the last village this side of the German border on the road to Aachen. I had been through these numerous times. The Burgemeister's name was H.W. Hackens and he drove us around the country side and finally to the United States cemetery at Henri Chapelle.

It was about two miles from the main road and here lies approximately 18,000 American and some 200 other allied dead. Then across the hedge row lie 10,000 Germans. The surrounding country is beautiful - the cemetery is being beautified so that by the time people from the States start coming over it should look very nice. The lots are neatly arranged and have 240 bodies to a plot. The white crosses are row on row - there is a little chapel - and the American flag overlooks those who gave their lives in this war, awe inspiring scene and I was very glad to have made the effort to visit this grave site.

The records are all on file and so I checked for Karl Eschen's grave site. It would be folly to try and make out that this is a fitting end for any man. All graves are exactly alike, rank means nothing. The only way to tell an officer from an enlisted man is by the serial number. I shot about 18 pictures of Karl's grave, the cemetery, surrounding country and other little particulars that the Eschens might enjoy. So, I finally did one good deed! I also checked on one of the guys killed in my squad on December 11, 1944. That was the day I was wounded in action. He was lucky - buried three days after his death.

We grabbed a ride all the way to the Liege Red Cross with a Lieutenant Colonel. Had a bite to eat and headed for the G.I. Beer Garden

9th Air Force - 365 Bomb Sqd. – 305th Bomb Grp. - APO 140

where we spent about three hours. It was after that when we had the enclosed photographs taken. A bunch of us met at the G.I. Night Club, and then spent the rest of the evening there. The latter is a delightful place to spend an evening which we frequently do. Anyway, today was quite a day and night.

Guess I'll go to work this afternoon before I am officially canned. Enclosed is a plan of the cemetery which you can put in the scrapbook. I have another one for the Eschens when I write them and send the pictures. Not much else has been going on. Quite a few guys are leaving. In fact, Eric Heintz will be going in a week or so. Will keep you posted. All my love...JACK.

August 22, 1945

Dear Mom and Dad:

Just a note to let you know that I am still alive and out of the guard house. However, the latter is beginning to appear more attractive. I took the afternoon off and read Betty Smith's "A Tree Grows in Brooklyn". Now I would like to meet that gal and see what she was really like. I have been doing a considerable amount of reading lately - some good, some bad. My next one is H.G. Wells' "An Outlook for Homo Sapiens" which is supposed to be good if you like some tastes of socialism and a few other isms. Anyway, I continue to try and improve my mind and maintain some of my intelligence.

My roll of films taken in Brussels and Liege will be done tomorrow and I'll try and send them and the other roll on home. Censorship of packages is in effect again. Of course, an officer can be thoroughly trusted - yeah, man!! Frankly, I've never seen such an irritated and disgusted bunch of G.I.s anywhere. Last night, one of the hangers burned to the ground, and it was probably! set by a Belgique. In the meantime, existence continues and morale is minus 100% for the troops. I hope it drops to minus 400% and maybe we'll see some action. No more news. Love to you both...JACK.

Dear Mom and Dad

August 23, 1945

Dear Mom and Dad:

Check the purple ink. Looks vaguely familiar doesn't it? Well, tonight has really been a quiet one. I took a shower and then on the way to our "home away from home" we picked up a case of ice-cold beer and brought it back. So, we just sat around the stove batting the breeze and knocking off the ale.

Went into town late this afternoon and got my pictures of Chelveston, Brussels and Liege. They came out pretty good except that I believe my range finder is a little bit off since some are slightly out of focus. On the whole, they are okey. As soon as the guys get what pictures they want, I'll send the negatives home so you can have those made that you want. I am really glad that I have my camera as it provides me with an opportunity to take some pictures of the scenery and some of the guys I work with.

Tomorrow - weather permitting - I may grab a pass and take off on a 24-hour pass to Maastricht, Holland. I would like to see that place as it was quite a battle ground not too many months ago - and, I understand there is a rest camp located there now. Didn't get any mail today because I didn't pick it up so I better get down there pronto. Am enclosing some stuff that I picked up here and there. Really no news. Guess I'll hit the sack and get a good night's sleep. Everything is okey. Love...JACK.

August 25, 1945

Dear Mom and Dad:

Things are mighty quiet around the office so I'll just sit down and give you the latest dope on my new escapades. Yesterday, four of us decided to take off and hitch hike up to Maastricht, Holland. So, we grabbed a 24-hour pass and thumbed into Liege and from there due north to Maastricht. All along the way we followed the Muse and Maas Rivers and also the famous Albert Canal. The canal is really a masterpiece. The trip was quite scenic - beautiful country and many pill boxes which had been a part of the Dutch defenses.

9th Air Force - 365 Bomb Sqd. – 305th Bomb Grp. - APO 140

When we reached Maastricht, I expected to find the city hard hit with the effects of war as there had been some severe fighting in that sector, but I was greatly surprised to see very little, if hardly any, damage. The city is old and very beautiful - many large trees and the countless canals running here and there. Maastricht has a population of around 70,000 and there are quite a few famous old sights. As an example: the caves around the bluff overlooking the Maas River, and a couple of old churches.

A large rest camp is located there so we registered in and got a bed and meal tickets. This rest camp is definitely not for guys like us who just came up for a short 24-hour period, but we talked our way in and got all the accommodations. Had dinner and you would almost think that you were a civilian. The dining hall was very nice. Clean linen on the tables and the Dutch gals served and waited on us. The amazing thing was that everything was absolutely FREE. Someday, I'll have to tell you a story about this trip that is really rare. For now, though, all I can say is that I didn't spend a single cent the whole trip - I'll take it back, I spent one Guilder for a round of beer, and that was only about 37 cents. Everything in Holland is strictly rationed so one cannot buy anything except a few little nicknacks here and there. Most of these, look inferior. I bought a post card or two but that was all. Walked around and looked in the shop windows. Since we weren't on 3-day passes we weren't allowed in Danceland - a G.I. dance floor and beer garden. We did run into Duffy's Tavern for a few short beers. Most of the best places to go have been taken over by this rest camp project and are run under their jurisdiction.

Had a good night sleep and then got up at seven this morning for breakfast. Hit the road and immediately caught a ride into Liege in a command car. We really made record time. This guy was driving like the proverbial bat out of hell all the way and even through Liege. The amazing thing was that we were only picked up by the MP's once and that was down in Liege. Didn't get a ticket - only a warning. Hopped out of that vehicle and climbed into a weapons carrier that brought us right into St. Trond. the whole trip from Maastricht back took about an hour and fifteen minutes. Really excellent time.

Dear Mom and Dad

I am on duty this afternoon and tomorrow morning, and then I think that I'll take off for 48 hours and go back up there to check over a little deal. Then I'll hitch hike on over to Aachen, shoot a few pictures, and then drop in and see the Burgamiester of this little village of Hergenrath which is about 4 miles southeast of Aachen. Then I'll come on into Liege to spend the night. Well, it sounds mighty good whether I get around to doing it or not. On the whole it has been pretty nice whenever we were taking these sorties to Holland. The people are pleasant and the country seems to have survived war conditions quite well.

Have to take a typhus shot this afternoon among other things and frankly, I am not at all interested. In fact, I am very tempted just to forget to go altogether. Every time that 3-month period comes for those booster shots I am tempted to take off for a couple of days.

Can't think of any more news good or bad. Again, let me remind you to put away all foolish thoughts of your traveling son coming home because just AIN'T!! The war might be over, but did you ever hear of the occupational forces - well, that's those forgotten bunch of sad sacks that have to remain to take care of the women and drink .001% beer instead of water. If we get out of here and back to the States within two years I'll consider myself mighty lucky. Hope everything is okay with you two. I still think that I could run this show better than its being handled, so I guess I am still in good health. It is when I stop moaning about everything that you'll know I am ill. Love...JACK.

August 29, 1945

Dear Mom and Dad:

I have been running around a lot the last few days so that is the reason for not writing. Guess I'll go to work this afternoon for a change. Spent a couple of afternoons and evenings in Liege; then, yesterday, I took another flying run up to Maastricht and shot a bunch of pictures.

9th Air Force - 365 Bomb Sqd. – 305th Bomb Grp. - APO 140

Then hitch hiked on back into Liege where I took a good old tub bath and headed for the G.I. night club.

The one bad thing about this big excursion was that I only had one meal in 48 hours. The rest of the time I lived on coffee and donuts at the Red Cross. Since I was only on pass and not on furlough I couldn't sit at the transient mess hall in Liege. It's raining out and looks very miserable so there shouldn't be much flying this afternoon. That's pretty good because it means we won't have too much to do up at the control tower.

Rumors are running wild again and the latest is that all men with 45 or more points will NOT be moved on to Frankfurt when that field is ready for us. Naturally, the optimistic one's figure that we'll go home, but I know we won't. We just won't be getting home for years and years and furthermore I am beginning to like the freedom of European life. Am still sweating out my furlough to Switzerland. No orders as yet and I have no idea when they'll come through.

By the way don't send any Christmas packages until almost the very last possible date. That is a long way off, I know, but time does fly and I thought I'd better warn you. Everything is okay on this end. Love, always...JACK.

August 31, 1945

Dear Mom and Dad:

Your letter with the money order arrived and I was mighty glad to see it. The fact still remains that I won't get paid until about September 20th due to a slip up in the orderly room. However, right now, at this precise moment my finances are in excellent condition. In fact, I have in my possession approximately one hundred and twenty-five dollars. If and when that furlough comes through, naturally there will be a slight dent put in that tidy sum. However, don't be surprised if you find a money order coming your way for a change as I'll send home all that I won't be needing. The trouble is that money just doesn't go anywhere over here. Prices are terrific and that's no kidding.

Dear Mom and Dad

Glad to hear that Woody (Woodnorth), Milt (Kapp), Don (Heitzman), and a lot of the other fellows are getting home. Hope that they are lucky enough to get discharged and don't have to stick around for a lot of home duty. Frankly, I'd much rather be overseas than in the States until I can go right back and get discharged immediately. I'm having one heck of a good time raising all kinds of Hades so why be in a hurry to get back - especially with my flimsy 55 points. This is a joke army!

Got a letter from Herman Eschen and it was from good old San Francisco. I sure do envy him. I had some mighty good times down there! In case you don't remember it was due to a little trip to Frisco one weekend that five of us waltzed back into San Luis Obispo about 4 hours AWOL and almost got a court martial. That was a real weekend - one I'll never forget. Herman is going to spend seven months in school out there and then who knows where he'll be sent. Obviously, he has a lot of time to spend in the Navy. When it comes to points he certainly doesn't have very many.

Time really flies. Here it is September and I have already been over here one year. Some people would pay a fortune to stay over here for that length of time - as for me I've just spent one of the best years of my life. Not much else to report. Hope you are both fine. Love... JACK.

September 2, 1945

Dear Mom and Dad:

Just a quick note to let you know everything is okey. A couple of the boys leave for home tomorrow and the head of the department, Captain Cox, a really good guy, is also leaving. That will leave some other joker in charge who doesn't know anything so we may all quit flying control. Am enclosing a few snaps. The one of Roscoe (Wells), Carl (Camp), and me is really sad. We didn't feel nearly as bad as we looked.

One of the boys left on furlough to the UK to get married to a Limey gal and another guy put in papers so he could marry an English girl in three months. Personally, I think they are both nuts. I am now

9th Air Force - 365 Bomb Sqd. – 305th Bomb Grp. - APO 140

passing through the state of mind, etc., where marriage is the last thing I want or need at the present time. This is because of the fact that I like the variety and active life I am experiencing. Suppose about a dozen of us will go out and celebrate tonight in honor of the guys leaving. That's okey except I am working tomorrow morning. Oh, my aching head! Gotta go over and eat and get to work for a change. Hope you two are fine - I'm tops. Love…… JACK.

September 5, 1945

Dear Mom and Dad:

It appears that I haven't written for about two days so I better get on the ball and knock out a few lines while things are still a little quiet. We just loaded 18 ships with guys heading back to the good old USA. I don't know just where that place is, but they tell me "Go West Young Man, Go West", and you'll eventually find it!

In the meantime, I have been continuing to knock myself out having a nightly spree down in good old Liege. Frankly, if we didn't go down there we'd go nuts sitting around the barracks, and if we go into St. Trond there is absolutely nothing to do. Last evening, we really had a spree and started out with a delicious dinner of real Italian meat balls and spaghetti. It was mighty good! I am trying to gain back a little weight that I lost the last few weeks. A little is putting it mildly - 10 pounds to be exact. That's the result of the food we have been getting lately. Just call this joint "Little Belsen". I don't know who is getting the food over here in the ETO but it isn't the troops. That is also one reason why I spent well over a thousand francs last month for food alone. Such is life and I am having quite a time living it up.

Today I started out in ill humor so I decided to raise a little general hell. Result I blitzed Group Headquarters and got myself five more points plus the extra eight authorized for the time between VE and VJ day. I now have a sum total of 63 points. In other words, I may never get out of this army. Now what I am hoping is that I'll be in ill humor tomorrow morning and then I'll go and storm the orderly room and demand

Dear Mom and Dad

that furlough to Switzerland. Somebody had to use the typewriter for "business" reasons so now you'll have to put up with my handwritten scrawl. It might be a problem but bear with me! It is at least some form of communication to let you know I am not in the brig.

Next Day - September 6, 1945

Dear Mom and Dad:

Well, I am still hungry. Went into St. Trond and picked up a bunch of my pictures. It cost me exactly 500 Francs which is $11.00. That will give you some idea of just how high the prices are. I'll send them all home as soon as I get a few spare minutes.

Things are really going to the dogs around here. Everybody is going home and all of the departments are short on manpower. There is a possibility that I'll be put into AACs (Army Airways Communications Systems). We're sweating out that deal right now. I am going to take a run down to an airfield near Namur today to see what kind of a set up AACS would be and if I find it not to my liking I am going to pull strings and get out of flying control and into group operations. As long as I have a 552 Spec. Number (Control Tower Operator) I can't make any stripes and right now I could use the extra money.

Today I go off for the usual 48 hours much to my relief. Whenever I think about it I have to laugh. I really have a terrific racket. Got a nice letter from Grace Richards the other day and she spoke of having a visit with you, Mom. She was quite anxious about Bob, and frankly I don't blame her. There's not much news so I had better close and get ready to head out on my 48-hour pass. Love...JACK.

September 8, 1945

Dear Mom and Dad:

Today the first package arrived and the contents were okey. That is all of the stuff I'll be needing. As far as sending more packages I don't advise it. Don't bother with any Christmas boxes; just salt the money

9th Air Force - 365 Bomb Sqd. – 305th Bomb Grp. - APO 140

away. It is better that way rather than having the stuff chasing me all over the world. Don't let that get you too optimistic because frankly the outlook is lousy, but one can never quite tell what might happen. That's one of the great things about the military - you never know from one day to the next what kind of new surprise might be coming your way.

Sorry to hear that Morrison Bros. Co. is on strike. Looks like labor is really getting a terrific grip on things the world over. England has seen the labor movement take over, and I wouldn't doubt but what the USA will be running under the same type of government. We never seem to learn from the mistakes that the British make - we simply follow down the same path. I can well imagine what the old homestead looks like with office files and so forth moved in. Bet it looks like we were really going into business. Just hope everything gets straightened out soon and in good shape.

The pictures of Karl Eschen's grave are due tomorrow and I am hoping that they turn out really good. Will send them on to the Eschen's immediately and the negatives to you when I send the box of stuff that I have accumulated. In the meantime, everything is okey and I am still running on the hope that a few rumors around here will come true. I think I'll hit the sack. Love...JACK.

September 9, 1945

Dear Mom and Dad:

Just a quick note to let you know that I am still well and out of the guard house. The latter may come soon, however. I can't give you the full details right now, but those of us in flying control have had a showdown the last few days with the result that I've been raising hell with everything from a first Looey to a Major. I just took over a new job and told them I would take it on with one provision and that was that I made T/Sgt. in the near future. Frankly, I gave them all a rude awakening to a few general facts of life. I all but demanded some stripes. The story is yet to be told, but I know that a letter went in recommending an urgent raise for J.R. Dauner to Sgt. immediately and it was signed by Lt. Col. Collins, the operations officer. So, there is a possibility that your son may raise himself from those pleasant years as a buck private in the rear ranks.

If I do make the jump from private to Sgt. I am not going to let up on them until they give me S/Sgt and/or possibly T/Sgt. depending on how much I feel like doing the work. I have taken over all the administrative work in flying control at this time. My office hours are such that I work damn well when I please, and can take as many passes as I want. That, too, was arranged before I said I would take over this work. So, I am feeling great. Will give you more "poop from group" in the near future. Love…JACK.

September 13, 1945

Dear Mom and Dad:

Thought by this time I would be writing Sgt. on this letter, but the orders haven't come through as yet so I'm still sweating it out. I better make it soon or I am starting all over and re-raising all necessary hell. Then, too, I just won't work so they can change my initials to W.W. (won't work) Dauner. So far everything is going along okey as far as my new duties

Received another package today. Thanks a lot. You don't have to send any more of that stuff as prices have gone down on most of it. I still advise against sending any Christmas packages. I know that I won't be coming home, but something might come up. Then, too, we'll be moving again soon. I imagine it will be to Frankfort. Last night, a buddy of mine and I went into Liege and really had a time. Had a table at the G.I. Night Club and what a night it turned out to be. Plenty of wine, cognac, and song. I sure do like that city of Liege. Guess I will check out and go down to St. Trond tonight for the weekly dance. Met a sweet little gal - her father owns a pub which is right down my alley. Her name is Paula Niesen and the beer they serve in her father's tavern

9th Air Force - 365 Bomb Sqd. – 305th Bomb Grp. - APO 140

is excellent. 1 don't go with this gal for her love or money - it's for her BEER!!

Had an excellent USO show the other night. Best I have seen. Most of these USO shows aren't too hot - but, this one was absolutely great! It was amazing to all of us. We've moved again. All of us in flying control are living on line right next to base operations. Very convenient, you know. Aside from that I am going to learn how to fly on the side. I got one of the pilots around here who said that he would check me out in a Piper Cub. I'll probably get us both killed or in the guard house, but that's the least of my worries. Anyway, we have a date to do some flying and I hope that I can get checked out in good shape. News is scarce - am sending a box of stuff tomorrow. I imagine it will take a month to get to you. Everything is fine here. A couple of us are trying to line up an interesting trip on a mission to the Italian Theater of Operation. Love to you both…JACK.

September 16, 1945

Dear Mom and Dad:

Hold on to your high hats now and relax. I just got back from a little journey. I flew in tonight from Foggia, Italy - way down on the south eastern coast. Yesterday morning Pete Scatura and I cornered Lt. Col. Collins, group operations officer; Major Schubert, our group adjudent; and Major Shelton, my squadron C.O., and got the necessary permission to fly down in one of the B-17's and then return when it came back to base. After some forgery here and there and a little running around we grabbed a couple of parachutes and harnesses and boarded the ship. The ride was one of those once in a lifetime trip!

We left at two o'clock - flew over Liege and then set a course for Brenner Pass. When we crossed the Alps we went up to 15,000 feet and naturally went on oxygen. That was the first time I had gone to that altitude and had to use the mask. I was really amazed - there was nothing to it. It was a beautiful day - the sky was clear as a bell and we could see the beautiful little country of Switzerland with her famous Alps. I shot pictures all along the way. The Alps are really rugged - sharp peaks and treacherous caverns. Was on oxygen for about an hour and then we got out of the mountains and came down to an altitude of 1,500 feet as we passed over Bologna.

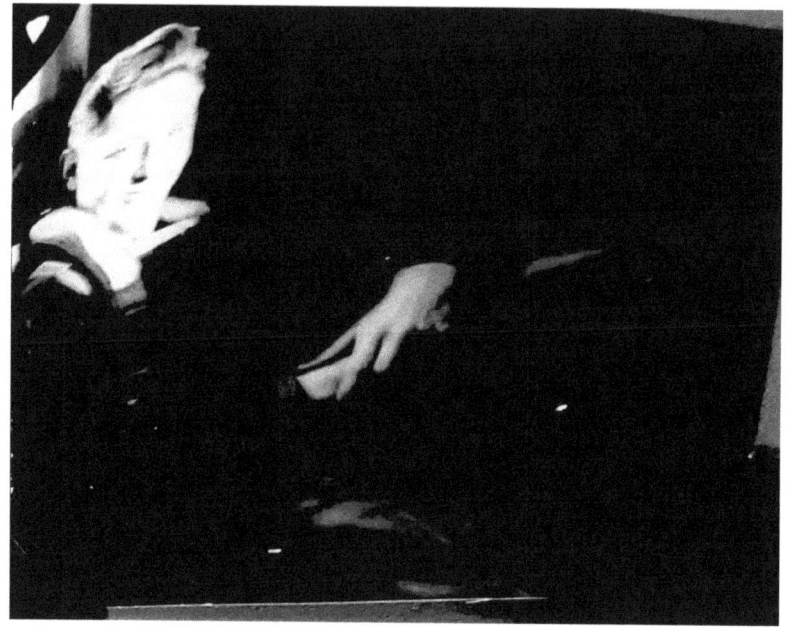

Jack strapped into his airplane seat.

From there we headed straight to Venice and here I received the thrill of my travels. I have never in my life seen a more picturesque nor beautiful city - at least from the air. It is indescribable. We buzzed it at about 500 feet and made a couple of 360's around it. I shot about five pictures. I think I'll chalk that place up as one of the spots I would like to visit as a civilian. Parting from there definitely was sweet sorrow. We then flew on down the eastern coast of Italy passing over many quaint sites and finally landed at Foggia. From the air it looks like a very interesting place.

9th Air Force - 365 Bomb Sqd. – 305th Bomb Grp. - APO 140

Got some food and then pulled a fast one and got a week's beer ration. What a luxury. seven cans of BUDWEISER BEER! It was superb. We then got a truck to take us into the city where we were met by beaucoup Off-Limit signs, millions of kids, and an oversupply of men. All that you've ever read concerning the filth of Italian cities is true. Meat products hang right on the streets. That famous Italian hot sauce is squeezed from the tomato - then mixed with other ingredients before being baked in the warm sun under a full exposure of flies, gnats, and kids with dirty hands.

But to continue - cigarettes were worth about $2.00 a pack. In the end, I bought Mom a very pretty bracelet for a souvenir. It set me back beaucoup Lira and I think I was hosed as it is delicate that it will no doubt fall apart enroute. Oh well, the sentiment is there any way!! But to continue - the women are buxom and built fairly well, but they won't even look at an American. Mussolini's campaign for kids really went over very well. There are millions of them and besides that seven out of every ten women are pregnant so the population of Italy is still on an upward trend. The male population down here is tremendous in comparison to France, Belgium, and even England.

After checking the city over on a Saturday night, we came on back to the base and had a few more cans of that good, old, delicious, mellow, refreshing, spirit lifting BUDWEISER. Then to bed. Got up this morning and decided we wanted to do some running around. Not knowing just who we could get, or should I say borrow a jeep from we headed for the base C.O. Pete and I went on the offensive and walked into the base commander's office and announced that we needed a jeep to see the neighboring country side. He sent us over to a Major who was still in the sack. We woke him and said we wanted a jeep to use for the morning. We got it!!

I guess the very nerve of two lowly privates demanding a jeep overwhelmed him. So, we gassed and oiled the buggy and took off to see the sights. Our first spin was out about 15 miles to Ventura where there stood an old castle built by Frederick II. There was also a famous old

Dear Mom and Dad

cathedral close by. Then back to Foggia where we really did that city up right. Foggia was bombed severely and about 30,000 people were killed. That's one reason Americans are disliked. It seems that some American airmen were shot in this area so the boys got slightly irritated and strafed the devil out of the town for 8 hours and during that time dropped two runs of bombs on the fair city.

To continue - we drove on back to base for dinner and then got ready to take off. We left at two o'clock and the pilot decided to go back via the longer route. Went direct to Naples and flew right past old Vesuvious. There is nothing pretty about it at all - so let no one kid you. Naples is a beautiful city and the Lake nearby is magnificent. From there we went on to Rome and here is where Miss Reu (Dubuque High School Latin teacher) would go mad with delight. We buzzed the city at about 700 feet. I got pictures of the Arch of Septimius; the Collesium; the Rostra; the Papal City; and many other famous points. The Tiber River winds all through the city. I think the most outstanding structure is the pure white marble Rostra - though the old Collesium stands out significantly.

From Rome we flew over the Isle of Monte Cristo - then on to Corsica. The Island of Corsica is terribly mountainous and we flew over at about 12,000 feet. Most of those islands are rocky, mountainous, places with very few inhabitants. Then it was nothing but water until we hit Toulan, France; then on to Marseilles. Here, there were beaucoup troops boarding ships for home. Marseilles is also a very lovely city. Then we set a straight course north for good old St. Trond, Belgium. The trip back took just a little over 6 hours while going down over the Alps only 4 hours.

All in all, it was a terrific trip. We were gone a total of 36 hours and in that time, I saw enough sights to make any man's head swim. As I said before it was one of those things you dream about.

Pete and I just pulled the right strings all the way along, and so Dauner has conquered one more new land. In the last 36 hours I was in

9th Air Force - 365 Bomb Sqd. – 305th Bomb Grp. - APO 140

the following countries: Belgium, France, Germany, Switzerland, Italy and Corsica. Not a bad 1 1/2 days' work!

My promotion didn't come through yet so I am going in and start raising all necessary hell over again. By the way, that stuff on the board was strictly an error in my favor. Think nothing of it until I write such forbidding words on the outside. I am going to make ratings or else someone is going to have the hell pestered out of them daily until i get them. At present, I am sweating out my furlough. The Switzerland deal is fast falling out of the picture so I may go to the Riviera instead. The latter is a paradise. You live in all of the luxurious hotels - dine in the famous dining rooms - and it is FREE as long as you are on furlough. It is truly a paradise.

In the meantime, I am sleeping as much as possible - working practically nil - and having a great time at night. What a life - and me, only a buck private. That shows what a joke the army really is. I better close and get this in the mail. All my love...JACK.

September 20, 1945

Dear Mom and Dad:

Just got back from Brussels and had quite a day of it. Went in this morning via the thumb. Caught a jeep and made it within an hour. Had donuts and coffee and then took in a two-hour tour of the city via a soft seated bus with skylights. We saw a lot of other points that I hadn't seen on the other trip. Went out to the famous Brussels Park; the Infantry monument; Sablong Square; Fifty-year Jubilee Memorial; and the King's Palace. It was really a mighty nice tour and I enjoyed it a lot. Then I took off by myself looking for some laces and linens for you, Mom.

The prices were very high. I was planning on getting you a beautiful table cloth - the type that is handmade like lace dollies. The one I picked out was priced at 7,500 Francs. I almost fell over on the spot. That, my dear family, is exactly $170.46 which is a little high. The next thing was a handmade linen lace blouse which came to 1,500 Francs

Dear Mom and Dad

or approximately $33.60. Of course, everything was absolutely beautiful - that's the truth. 1 ended up buying three hankies and a little lace broach the price of which I won't divulge. I I will say one thing - quote: "Mom, if you lose one of them I'll fairly well turn you squarely over my knee!" I have never seen such beautiful work. It is too bad there's a war on and prices are so high.

Looked around a little while and then headed for the highway to start hitch hiking. I thought we had better get out of town before it was too late. The truth is that we had no legal pass to Brussels - only our Class B which is good for only 25 miles. Caught a civilian car and came straight through to St. Trond. Sunday - Pete Scatura, Carl Camp and I are going to try and borrow a jeep or weapons carrier for the day and go to Margraten, Holland, and shoot pictures of Ben Pickard's grave. If we can't work that out I may have to give up the idea as it is really off the beaten trail. I'll do my best to get there.

A flash just came over the radio that all men with 70 points or more would be on their way home by the first of October, and those with 60 points or more by November 1st. It was supposed to have come from General George C. Marshall. It really sounds good if it is true. I would like to get back for Christmas this year, but am definitely not planning on it. Of course, then I might re-enlist - who knows? In the meantime, the food here is getting unbearable. I do less and less work and it rains more and more.

Had a very good sketch made in Brussels. Sure, am a handsome guy - at least by way of the sketch. Guess that comes from having such good-looking parents. Lucky me! Anyway, I mailed it from Brussels so you ought to get it anywhere from two weeks to two years. News just is at rock bottom. Hope you two are mentally better off than me. I lost a few marbles I think with all my traveling. Everything is okey over here. Love......

JACK P.S. I almost went to Iceland today. I had a chance to sign on but decided against. it.

9th Air Force - 365 Bomb Sqd. – 305th Bomb Grp. - APO 140

September 22, 1945

Dear Mom and Dad:

After a period of about 48 hours since my last letter, I'll sit down and give you the latest dope. Worked a little yesterday - a very little and then took off for Liege with one of my old cronies. We started things off right with a good tub bath and believe me I really soaked. Sure, did feel great. Then on down to the GI beer garden where we had sandwiches and beaucoup beer. After about two hours in the G.I. club we took off for the GI Nite Club and got ourselves a good table. The music was excellent.

Came on back to base on the liberty run trucks and hit the sack. It wasn't until this morning though that we learned about the crack-up that occurred only about a half hour after we got in. One of the squadron commanding officers, Major Brooks, a really swell guy, went up on a routine instrument flight from here to London, to Paris, and back to base. The visibility became pretty bad and he racked the ship about 10 miles from the field. Everyone on board was killed. He was one of the best officers on the base and the guys were all top drawer. The strange part is that they were the same group of guys that Pete Scatura and I flew to Italy last week – except for Major brooks. The co – pilot was the pilot on our flight to Italy. The two enlisted men on board, the engineer and radio operator, were the ones who went with us down to Foggia when we commandeered that jeep and took the excursion all over the country side. A couple of really nice guys!

I was talking to them only yesterday. It sure does seem odd when you think of it. They are trying to determine the cause - whether it was mechanical difficulties - or just what. He was a mighty good pilot so it all doesn't add up. Anyway, it sure was a shock. It cost the lives of five officers and two enlisted men. I sure am glad that I wasn't in the office about the time Major Brooks came in for his clearance as I might have decided to take that flight and then would have gotten a perpetual furlough somewhere out in space.

Dear Mom and Dad

Well, I am definitely going on furlough. I decided to take advantage and not wait any longer for the Switzerland deal. So, I am going down and spend the week from October 3rd to October 10th at the beautiful Riviera. I know it will be a swell deal and besides that I get an extra 850 Francs the minute I hit the place. One stays in the very best hotels - eats in the best dining rooms and it's all FREE since the Riviera is a US Army rest area.

No mail again today. In fact, there was very little for the whole group for the last few days. It just isn't coming through these days. Guess the troops are taking up all available shipping space. There is very little news - it's raining out now and looks like a generally miserable night. Glad I am staying on the base for a change. No more for now - will keep you posted on all of the latest news. Love...JACK.

September 27, 1945

Dear Mom and Dad:

Thought I had better sit down and drop you fellows a letter as it has been a few days since the last one. As far as anything new occurring there has been absolutely nothing - well, except that I have now moved from the status of private to the soaring rank of Corporal. Next month, providing I don't get busted which is highly probable, I should reach the lofty realm of sergeant. At present I am working so little that it is pitiful that I even draw the pay of a private. Such is this life over here in the ETO. Those who work hard get nothing and those who do absolutely nothing get all of the benefits. I happen to be in the position of the latter.

Yesterday afternoon I was supposed to have gone out to Kerk de Stadt, a town about 14 kilometers away from. Naturally everything would roll in here at the office, and I couldn't get away until about two o'clock which was too late to catch the tram. So, I guess that I'll just have to try and get another invitation. There is absolutely no news. Might be on my way home some time in November or early December, but I wouldn't guarantee it. Please don't send any Christmas packages and warn everyone else of the same. There's no sense of having

9th Air Force - 365 Bomb Sqd. – 305th Bomb Grp. - APO 140

that stuff getting lost or following me all over the world again this year. In the meantime, keep your fingers crossed and you might be seeing your traveling son again in not too many moons. Love…....JACK.

October 1, 1945

Dear Mom and Dad:

Well how's everything on the home front today? Things over on this side of the pond continue the same. Haven't done anything constructive during the last week; yet, it seems as though my letter writing time has been nil. Yesterday, I abandoned all work and we took off for St. Trond to watch the big celebration. It was a big Catholic holiday in honor of Ave Maria and the people really outdid themselves. The streets were decorated beautifully and every window was filled with religious scenes. The color scheme was all blue and white. I had planned to shoot a bunch of color shots, but the sun refused to come out so I settled for black and white.

As per usual I did not get up until ten o'clock. Went into the office and started making up the monthly report. It took me a little over an hour - on up to chow where we "got no bread with one meat ball" and then on back here. No mail again! The stuff absolutely isn't coming through these days. By the way, I finally sent that box with a few odds and ends. I bought some other stuff for you the other day, Mom, but I won't send it until I've gotten another load to go home. It is a good idea to send smaller boxes than on large.

In the meantime, I leave for a seven-day furlough to the Riviera on Wednesday. Naturally, I'll have a rare old time. Then about the 15th of October I am going to put myself in for Sergeant. Maybe just the fact that I had enough intestinal fortitude to do it will get the stripes for me. Of course, I might lose what I have, but who cares - double or nothing on this roll! News is scarce - just thought I'd better drop you a line and keep you posted. Hope everything is okey.

Love....JACK.

Dear Mom and Dad

October 2, 1945

Dear Mom and Dad:

Mail continues to be delayed and it has been about four days since my last letter from anyone. I don't know why it isn't getting through. Have been wondering if my letters are coming through just as slowly or if they were making better time.

Rumors are again on the bloody loose around here. Some say that we will all be on our way home by the fifteenth of next month. Others say that we will be moving on to Frankfort by the same date so take your pick. Anyway, it looks as though we will be moving somewhere, sometime, when someone gets a brainstorm. One thing, however, a government inspector came and condemned the huge chateau where all the guys stay and also the mess hall. So, something will have to be done soon.

Everything is the same as usual. I am still getting all my beauty sleep - most of it in the morning and working just as little as possible. Hope everything is okey back on the home front. Will try and drop you a line from down on the Riviera. All my love, JACK.

October 3, 1945

French Riviera - D'Angleterre Hotel

Dear Mom and Dad:

Well your traveling son is at it again. After sweating out poor weather all morning we climbed aboard an Air Transport Command (ATC) C-47 and hopped down here this afternoon. It was a good flight and we passed over the southern French Alps on the way. I'll say we did!! We flew at 14,000 feet with no oxygen and we all darn near froze.

Landed and got checked in at the D'Angleterre Hotel. This place is the most marvelous set up I have ever seen. The government has taken over all of the best hotels complete with staff for the use of leave personnel as part of reverse lend-lease. The meals are terrific and you can get anything from a single, double or suite of rooms depending on the number of guys in your own clique.

9th Air Force - 365 Bomb Sqd. – 305th Bomb Grp. - APO 140

The old Mediterranean Sea is right in front of us and the view is absolutely beautiful. Went dancing in the lovely main dining room tonight and there was an A-1 floor show. Really good talent and taste. They are actually exquisite - need I say more. I am planning to go out to Monte Carlo tomorrow on a tour. Otherwise it is "off Limits" to G. I's. Guess they're afraid someone will break the bank!! Must close. Will write soon. Everything is tops! Love...JACK.

October 6, 1945
French Riviera

Dear Mom and Dad:

Forgot when I wrote last so I'll start the day after I arrived. So far this has really been something out of this world, so hang on to your fur coat and listen to the tales of your "Traveling Son".

Thursday, we had breakfast and hopped a bus tour of three hours out to Monte Carlo. The trip out was made on the Middle Corniche Road which is about half way up the mountains. The scenery was beautiful and we passed such spots as King Leopold's Villa and also one of Gloria Vanderbilt's homes. Passed through Eze, La Turkie, Roguebrune, and finally down to Monaco and Monte Carlo. The city itself is "Off Limits" to American troops. However, we could easily see the famous casino with its green roof. Also, the Prince of Monoco's Castle - the museum - and numerous other points of renown. The trip back was on the lower Corniche Road and followed right along the old Mediterranean Sea. Really it was a lovely trip.

Then yesterday we got up and took a tour to Grasse. It is here that many of the famous perfumes are made, and also where the flowers and extracts are produced for the big outfits in Paris. This trip took us from Nice to Cognes where we drove up into the mountains to Villeneuve Loubet, Roguefort (Not the cheese), and on to Grasse. Had dinner here at Grasse and then went to a large perfume factory. It was all very interesting and also costly. The perfume I bought for you, Mom, is on its way. I imagine in the States the bottle would be worth beaucoup

Dear Mom and Dad

Francs. It is over here, too! I was going to get "Habanita" for you. It is "The Thing" over here, but I don't like it so I bought what I thought smelled the nicest by my standards. By the way - they have something new on the market. Its commercial name is "Concreta" and is the genuine wax of the flowers used directly as perfume. I have an ad showing it which I'll send to you later.

Came back via Cannes which is where the officers are housed. Personally, I believe that Nice is nicer. From Cannes we proceeded to Antibes and finally on into Nice. Then last night we went up to the Casino Club and saw a stage show which was quite good. Then back to the hotel where we had a few dances and on to the game room where and I hit the gold star award on one of the "one-armed bandits". And so, we hit the sack and today was a new morning, noon, and night. Headed for the Anchorage at 9:30 A.M. and caught a speed boat ride down to Monte Carlo. It was a beautiful trip and I got some lovely color shots of the Casino and other points. It was about a three-hour trip and well worth the time. After dinner which included steak and chips, we headed for the beach. Yeah, man! There for the first time I had it proven that the hand was quicker than the eye! If you have any doubt just read on!

Guess, I am pretty lucky to have seen about all there is to see here on the continent. Just two spots I would like to visit: Berlin and Vienna. Then I'll have seen about everything. Hope you two are fine. I never felt better and am hitting the scales at a record breaking 160. Love......
JACK.

October 11, 1945
French Riviera

Dear Mom and Dad:

Greetings from your AWOL son. At present I am about 15 hours over due and I am not in the least bit worried. No plane has shown up as yet to take us back so we're quietly sweating it outs. The ship that was supposed to take us back off blew a tire on takeoff so here we are.

9th Air Force - 365 Bomb Sqd. – 305th Bomb Grp. - APO 140

As usual it is a lovely day out on the beach. The sun really comes down and not a cloud in the sky. Such is life on the French Riviera. We all ought to come back here in civilian life. Prices really aren't to terrific for travelers in normal times. Of course, now they are high because everything is on the black market. No more news. I'm fine! Love……
JACK.

October 15, 1945

Dear Mom and Dad:

Here I am back in St. Trond after a grand and glorious vacation. Of course, you don't know how close you came to having a son six foot under or maybe more - but then that's past history. Came back Friday only about 72 hours AWOL. A plane from our base came down and we took off from Nice at 11,30. All went well until we were about a half – hour out and flying over the French Alps. Suddenly we began to smell gas throughout the ship.

Then we started losing a little altitude and all of a sudden, the pilot gave the ship full flaps. By this time everyone was looking at everyone else. There were 25 of us on board and no one had a "chute". (But we don't talk about that). Then by chance I put on the earphones and heard the pilot giving instructions to the navigator in case we burst into flames. Anything for excitement, you know! In addition, when we got over our base there was a dense fog; however, we landed safely and got back to base okey!

Came back to the hotel and saw the floor show in the Club D'Angeleterre - then a few dances and some good Vermouth. Finally, on to the sack for a good night's sleep. Had 12 days' work waiting for me when I walked into the office, and it took exactly a day to clean it all up. Everything was the same old routine. Have been put in for sergeant and it should come through in about two weeks.

Had hopes of being home for Christmas. If luck holds, I will. The group is leaving for the States on December 15th, but I imagine I'll leave before then. The outfit is scheduled to fly back via the southern

Dear Mom and Dad

route - that's why I'd like to stay with them, but if my orders come I am not going to wait.

Am sending home $100 in about a week. It will be under my buddy Wendell Houck's name so you'll know why you're getting it from an unknown person. I am going to hang on to about $150 so I won't be short if and when I hit New York or Boston. Don't send anymore boxes or anything of value - particularly money orders or the like as I may leave here anywhere between a few weeks to a couple of months.

In the meantime, hang on to your hats - and don't get too optimistic. If the darn Limeys hadn't taken the "Queens" (The Queen Elizabeth and the Queen Mary) from us I would have been a cinch for getting to Old Dubuque, by Christmas! Cheers for now - I've got to go. Will keep you posted on all new developments, and along with the rest, I'll try and keep out of jail. So far, I have been able to avoid getting into any trouble with the local MPs. Love.... JACK.

October 18, 1945

Dear Mom and Dad:

Just a note to let you know that I am still alive and out of jail. So due to all of this I am enclosing the miserable sum of $100 to be used in any way you all see fit. Best you see fit to either put it in my account or else invest it in something which will make a quick million.

Yesterday Lou Rotella and I went out to a little village about 10 miles from St. Trond with Paula (Niesen to see her aunt and spend the day. Her aunt is really a live one and has a darn cute little daughter by the name of Marie Therese Niesen They have a very nice home and the hospitality was great. She had baked two pies which we put away like the magician pulling the rabbit out of the hat. Then we sat around, visited and listened to AFN Paris. We took the five o'clock train back to St. Trond; but before leaving we were given an invitation to come out and spend a couple of days with the family.

Last night two of the boys got into a row and one of them teed off and clipped the other one. This other joker, who nobody likes, got

9th Air Force - 365 Bomb Sqd. – 305th Bomb Grp. - APO 140

up and called the MP's. So, we framed the son-of-a-gun and all of us appeared as witnesses at two o'clock A.M. that this one guy didn't even touch him and that the other joker must have gotten cut up from falling as he was pretty drunk when he hit the barracks. Case immediately was ended and our man let loose. The other joker was seriously reprimanded. Thus, you see the benefits of "framing" your enemies and having friends.

My pictures came out pretty well and I'll send a few along. They've all been going to you. By the way, my camera is off kilter. The range finder is knocked out and the pictures have been out of focus. Guess old age is creeping up on it. Maybe I'll sell it before I leave. No more news. Hope you are fine. Love...JACK.

October 27, 1945

Dear Mom and Dad:

Haven't written for a day or so, so I'll cut loose and let you know the latest. All of us with 60-64 points were scrubbed from this last shipment. The 65-70 guys are leaving in a day or two. I think that I'll be out of here within the next two weeks. By that time, I'll make buck sergeant. The orders are in personnel now and should come out in a day or two. Then I am having my specialist number changed so that if I am here another month I can make staff sergeant. Just in case!!

The weather has been lousy, but Lou Rotella and I have been going out regardless. Every night we go down to Paula's and play this Belgique card game "Kwoena" with her old man for drinks. Tonight, Lou and I beat him two straight games; then another old Belgique came in and Lou and I played the two of them. We won two and they won two. The son-of-a-guns talked back and forth in Belgique and hosed us - so we worked out signals that Paula couldn't even understand and put the ream supreme to them. A good time was had by all and it was really good to see the expression on their faces.

My trip to Tunis has had it. I should have gone down a few days ago with Major Cook. He spent a day in Tunis and two days in Rome.

So, I snafued - but how was I to know? Maybe I'll make it yet but I am getting leary of flying as the ships are in poor shape and the weather very bad.

Tomorrow is the Sabbath and if I get up in time I may go to church. Haven't been for ages so I should try. Have quite a bit of work in the office, but that can wait until I feel like doing it. Then, tomorrow we'll either go to Liege or beat Paula's old man in "Kwoena". No mail on the base for four straight days. I hope someone is getting a big kick out of holding it up. Too bad they don't string-up a few of those dock workers.

Can't think of anything else - just the same old stuff and routine. Up at 10 - an hour at the office - dinner and then into town. I'm just getting fatter and lazier. Hope that you are both fine. Love…...JACK.

October 31, 1945

Dear Mom and Dad:

Today was pay day and I drew a little more due to the promotion. My sergeants rating is down at personnel now and should come out on orders very shortly. I am sweating it out right now. Maybe I ought to start raising a little general hell once again. Was informed by the squadron this morning that I would find myself on guard duty in a couple of days so I promptly pulled out a letter from our files that dated back to September 1943 from General Hap Arnold stipulating that no man in flying control will pull any kind of detail. This was immediately presented to the Colonel when he walked into the office this afternoon with the result that flying control will NOT pull any guard duty.

Everyone on the base pulls it except first sergeants; crew chiefs; and flying control. That's just a small idea of how much weight we do carry here. And, that's just the reason I can come and go as I please. By the way, I have my replacement now and have been checking him out the last couple of days. Soon I won't do any work at all. Or at least just enough to get by the barest minimum in order to say that I am still in flying control.

9th Air Force - 365 Bomb Sqd. – 305th Bomb Grp. - APO 140

The weather has been terribly poor the last few days. Fog darn near the whole day and hence very little flying. Which is okey by me. Think that I'll break loose and take that three-day pass to Paris or Brussels either this weekend or the next. Just depends on how this guy I am checking out catches on to his duties. He appears; very conscientious and that is my meat - just the kind of guy I want to unload the job on.

No information whatsoever on whether we are going to get out of the group - whether we'll stay with them for a while - or just what. That's what I like about the army - one never knows, does one?? If I do leave for POE (Port of Embarkation) sometime this month it looks like I'll probably ride home on an aircraft carrier as I see where they are sending a few of them over to pick up the troops. Really no news at all. Just thought I'd let you know that I am still here. Love...JACK.

November 7, 1945

Dear Mom and Dad:

Just a quick note to let you know that I am on the alert, and that I'll no doubt ship out of here around November 12th. I'll proceed from here down to San Quentin, France, to join the 397th Bomb Group which is now in Category IV, and will be on my way home somewhere between then and the first of the year -- probably around December 1st from all indications. So, with a little luck I should get home by the holidays. Don't start planning 100 much on it; however, the chances that I will make it are better than the chances that I won't.

Enclosed is a money order for $50 to toss away in the bank for when I get home and will be needing it. Think I'll keep whatever money I pick up from now on with me unless I get way too much. Right now, I have about $80 and should have around $130 before I pull out of here. That ought to take care of me until I hit the States. If I have the time I may knock off a couple of days when I hit New York...that is if I am not shipped to Jefferson Barracks which I imagine will be my Separation Center. Again, I must repeat please don't let my momentary high spirits arouse you too much. The army is like a house of cards when it comes to news - everything can easily fall apart at the last minute!

There's little more to report. From now until we leave I imagine there will be some real celebrating. In fact, we're starting tonight with a sortie into Liege. Love...JACK.

The Air Inspector checked my files yesterday and naturally couldn't find anything to raise hell about. Of course, look whose files he was checking. What really slayed me was that in my squadron there are only two men who don't pull details of any kind and one who absolutely can't be put on anything -- that's ME, and the First Sergeant. Yes sir, as a lowly corporal, I am a wheel! I've got such a neat set up that I almost volunteered for 6 more months overseas duty. With the pension time now down to 20 years, I could be drawing that when I am 38 years old. Something to think about! Who knows I may go right back in, but one thing -I'd never serve that time in the States. I'd volunteer immediately for overseas duty. I like this life, and I still have the wanderlust and plenty of sand in my shoes.

I'd like a year in Africa - a year in Panama or South America - a year in Hawaii - one in China and one in the Asia Minor regions. Of course, a life like the one outlined above is a simple formula of "How not to get married in one easy lesson". How would you like a nice big buck toothed double breasted Zombie for a daughter-in-law? That's what my time in Africa might net. There is no rest for the wicked, they say - but, I am disproving that. I am still putting in 12-14 hours of sack time daily.

I have been including in my correspondence some of my Continental loves, lies and laughs. That will all have to be straightened out if and when I ever get back to the States. Of course, there is always the possibility that we might fly and the plane might have to ditch somewhere in the middle of the Atlantic. But I feel lucky so I don't care. A few days in a rubber boat would be just another experience to chalk up.

9th Air Force - 365 Bomb Sqd. – 305th Bomb Grp. - APO 140

Can't think of any more news or views so best I say Amen for the night. Suggest that you stop writing me as soon as you get this letter as my mail will be all over and probably won't catch up until I get home. Cheers for now. Love....JACK.

November 11, 1945

Dear Mom and Dad:

Just a short note to let you know that I am on my way to the new outfit. We leave tomorrow morning via truck for the 397th Bomb Grp. My advice is that you simply discontinue writing letters and inform all other people who might try and write or send packages of the same. I only hope that you've taken heed of my prior advice and have sent absolutely no packages. If you did you can't say that I didn't warn you. Took a physical - that's what they called it. Checked my clothing forms and so I am already to go.

Naturally, it is raining today and likewise the same for tomorrow so we are looking forward to a very pleasant trip. With the new restrictions on flying in this group they can't even fly us down there which browns all of us off highly. However, I don't mind in the least if there is only some guarantee that we won't have to wait ever and a day down at the 397th before getting to a POE. Anyway, I am on my way home - regardless if it takes me anywhere from six months to six years to make it to 1726 Overview Court in Dubuque, Iowa. By the time I get there I'll probably be grey haired and carrying a cane.

Frankly, no one is very excited about this going home deal. If we don't have to sweat it out here and there and everywhere along the way it will be okey, but if we get held back for quite a while I am going to be highly agitated because I am really having a dam good time right here. In a few more months I'd probably be a Belgique myself. In fact, with the racket I now have - and since I could make Staff Sergeant; I have been mighty tempted to sign up for another three year and just stay in. If I do decide to stay in I'll take a shot at OCS and try to pull a commission. Can't make any money as a Looey, but it is a better life. So

Dear Mom and Dad

much for that - at present all I want to do is to get the hell home and see just how bad conditions are in the good old USA. If it looks too bad I am heading for new lands.

No more news for now. Will drop you a line as soon as I get a little time down there and let you know just how bad things are in the new location. You've heard of San Quentin Quail, no doubt. Well, you won't have to worry as there are only about 20 of them down there to take care of about 2,000 GI's. At least that's what we've been told and due to that old thing known as supply and demand - well, as any fool can plainly see the demand is terrific so the prices concurrently are exorbitant. this bit of information comes hot off the SNT wires (Stool Number Three). No more news for now. Everything is under control over here - hope you are both fine. Love...JACK.

Chapter 22

Hqs. & Hqs. 397th Bomb Group APO 140 - c/o Postmaster, New York, N.Y. Point of Embarkation Base A-42

(Located about 30 Miles from Perrone, France, November 15, 1945 - December 10, 1945)

November 15, 1945
Perrone, France - A-72 Airstrip

Dear Mom and Dad:

    Well, here I am beaucoup million miles from nowhere, and that my dear parents is no lie! What a God forsaken hole this is. The food is very good in comparison to that of the old 305th, and the recreation facilities are okey. The nearest towns are St. Quentin and Perrone, but they are both about 30 miles away.
    We came down in trucks. Stopped off at Chaleroi for lunch and then proceeded on to this base. We were immediately put in a casual pool where we remained all night and then we were processed the next morning. This was very much like the usual routine that takes place in any processing area except this time we were given a new type of flu shot - and what a shot! It didn't bother me too much until last night and then my arm began to swell and ache. I've had so many shots since I have been in the army that one more shot or less doesn't mean too

much. The rest of the day we took it easy, and then the next morning we had to report to find out just what our assignments would be on this particular base. Since I had that confounded 405 (Clerk Typist) I got tossed into the S-4 office which is Supply. So here I am knocking myself out at a typewriter. I hate this kind of work but at least I am back behind a desk again.

Someone felt the need of using the typewriter so you'll have to put up with a pencil. The reports are, and I believe they are correct, that the 65-69-point men will leave on November 22nd and the 60-64-point men on November 28th. The question then is how long it will take before we get on the boat. So, you see I may never make it by Christmas. Therefore, don't plan too much on it. With luck though I might be able to do it. Nothing at all new. Just sweating it out. Will write when I can. Don't bother to write me - there's no need nor sense of doing it! Love...JACK.

November 18, 1945
Perrone, France - A-72 Airstrip

Dear Mom and Dad:

Here I sit with pen in one hand and caressing a bottle of Queen Anne Scotch with the other. They got a few bottles in and I pulled the lucky number. So, in a couple of nights we're going to have a real celebration. As for as my activities the last few days I haven't been doing a great deal of work as usual. The food is still okey so no one can complain.

Every night so far, we've gone down to the bar in the 397th Sqdn. and spent the evening playing cards. Made about 500 Francs in a good poker game last night. Night before last I won about a 100 Francs playing knock rummy. As yet I haven't gone into town and rather doubt if I'll get around to doing it. It holds little, if any, interest and I am not about to get into any trouble at this stage of the game so I am staying right here and finding cards, beer and what other form of booze that might be on the shelf at the club as my primary form of dissipation.

397th Bomb Group, APO 140, Point of Embarkation Base A-42

We are still scheduled to leave here on November 28th and the port is now Le Harve. I only hope that there isn't any delay and that things don't SNAFU.

Again, I remind you not to write or send any packages as they will only be going all over the ETO. Everything is okey so don't worry. Cheers for now. Love... JACK.

November 20, 1945
Perrone, France - A-72 Airstrip

Dear Mom and Dad:

Here I sit with nothing to do so I might as well drop you two a short line to let you in on the latest or should I say the best rumors at the present time. We are still sweating it out here and Lord only knows when we'll move to POE. The latest dope is that those with 60-64 points will move to Le Harve somewhere around the tenth of December and be on the boat within 48 hours. This means that only sheer luck can possibly get me home for Christmas so my advice is that you do not make any plans whatsoever. I believe that you can expect me home for New Year's if things work out at all according to schedule. At least that is the way things stack up right now. Of course, one never knows what will come up in the meantime. One thing I'll guarantee you is that there is no chance of anything but a delay! As I've said before it is all a matter of waiting and sweating it out.

In the meantime, there is little to do. I have been into Perrone a couple of times but there is nothing of interest. Haven't even bothered to go into San Quentin and doubt if I will - and, last but not least I haven't the ambition to go down to Paris. So, I have been content to spend the evenings here on the base at one or the other of the Clubs. Hit a few good licks in a poker game the other night and since then have been going up and down like the preverbal see-saw. Anything to pass the monotony. No sense trying to write letters as they are no good. Too many other things on one's mind to worry about writing.

Dear Mom and Dad

Bought a very good looking lighter this morning. It set me back 340 Francs which is about eight dollars in cold, hard, USA currency. French Francs aren't like good old American currency. The French Franc is such good currency that I've seen many a guy uses it for toilet paper. In fact, I've found it good for that use a few times myself when I was really hard pressed. Things are tough all over these days!

Now if I was an arm chair general with my own special train, I think I'd parti tute suite for the Riviera for a couple of days and sweat out all this nonsense down there. Unfortunately, I am not an arm chair general - if fact, I don't even have an arm chair. There is absolutely no news as you can see. Will keep you posted. Love...JACK.

November 26, 1945

Perrone, France - A-72 Airstrip

Dear Mom and Dad:

Just a quick note to let you know that our outfit is really getting good and hot. If all works out okey we should leave here on Friday or Saturday and head for Le Harve. Of course, we don't know how long we'll have to stay at the POE, but we do know that we're supposed to be at the port by December 2nd. It is very possible that we'll have to sweat it out down there for a short period of time. That's something that we'll just have to wait for final developments.

In the meantime, we've been knocking ourselves out night after night with the same old routine. They say that a clean ear never decays - well, things equal to the same thing are equal to each other - therefore, we all ought to have clean kidneys with all of the beer we've been consuming. In the meantime, this new finance deal has gone into effect and at present I have exactly what I'll be able to exchange. You can take back or I should say exchange into American dollars the equivalent of three months' pay.

The month before last I drew two months' pay, then last month I drew one month and finally I'll draw pay for this month. That gives me a total of around $150 and that is exactly what I'll have when I draw

397th Bomb Group, APO 140, Point of Embarkation Base A-42

this month's pay. This is one time when it is too bad I have any of those allotments because that cuts down on the amount I can drag back. You should get a load of some of the big gambling going on around here. The guys are stuck with thousands of dollars' worth of Francs and no way of getting the stuff converted and sent back home. Hence, they are going crazy throwing it away. A lot of them are going on buying sprees and picking up watches, cameras or anything else with some type of material value. It is really amusing - the GI's are outbidding the French on certain articles like the above.

Things are terribly quiet around here. Two of the squadrons have moved out to Marseilles already. That is one of the reasons we are so confident that we'll be able to get out of here in such quick order. I was afraid that this office would be a madhouse closing everything up like we're doing, but so far hardly anything has come up and I frankly doubt if it will. Then, too, one fortunate thing is that we're going home with all the wheels so there is a possibility of getting a big ship. You know as well as I do that a Commanding Officer will always arrange for the best possible deal when he himself is going along. Therefore, I am hopeful it will be an aircraft carrier.

Not much to tell you. Just thought I'd give you the latest and let you know how the situation looks. Doubt if you'll get many more letters. Meantime, love to you both......JACK.

December 3, 1945

Perrone, France - A-72 Airstrip

Dear Mom and Dad:

As you can see I am still here in this place of desertion and dissipation. The latest dope is that we'll leave for the POE somewhere around December 7-15th. In other words, the possibility of getting home for Christmas is getting rapidly out of the question. New Year's Eve looks like a better bet and if I do get home it would be a great celebration!

In the meantime, I have been raising the usual amount of hell. The other night a couple of my old cronies and I went into San Quentin

Dear Mom and Dad

with Major Agan and hung a good one on. Or did I write you the grewsome details of that already. Saw a couple of good movies in the past few days. The best being Bogart and Bacall in "The Big Sleep". Yesterday, I arose at the early hour of eight o'clock and went to breakfast and then hauled Bob Britt to church. I thought it was about time for me to have my presence grace a church pew again.

Lou Rotella came down in the afternoon and we shot the breeze for a while, and then headed for the Red Cross. After dinner, we all went up to the NCO's Club and spent the next five hours drinking beer and playing pinnocle. I've now learned almost every card game in the deck, I think. I learned to play the latter about a week ago, and it is a pretty good time passer. The days are dragging terribly and time hangs heavily on our hands. I have never seen hours pass so slowly. It is getting rough and you can see that it is beginning to tell on the buys.

There is no more news to share with you at present. Just sweating it out and that is about all. Hope both of you are okey - I am still breathing and not in the guard house. Will write when there is some development; otherwise this writing letters has had it. Love to you both……JACK.

December 25, 1945
Aboard the *S.S. Walter E. Ranger* (a Liberty ship)
The Azores

Dear Mom and Dad:

What a hell of a place to spend Christmas!! Well, anyway Merry Christmas and here's hoping that we will all have a happy and prosperous New Year. In case you've been wondering what in the devil has happened to your traveling son - well, he has been traveling. We went from Perrone down to Le Havre and rushed through processing in three days. Then at two o'clock in the morning on December 16th we boarded the S.S. Walter E. Ranger which is a Liberty ship that carries only about 500 persons.

It is on this slow moving tub that I have confined my activities for the last nine days. We average about 160 miles a day. The only reason

397th Bomb Group, APO 140, Point of Embarkation Base A-42

we are docking in the Azores is to dump a guy off with acute appendicitis. With luck and plenty of it maybe we'll make New York by January 7th or 8th. What a life. I really don't care how long were on the sea now since I can't make it for Christmas or New Years. Besides that, as usual, I've got a racket. Two of my cronies who are both medics moved into the ships hospital and so I moved down there also. We have a private room with lavatory, beds with sheets and the works. Even better than the Officers' quarters, by golly. The troops live in the various holds and sleep on hard canvass bunks which are five bunks high. Besides that, I picked up a special chow pass that allows me to buck the line whenever I care to. Quite a handy thing, you know. Then to pass my time I am a reporter on the ship's newspaper, so I don't pull guard, KP, or any of those other meaningless tasks.

So far, my gamboling has been darn near zero. Just a few cheap games of pinnocle which I've won. I have about $200 on me and that is what I plan to get off the boat with so rest at ease on that score. Last night Britt and I became bottle babies with my quart of Haig and Haig Scotch. Then, we got in on a wild party up in John Zieries room. He is Chief Boatswain on board - been sailing for about 20 years. If I am not mistaken he ran around with Dick Bissell, Tom Roshek and that gang of guys back in Dubuque. Anyway, a good time was had by all and the only damage was a panel in a door which got busted out.

However, on to more pleasant things. During the first five days we had very bad weather. One night the gales got up to 75 mph. The rail was continually loaded with the men tossing their cookies which delighted all of the fish in the ocean. Johnny, Britt and I disappointed them since not one of us got sick. I haven't missed a meal as yet - the food is okey. Tonight, we get turkey and the trimmings, ice cream and mince pie to boot.

There are 500 of us on board so you can see what a small ship we're on. Maximum speed is 10 knots, but the most we've gotten out of her is 8 knots. A snail's pace you might say - or in the words of Paul Revere - one by land; two by sea; and 20 by the S.S. Walter E. Ranger. Time really hangs heavily - no kidding. We're all on the verge of blowing our out. Unfortunately, they confiscated all guns and knives. By the way, I hope the radiogram got to you okey. That cost a small fortune and notice that it wasn't Collect!!! Will probably go to Camp Kilmer, New Jersey, after getting off the ship, and then head for Camp Grant, Illinois, where I'll be discharged or given a furlough. Personally, I am bucking for a furlough (30 days) so I can draw an extra month's pay.

There is a chance that I may go back to Shick General Hospital for a while and get a good physical check over. In the meantime, just keep the home fires burning and I'll see you soon. Haven't gotten any mail, naturally, for over two. Gotta close and start getting this smuggled off the ship. Here's hoping that you have a very MERRY CHRISTMAS!

All my love...JACK.

January 3, 1946
Aboard the *S.S. Walter E. Ranger* (Somewhere in the Atlantic)
Dear Mom and Dad:

This won't get mailed until we land in the States but I did want to bring you up to date. Well, we had Christmas dinner on board with all of the trimmings. However, the cooks all got drunk and pulled the turkeys out of the freezer too early with the result that the meat got tainted and the whole ship came down with the "G.I. Runs". It was a mess. Since the three of us had private sleeping quarters with a toilet I sat on the stool most of the time with my head in the wash basin. Believe me, it was coming out of both ends. There was sickness all over the ship and not enough places to go to the toilet. Finally, after a couple of days things did settle down.

Then, among other things we had two emergency appendectomies on board which meant that the call was put out for all of the medics to report to the dispensary with our make shift operating room. I decided to make myself scarce since I didn't feel that I could face up to assisting in an operation. The first time it worked since I pleaded sickness when I was called on the carpet. However, on the next emergency I

397th Bomb Group, APO 140, Point of Embarkation Base A-42

was paged over and over again to get down to the operating room. I didn't show up once again. This time the doctor who was a Captain put it to me point blank. He said: "Dauner, are you or aren't you a medic?" I had to reply that I wasn't and he told me in no uncertain terms not to show my face around him anymore. However, I didn't have to move from my luxurious quarters, thank goodness. Am just glad that both of the operations were a success without me. I might have been the cause of some poor guy dying on the table if I'd been in the operating room.

The seas are a little calmer but this has really been a rough trip. For three days we made absolutely no forward progress. This was all charted on a huge map down in the main lounge area. We just held our own against the stiff North Atlantic winds. Am not sure that I ever want to get on board another ship again although I have to admit our trip on the old S.S. Mariposa going over to England was a great experience.

They are projecting that we might get into New York within the next several days. Nobody knows for sure but at least we are making progress. Will mail this as soon as I get off the boat. Who knows, with a little luck I might even beat this letter home. Anyway, it will probably be my last letter while I am still in the military. Let's hope so. No more news for now. Love....JACK.

Author's Summary of His Final Days in the Military.

We arrived in New York harbor on January 7, 1946. It was a sunny but cold day. The Red Cross was on hand to serve hot coffee and donuts which really hit the spot. All of us were grateful just to be on American soil again. In fact, many of the troops actually got down on their hands and knees and kissed the ground they were standing on. After some delay in getting the ship unloaded we were taken by truck to a train for transportation to Camp Kilmer, New Jersey.

After processing we were then transported to another train for our departure to various sections of the country where we would then be processed and given our Honorable Discharge papers. My orders were to proceed to Camp Grant which was near Rockford, Illinois. On the

Dear Mom and Dad

evening of January 11, 1946, I was given my official Honorable Discharge from the United States Army along with all of the pay which was due me. I was also provided with the opportunity to file a claim for any disability income as compensation for wounds or any permanent damage which I might have sustained while in military service.

Since I was in excellent physical and mental condition I opted to make no claims. Many of my friends and other personnel did make claims and were given awards of anywhere from 10% to 100% disability. It was my personal feeling that unless an individual really sustained permanent injury no claim should be filed. (I later learned that my honesty and false sense of well-being cost me some well-deserved compensation) That same evening I boarded a bus from Camp Grant, Illinois, for my home town, Dubuque, Iowa.

For me the nearly three years which I spent in the military was a tremendous learning experience. I had the opportunity to become an officer, but preferred to bail out of the Meteorology Cadet program in which I had been readily accepted. I learned later that life would have been much more enjoyable as a Meteorology Officer on an air base. However, I am proud to say that I served my country as a combat soldier and later as a control tower operator. I watched men give their lives for their country both on the ground and in the air; and I learned a great deal from the outstanding leadership qualities of many officers I served under. However, all too often the enlisted man had to endure the complete ineptness of a lot of pompass officers who without their bars and the "Army Book" would be destined to failure in any other field. Most of these egomanics never saw any combat, treated enlisted personnel as slaves, and personified the very worst in leadership qualities.

Thus, ended my military tour of duty which lasted just a couple of weeks short of three years. Without a doubt, it was not only one of the truly great experiences which occurred during my younger days, but also one which I have cherished throughout my life. I have often said that every young man should be required to serve his country for

397th Bomb Group, APO 140, Point of Embarkation Base A-42

a minimum of two years in one of our military branches in order to effectively learn the essence of discipline, leadership, and team work. As far as I am concerned, these qualities are essential ingredients in any type of successful business, government, educational or military organization.

B-17 Bomber Flights Taken in 1945

March 15, 1945: A five-and-one-half hour flight on B-17 (809-S) of the 409th Bomb Squadron with Major Collins from Chelveston to Paris, Rouen, St. Lo, Le Harve, and back across the English Channel to base. Circled Paris twice. St. Lo was in ruins. Sunken LSTs still visible at beach head from D-Day. Passed over Caen, which also showed heavy damage.

March 29, 1945: A five-and-one-half hour flight on B-17 (964-K) of the 364th Bomb Squadron with Lt. Bakula from Chelveston to Padington Cambridge, Norwich, Spalding, Nottingham, Oxford, Leicester, and Northampton. We flew at 2000 feet and it was a plenty rough trip.

April 12, 1945: A three hour cross-country flight on B-17 (924-E) of the 364th Bomb Squadron with Capt. Sherman from Chelveston to Swindon, Staunton, Exeter, Burton, Stratford-on-Avon, Northampton, Plymouth and much of the west coast before returning back to base.

April 15, 1945: An eight hour flight on B-17 (034-X) of the 365th Bomb Squadron with Capt. Clark. The flight plans were as follows: Base (Chelveston), Corridor No. 4, Entretat, Le Harve, Rouen, Paris, Orleans, Tours, Le Man, Laval, Rennes, St. Malo, Cherbourg, Hague, Corridor No. 8, Charistchurch, Base (Chelveston). We flew over Paris at 700 feet. It was a clear day and we buzzed almost every city enroute at 3–500 feet. Our flight took us over many old castles, both in England and on the continent. Out of St. Malo over the water the altimeter read "0". We could have hung the washing on the tail of the plane very easily. Paris was really in bloom and famous landmarks very visible.

B-17 Bomber Flights Taken in 1945

April 18, 1945: A two-and-one-half hour flight on B-17 (860-P) of the 422nd Bomb Squadron with Capt. Bingham. The flight left base (Chelveston) to Great Yarmouth, Jetison Point "A" at 5225N 0220E, Great Yarmouth, Thurley, and back to base (Chelveston). We dropped five 500 lbs. fragment stick bombs.

April 19, 1945: A three-hour slow time flight on B-17 (015-H) of the 366th Bomb Squadron with Lt. Artman. We flew from base (Chelveston) to Southampton and back to base (Chelveston). We buzzed "Flak-Home" with altimeter reading "0". Waved to everyone and gave them about five buzzes before heading back to base. Flew very tight formation with another plane from the 366th Bomb Squadron.

May 9, 1945: An eight-hour flight on B-17 (809-S) of the 422nd Bomb Squadron with Maj. Parks having the following flight plan: 0825 depart base (Chelveston); 0856 arrive at Gravesend; 0915 at North Foreland; 0949 at Ostend; 1009 at Brussels; 1039 at Aachen; 1046 at Duren; 1055 at Cologne; 1100 at Hamburg; 1122 at Dortmund; 1134 at Munster; 1143 at Hamm; 1228 at Frankfurt; 1242 at Bingen; 1254 at Coblenz; 1307 at Bonn; 1354 at Brussels; 1441 at Cape Griz Nez; 1452 at Dungeness; 1519 at Guilford; and 1545 at base (Chelveston).

Major Parks set the flight plan of May 9, 1945, so as to pass over the spot where I had been wounded back in 1944 while I was serving in Co. K., 60 Infantry, of the 9th Frankfurt was in very bad shape. Munster was also very heavily bombed. However, Aachen was the worst of all for its size and the amount of destruction. Brussels was very well preserved and remained a beautiful city with little damage.

July 7, 1945: A one-and-one-half hour flight from Chelveston to St. Tronds, Belgium (A-92) with Lt. Scarpula. We took a direct route and shot a few pictures en route to our new air base with the 9th Air Force.

Dear Mom and Dad

August 14, 1945: A five-hour flight with Capt. Clark in (707 JJ-N) of the 365th Bomb Squadron with Capt. Clark from St. Trond (A-92) to Bordeaux. We landed and then buzzed the city after take-off. Saw the submarine pens along with many sunken ships in the harbor. It was a most interesting trip - a beautiful city - and a fantastic sight from the air.

September 15, 1945: A twelve-hour flight with F/O Strayer from A-92 over the Swiss Alps; Venice; and Foggia, Italy. On our return flight two days later we flew over Naples, Rome, Corsica, Toulan, Marsellies, and back to base (A-92). F/O Strayer and his crew were killed in a crash a few weeks after we made this trip to Foggia, Italy. An outstanding pilot and fine crew who were missed by all of us on base.

October 3, 1945: A group of us flew from base (A-92) to Nice, France, in a C-47 from the 477th Bomb Squadron. This was a one week furlough. Fortunately, our leave was extended a couple of extra days because of weather conditions.

October 13, 1945: A three-hour trip with Lt. O'Rourke from Nice, France, to St. Trond (A-92). One engine gave us a lot of trouble; however, we made it back to base after a couple of trying hours.

October 31, 1945: Lt. Soskin and I flew an L-4 N-6 to Liege, Belgium, and back. He gave me a flying lesson and after chasing some of the cows in the field we did a few loops and spins. He was one of the really good guys on base, and he checked me out pretty well in the L-4 after about one-and-one-half hours in the air. Apparently, he recognized my love of flying and how disappointed I was that my 20/30 vision had kept me out of pilot training.

B-17 Bomber Flights Taken in 1945

The ARC Casino Club on the Prominade de Anglais on the French Riviera at Nice. Prior to the war it was a huge casino but then taken over for a Red Cross Club.

An aerial view of Paris taken on a flight the author made on a B-17 bomber from the 305th Bomb Group.

Arc de Triomphe
Paris, France

Cathedral and panoramic view of Orleans, France

Notre Dame Cathedral
Paris, France

Castle at Tours, France

Chapter 23

Post-War Academic and Professional Life[1]

Jack and Carolyn.

Jack returned back to finish work on his Bachelor of Science in Commerce degree at the University of Iowa. Jack was an active member of the Phi Kappa Psi national fraternity. In the fall of 1946, Carolyn Lee Wells was introduced to Jack and they dated throughout the fall and spring semesters at the University of Iowa. Carolyn was born on May 10, 1926, in Jacksonville, Morgan County, Illinois. She attended grade school in Burlington, graduated in 1944 from Davenport High School and received a Bachelor of Arts degree with majors in Art and English from the University of Iowa and the University of Dubuque on August 6, 1947. In addition, she also completed most of her work on a master's

---

1 Some of the information in this chapter was obtained from Carolyn Wells Dauner's *Wells Family Sketches: Our History in America 1682–1992*, published by Jack R. Dauner Associates, 1992.

Post-War Academic and Professional Life

degree in special education at the University of Detroit. Jack and Carolyn got married on May 12, 1947, at the Methodist Church, Troy, Kansas.

Jack finished his degree at the University of Iowa in the summer of 1947 and accepted a position as Assistant Manager of the Dubuque, Iowa, Chamber of Commerce in 1949. Jack and Carolyn moved to Davenport, Iowa, where Jack assumed broader responsibilities with

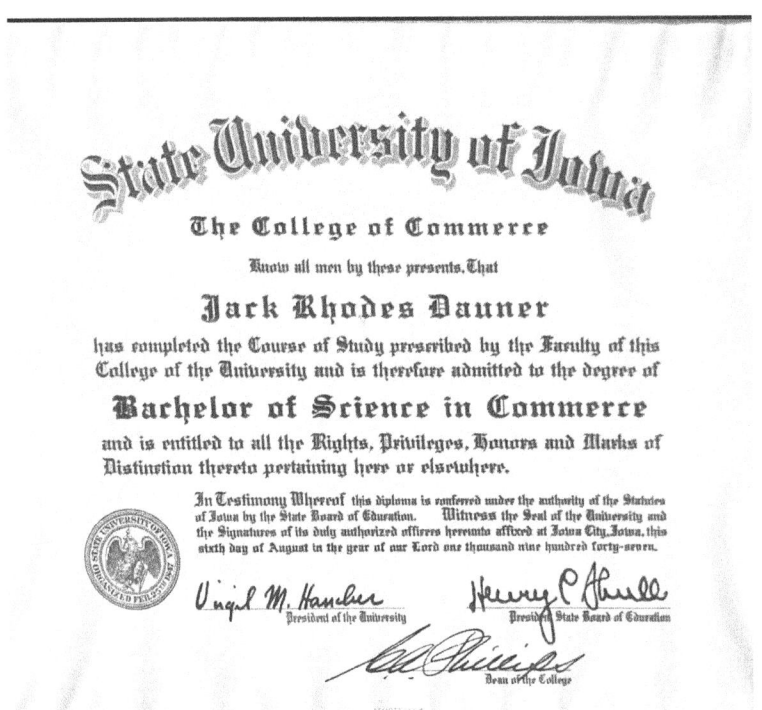

Jack's Bachelor of Science in Commerce diploma, issued by State University of Iowa.

the Chamber of Commerce. One of his many responsibilities was the supervision of everything related to the Chamber building and the Membership Committee.

In 1950, Jack was elected President of the Davenport Newcomer's Club and Carolyn was elected President of the Newcomer's Auxiliary.

Dear Mom and Dad

The organization had over 150 members and featured monthly dinner dances at popular locations throughout the metropolitan area. Both groups were widely recognized for the public service they offered to new people moving into the area. In 1951, the Dauners moved to Madison, Wisconsin, where Jack was associated with the Madison Chamber of Commerce and Foundation. One of Jack's early accomplishments was the organization of National Sales Executives of Madison, an affiliate of National Sales Executives, Inc. As a result of his efforts, the organization received national recognition for several of its programs during the 1952 International Convention, which was held in Atlantic City. In the spring of the following year, Jack was appointed Acting Manager of the

C. of C. Assistant Accepts New Post In Madison, Wis.

Jack R. Dauner, assistant secretary of Davenport Chamber of Commerce for the past two and one-half years, has resigned to accept a staff executive position with the Madison, Wis., Chamber of Commerce.

Dauner, who has served as secretary to several of the chamber committees and the Sales Managers bureau, will assume his new post Aug. 20. He has been active in many civic projects and is a past president of Davenport Newcomers club.

Prior to coming to Davenport, Dauner was assistant secretary of Dubuque Chamber of Commerce for one and one-half years. He is a graduate of the University of Iowa and a member of Phi Kappa Psi national fraternity.

Article announcing Jack's new executive position in the Madison, WI, Chamber of Commerce.

Post-War Academic and Professional Life

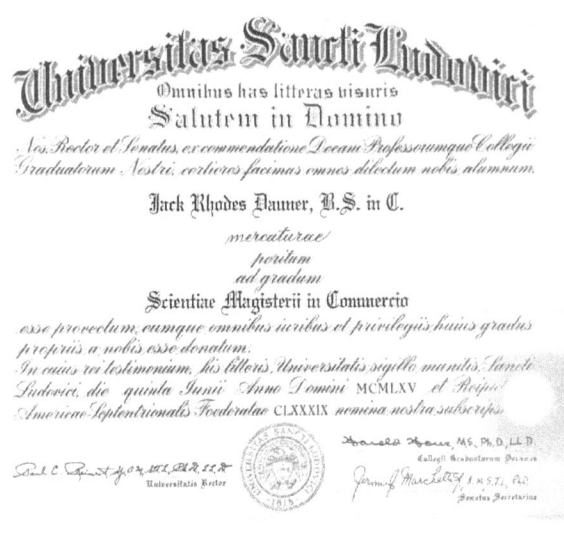

Jack's Masters Degree in Commerce diploma.

Madison Chamber of Commerce and Foundation.

In the fall of 1970, Jack assumed a teaching position as Associate Professor of Marketing at the University of Detroit. Jack returned to St. Louis to participate in the graduation ceremonies and received his Doctor of Philosophy degree in Business Administration ("A Comparative Analysis of Salesmen's Compensation: Plans, Policies and Trends") on December 13, 1970. This occasion was celebrated by a party given by Carolyn's parents, Delbert and Elsey Wells at the Clayton Inn which was

Jack's PhD diploma.

attended by Jack's parents, Bill and Pauline Dauner, all of the Wells family from Davenport and many faculty members and associates from the University.

Because of severe budgetary cuts at the University of Detroit that year, Jack negotiated a better contract and assumed similar teaching responsibilities in the School of Business at the University of Akron (Ohio) in the fall of 1971. During the academic year, Jack commuted weekly between Akron and Detroit until June of 1972. Jack developed a number of innovative programs in the classroom, including the use of a computer-oriented business simulation. At this time, Jack also became involved with Central Michigan University in the Institution's off-campus graduate programs which were conducted on the weekend at military bases around the United States.

Jack served as President of SME of Akron in 1974–75 while at the same time serving as Vice President of Career Education of SME International and as an International Director. He also became heavily involved in the presentation of seminars for corporate and university executive development programs.

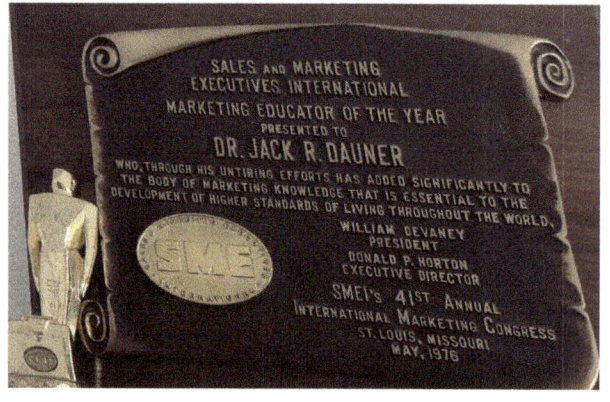

Jack's Marketing Educator of the Year plaque.

As a result of these many activities, he was honored in 1976 as The Marketing Educator of the Year by Sales and Marketing Executives International during the organization's 41st Annual Convention which was held at the Chase Park Plaza Hotel in St. Louis, Mo.

In 1976, Jack and Carolyn moved to Pinehurst, North Carolina, on a leave of absence in order to check the climate and determine the long-term possibilities of living in the south. During the first several

Post-War Academic and Professional Life

weeks after arriving in Pinehurst, Jack checked a number of options and decided to take a contract at Fayetteville State University, an affiliate with the University of North Carolina system. For the next twelve years, Jack commuted between Pinehurst and Fayetteville through the Ft. Bragg Reservations to cover classes on Tuesday and Thursday.

Jack in his Chamber of Commerce days.

Jack assisted Campbell University in establishing their Masters of Business Administration program and frequently taught in their graduate program as Visiting Professor at the Fort Bragg Campus. Since 1973, he also served as an Adjunct Professor of Marketing and Management for Central Michigan University, and regularly flew all over the country on weekends to cover CMU graduate classes. On many of these assignments, Carolyn joined Jack, particularly those involving the Azores, Key West, Atlanta, Charleston and other very interesting and/or desirable locations.

Jack was the author of a book, *Salesmen's Compensation: Plans, Policies and Trends*, and coauthored *How to Plan an Evaluation Program and Conduct Sales Meetings*. He was a contributor to the *Handbook of Modern Marketing*, as well as having numerous articles published in professional journals in the business and trade fields. In 1981, Jack was invited to give the keynote address before the Annual Management Conference of Sales and Marketing Executives of New Zealand, which was held in Wellington. The invitation came from John Morrison. John served as the Southeastern Pacific Regional Vice President of SME International. He was also a past President of the New Zealand Association and General Chairman of this conference.

In addition to the academic assignments, Jack also set up his own consulting firm, Jack R. Dauner & Associates. As a consultant, Jack served a diversified list of clients ranging from those in banking, heavy equipment, recreation, food, airlines and many others. Jack had several years' experience as a trade association executive and consultant with management responsibilities ranging from department head to chief executive officer. He had extensive experience in the planning, organizing, coordination and promotion of various business-oriented seminars, conferences, conventions, trade shows and other educational programs. He was a frequent participant and speaker for company, association and university programs.

Jack and Carolyn moved to their beautiful home in Lake Forest Drive, Pinehurst, in 1985. They joined the Country Club of North Carolina and the Pinehurst Country Club. Unfortunately, Carolyn became very sick and Jack retired in 1989 to be a caregiver to Carolyn till she passed away on March 19, 1994.

Jack's business publications, listed in chronological order

Marketing Strategy and Purchasing

JACK R. DAUNER

The marketing man considers a customer either as a consumer or as a business firm. Within the past several years, both types of customers have increased their levels of sophistication. On the one hand, the consumer is better educated, has a higher income, and is more style and quality conscious than his counterpart in any previous generation. On the other hand, the progressive business firm, with its well established purchasing department, has implemented vigorous programs of *value* and *vendor analysis* that have contributed greatly to effective decision-making in selecting products, product lines, and suppliers.

Before going any farther, it would be well to define the three key terms in the title: Marketing, strategy, and purchasing. The American Marketing Association's Committee on Definitions defines marketing as "the performance of business activities that directs the flow of goods and services from a producer to a consumer or user." However, Paul Mazur[1] made what is probably one of the most expressive and all inclusive statements on modern marketing when he said: "Marketing is the delivery of a standard of living to society."

The term, strategy, is reminiscent of military experiences, since strategy is usually thought of in terms of the actions taken by an army to achieve certain military objectives. In the context of business, however, strategy refers to the plan of attack a marketing man will use to gain favorable acceptance of his product or product lines by a customer over competition.

Finally, and certainly not of least importance, is the purchasing function. The purchasing function can be considered primarily in the light of buying, but it is far more complex than simply exchanging the price of a product for the product itself. The purchasing function reflects not only the need, desire, and ability to buy, but also the search, examination, negotiation, and final purchase of the product or products that fulfill these requirements.

Purchasing Objectives vs. Marketing Objectives

The objective of sound purchasing is to buy materials of the right quality, in the right quantity, at the right time, at the right price, from the right source, with delivery at the right place. This same statement can be made marketing-oriented simply by substituting the word "marketing" for "purchasing" and the word "sell" for "buy." The objectives of both purchasing and marketing are compatible in what might be known as a bill of rights for purchasing and marketing.

Some experts in business are stressing the importance of continuing specialization and concentration for the field sales force in their work to meet marketing objectives. The idea of systems selling is fast becoming a marketing status symbol. However, in all fairness, it has been found that, by organizing and responding properly to the growing complexity of selling in a highly industrial environment, an organization may be able to meet the "systems" challenges of the space age.

Some businessmen and academicians feel that computers may someday replace salesmen. However, present recruiting activities indicate that nothing could be farther from the truth. In fact, most sales and marketing executives point to an ever-expanding need for good salesmen. In addition, salesmen today are better trained than their predecessors and certainly much better paid. For example, young sales trainees, freshly graduated from college with only a bachelor of science degree, are commanding from $625 to $750 per month, plus fringe benefits and expenses.

The Marketing Umbrella

Most people, including many purchasing agents, use the terms *marketing* and *selling* interchangeably. Although differentiating between the two may seem academic, it is advisable.

Marketing, as defined earlier, is the performance of business activities that directs the flow of goods

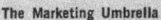

Mr. Dauner is professor, department of marketing, St. Louis University. This article was adapted from his speech at The Catholic Hospital Association's annual convention, held in Minneapolis, June, 1969.

Dear Mom and Dad

Purchasing is directly related to marketing strategy in that it represents the customer to whom marketing strategy is geared. The best benchmark for successful marketing strategy and purchasing is finding out what customers want and then helping them get it. This article discusses the "marketing revolution" in relation to this benchmark.

and services from the producer to the consumer or user. It is a total system of interacting business activities designed to plan, price, promote, and distribute want- and/or need-satisfying products and services to present and potential customers.

The marketing system is often looked upon as a massive umbrella which shelters a whole series of subsystems, including marketing research, product planning and development, packaging, channels of distribution, pricing, advertising and sales promotion, personal selling, and sales forecasting and analysis. The crux of the selling function is to interrelate with all of the various subsystems within the marketing system and, at the same time, serve as the dynamic force that is designed to personally interact with the customer.

The Marketing Revolution

As an example of how the marketing concept has developed within the framework of the corporate structure, Robert J. Keith[2] described the classic case of the Pillsbury Company. According to Mr. Keith, the Pillsbury Company has passed through three distinct marketing eras and is now entering the fourth.

First came the era of manufacturing, which started in 1869 when the company was formed and continued into the 1930's. During this period, primary emphasis was directed toward the production and manufacturing of a high quality flour.

In the 1930's, management at Pillsbury became more conscious of the consumer as a key factor in the business equation. At this point, the company began to shift emphasis to sales, and thus Pillsbury moved into its second management period which was sales- and consumer-oriented.

At the beginning of the 1960's, the company entered its marketing-oriented era, which was guided by the philosophy that Pillsbury makes and sells products for consumers. This approach was reinforced by the introduction of the brand manager concept. Under this system, the individual holding the title of brand manager is solely responsible for marketing his specific product.

Today Pillsbury stands on the brink of the fourth major era: Marketing control. In this period, the company changes from one that espouses the marketing concept to a total marketing company. Marketing control makes marketing the basic motivating force of the entire company. When this stage of development is reached, the marketing revolution is complete.

Certainly this revolution in marketing is worthy of consideration by purchasing agents. In fact, purchasing agents might ask themselves the following question: How far have suppliers progressed in becoming marketing-controlled organizations and what are the short- and long-run implications of this development for our particular organizations and purchasing departments?

The Road to Better Understanding

Another example of in-depth marketing of which purchasing agents should be aware is the approach used by one of the largest producers of raw materials in the U.S. This company's marketing strategy is designed to reach all people whose decisions, reactions, and activities can affect the sale of its products. The company's strategy goes far beyond even the purchasing agent, who is primarily charged with the responsibility of placing orders.

This company's in-depth marketing strategy includes three phases:

1. Aiding customer industries to expand their markets, sell more of their present products, and develop markets for new products.

2. Working to get the company's raw material into the products being sold by telling the company story to numerous individuals in the customer's organizations, to the public, to government agencies, and to persons in other miscellaneous areas.

3. Reaching as many people as possible in the customer's and in potential customers' organizations and anyone else who may influence the source from which materials will be purchased once they have been specified.

The final problem in the marketing situation is the matter of bringing the buyer and seller together. Probably one of the most interesting approaches to this problem is the concept known as "sales situation management" which was developed by John J. McCarthy for the General Electric Company.

The SSM approach considers both salesmen and buyers as professionals engaged in an "exchange of need satisfactions." The basic hypothesis of this program is that the prerequisite for maximum success in any job is the conviction that the work one does is important.

One of the most unusual tools used in the SSM program is the "estimate of the selling situation," which is an essential part of the pre-sale preparation. It is an adaptation of the military battle strategy of estimating the situation. It requires salesmen to have well-defined short- and long-range objectives that are supported in depth by well-documented intelligence reports. These reports include information on the product, economic, and psychological needs of the purchaser. The program's objectives include helping the purchaser accomplish *his* goals.

According to McCarthy, the customer's self-image is present in every sale, and often, sales are lost because they present an unwitting threat to that self-image. Typically everyone has three "me's": the "me-I-think-I-am," the "me-I-wish-I-were," and the "me-I-try-to-project." Naturally, people prefer to do business with those who make them feel important and respected.

The purchasing agent may give as his reason for not purchasing a particular item the fact that the price is too high or the delivery is too slow, when his real, unspoken objection is to the manner in which he believes the salesman regards him. He begins to ask himself such questions as: Are my opinions respected? Am I treated as an individual or am I given a canned presentation prepared for someone with an entirely different problem? If a salesman is going to successfully reach this buyer, he must be perceptive enough to understand what the buyer's true objections are.

Selling Situations

The following steps are designed to provide a variety of responses to selling situations as they arise:

1. *Consider customer objectives and goals.* Before trying to get a customer's attention, the salesman should consider the customer and his problems and needs.
2. *Consider selling objectives.* If these objectives are multiple, the salesman should establish priorities. Since goals are short-range, objectives should be set first.
3. *Compare selling objectives with the customer's*

objectives. This comparison will indicate the basic selling problem.

4. *Consider selling goals.* The salesman should determine whether or not selling goals conflict with one another and whether or not they facilitate attainment of long-range objectives.
5. *Gather intelligence.* Major categories of intelligence information are the seller's products and competitors' offerings, knowledge of competitors and their employes, economic factors which affect the customer's business, and psychological factors that affect the customer.
6. *Analyze the intelligence.* Salesmen should examine areas of weakness and be prepared to answer customer's questions.
7. *Develop a sales strategy.* The effective sales approach should determine what alternatives exist, how competition is likely to react to these alternatives, and how customers will respond to the alternatives.
8. *Plan opening tactics.* The salesman should explore his advantages and anticipate, meet, and neutralize his disadvantages.

Some salesmen think that, by discussing this sales situation management program openly, a potential Trojan horse has been removed from the purchasing agent's camp. Nothing could be further from the truth. Successful buyers and sellers will both recognize this pattern as a professional approach to a successful buyer/seller relationship.

The real clincher to any discussion on marketing strategy and how it relates to purchasing is the suggestion made by Frank Bettger.[3] According to Bettger, the most important secret to a successful buyer/seller relationship is to develop a sales plan originated by the *buyer*, not one originated by a salesman. In essence, this approach suggests that the salesman find out what a customer wants and then help him get it. When everything is reduced to the simplest equation, this is the real benchmark for successful marketing strategy and purchasing. ★

FOOTNOTES

1. Paul Mazur, "Does Distribution Cost Enough?" *Fortune*, November, 1947, p. 138.
2. Robert J. Keith, "The Marketing Revolution," *Journal of Marketing*, January, 1960, p. 35.
3. Frank Bettger, *How I Raised Myself from Failure to Success in Selling*, Englewood Cliffs, N.J., Prentice-Hall, Inc., 1949.

Dear Mom and Dad

How to Succeed by Trying

by Jack R. Dauner*

MANY books and people talk about the secrets of success as though some deep, mysterious truth is involved. There are, however, no hidden secrets or no mysterious rules. The basic factors for success are plain and simple.

There are countless individuals who seem to have all the needed requirements for success; yet, they do not succeed. They have natural ability . . . education . . . attractive personalities . . . outstanding talents . . . but, they fail to make good. Why? Because they neglect certain simple fundamentals.

On the other hand, there are individuals who lack these advantages, yet make outstanding successes in business and in their family and social life. The explanation is clear. They have acquired habits of living by the simple rules that assure success.

I have learned over the past 25 years of business and academic life one interesting phenomena: People, with rare exceptions, do not fail because they lack knowledge, education or talent. They fail chiefly because of what they do not do . . . not because of what they cannot do.

Think with me for a minute and get this picture clearly in your mind. On one hand, people with nothing out of the ordinary in their favor achieve outstanding success. On the other hand, people with every natural advantage in their favor fail to make good. Why does this occur? All because the successes followed and the failures neglected a few simple rules.

Only 10% Try to Succeed

Alongside that picture note this important fact. Surveys made over the past 50 years consistently show that only 10% of all people are truly seeking to be successful. The other 90% are searching for a right to fail. They are not willing to go after success if it requires any effort.

Let me share with you a story of two brothers which will illustrate this point. They were born and raised in Flint, Michigan. Their name was Curtice. When they went to work, they both got jobs in the paint shop of the Fisher Body Division of General Motors in Flint. The years passed. When the older brother was ready to retire at the age of 65, he was asked by a reporter: "How come you didn't get any further in General Motors than the paint shop were you started?" He replied: "I didn't have the time and money to do the things essential to get ahead." Then the reporter asked: "Where did your brother, Harlow Curtice, get the time and money to become president of General Motors?" With a shrug of his shoulders, he answered: "Oh, he was always the ambitious one in the family."

What really happened was this. When Harlow Curtice decided that he wanted to get more out of his life than he could find in a paint shop, he took a course in bookkeeping at a local business school. When he graduated, he looked in the classified advertisements of the local paper and found that the spark plug division of General Motors needed a bookkeeper. He applied and got the job. He did not stop there but raised his sights. He continued his self-development until he was appointed General Manager of the Spark Plug Division. He put this division on its feet and moved from there to the presidency of General Motors.

Harlow Curtice would have been a success in any business that might have been looking for a bookkeeper that day he read the classified ads. He was one of the 10% of all people seeking out success, not one of the 90% looking for an excuse to fail.

One of the big reasons that most people go through life getting so little out of it is that they don't really know what they want. They take things as they come. They go after the idle pleasures of the moment instead of permanent satisfaction and assured happiness.

Six Rules for Success

I would feel remiss if I did not offer you a few ideas which might help you in being a part of that 10% of all the people who seek out success. Here they are!

1. *Analyse Yourself.* Set forth what you want in terms of the basic human desires of security, love, ego satisfaction, bodily comforts and possessions.

2. *Define Your Objectives (Goals).* As you establish your goals be sure that you clearly define your duties and responsibilities; the same time make sure that your goals are definite, realistic, and attainable.

3. *Develop a Positive Mental Attitude.* Let me illustrate this point with a short story. A young man came to an oasis at the edge of a town in the Near East. Approaching an old graybeard at the well, he asked "What kind of people dwell in this place?" "What kind of people dwelt in the place from whence you came?" asked the old man. "Ah! They were a bad and selfish lot," replied the youth. "I was glad to leave them." "You'll find the same here," said the old man.

The old man tarried at the well and later in the day another young man came to drink and seeing the old man, he put the same question to him: "What kind of people dwell in this place?" Again the graybeard replied with the question, "What kind of people dwelt in the place from whence you came?" Said the young man, "They were a fine lot: honest, friendly, hospitable. I hated leaving them." "You'll find the same here," said the old man.

Now a lounger at the oasis, who had

---

* *Jack R. Dauner (D. Sigma '65F, St. Louis) is an associate professor of marketing, University of Akron, Akron, Ohio.*

heard both conversations, challenged the old man: "How could you give two different answers to the same question from two different men?" "My son," the wise man answered, "each carries in his heart the environment in which he lives. The one who found nothing good in the place from whence he came will find the same here. The one who found friends in his former place will find friends here. People are to us what we ourselves find in them. Seek, and ye shall find—from within yourself."

Remember . . . everything in your life depends upon your mental attitude, and the important thing to remember is that you are the one who controls your own mental attitude.

4. *Learn the Art of Persuasion.* Learn how to get others to think and act favorably with you because when you win the co-operation of another person you double the resources working for you. You can do this through motivation— the art of arousing another's emotions so that he believes it is to his own benefit and best interests to do as you want him to do.

5. *Develop a Winning Personality.* The dictionary defines personality as "the sum of one's qualities of body, mind, and character; that which makes one human being different from another; individually." Some people are blessed with a magnetic personality . . . others find it difficult to make a good first impression. The important thing is for you to accept what you have and work from there . . . and to begin by thinking well of yourself. You must like yourself to live with yourself. And you must live every moment of your life with yourself. Therefore you must learn to live happily with yourself before you can live happily with others.

6. *Learn How to Manage Your Time.* Successful people work no harder than other people. They just work smarter. They get their work done. They have taken their cue from old Benjamin Franklin who said that "Time is money."

A $25,000 Lesson

Two of this country's most successful men were Ivy Lee, a noted management consultant, and Charles Schwab, the president of Bethlehem Steel. During an interview Ivy Lee said to Schwab, "With our consulting services, you'll know how to manage better." Schwab replied: "I'm not managing now as well as I know how. What we really need around here is something to pep us up so that we'll get things done." "Fine," said Lee, "I'll give you something in 20 minutes that will give you the action you are looking for. Try it for 30 days and then send me a check for what you think it is worth." Schwab said: "Let's have it." "All right," said Lee, "take this sheet of paper and write on it the six most important things you have to do tomorrow." Schwab did.

Now, said Lee, "number them in the order of their importance." Schwab numbered them. Then Lee continued: "Start working tomorrow morning on item Number one and stay with it until you finish it. Then tackle item number two in the same way. And so on until quitting time. If you can't finish all six, don't worry. You will have finished the most important ones. The others you can handle later." The outcome was that Schwab sent Lee a check for $25,000 saying that that was the most valuable lesson he had ever learned.

Well, that's your *Blueprint for Success.* There's no magic in it. There's no easy way to accomplish all of the things you want to attain over your whole life span. But if you will take to heart these six steps you cannot help but win from life the security, happiness and fulfillment that comes to that select group of 10% of all the people who are seeking out success. One of the Greatest Football coaches all time—Vince Lombardi—once said: That the *Quality* of any man's life has to be a *Full Measure* of that individual's personal commitment to excellence and to victory—regardless of what field he may be in.

That is my charge to each of you— make your own commitment to success —and it will be yours to keep!

Dear Mom and Dad

Akron Beacon Journal
Monday, June 21, 1976

Business Notes

By Larry Froelich
Beacon Journal Financial Editor

Corporate donations used against business?

Corporate dollars for anti-business pursuits? It sounds like sure suicide but Akron University's Jack R. Dauner says that's exactly what some businessmen are unwittingly doing.

The money is in the form of legitimate corporate contributions, and it is going to colleges and universities throughout the country to be used, ostensibly, to promote understanding of the free enterprise system.

BUT STRANGE as it may seem, says Dauner, "business has funded various programs which have sustained continued abuse by academic people (with anti-business attitudes).

"The name of the game today in many areas of higher education is to get corporate dollars under any subterfuge and then use them against the business community by supporting faculty and programs which are diametrically opposed to the concept of the 'profitable enterprise.' "

Dauner noted in the 1974-5 fiscal year, business shelled out more than $275 million to higher education. Even so a recent Gallup Poll indicated 62 percent of today's college students favor stricter government controls of business, he added.

DAUNER'S verbal punches at the business and academic communities were delivered during the recent international meeting of Sales and Marketing Executives-International held in St. Louis.

Dr. Dauner, who is an associate professor of marketing at Akron U, had just received the SME-I Marketing Educator of the Year award and used that opportunity to voice his concerns over the poor relationship between academia and business.

"I felt it was time to take a harder look at the

Jack R. Dauner

classroom and business," Dauner said last week. "Business is falling short in making itself available (to the universities), and my colleagues in academia spend too much time in their ivory towers."

DAUNER said he believes there's room for a lot of improvement in the relationship locally between the two sectors. "Businessmen aren't called upon enough to speak in our classrooms, and I know some rubber industry executives view our program as a little on the light side. But, we should all be working toward the same goal of making it a more viable situation."

"I'm sure that I tend to be a little too pro-business because of the 16 years I spent as a trade association executive, but I think it's important that we (in academia) work more closely with business, government and the community."

At the convention, attended by some 500 business executives, Dauner said the day has passed when corporations can afford to write a blank check to colleges and suggested ways to ensure their funds will promote a strong business curriculum:

Earmark funds for a specific purpose, such as a research project. Dauner commented that nearly three out of every four corporate dollars contributed to Akron U this fiscal year carry such conditions.

Get to know the dean of the college of business administration and tenured faculty and evaluate their professional contributions.

Study the curriculum and determine the quality of the education being offered and the end product.

Make a checklist of the institution's strengths and weaknesses to measure its effectiveness.

Use the local business faculty for placement of their students. This helps bring the teacher into closer contact with the business community.

As hard-headed businessmen concerned about bottom line performance, said Dauner, these executives can ill afford to gamble away such funds without some knowledge of how they'll be applied.

Post-War Academic and Professional Life

Medical Products Salesman — September 1978

Managers Need Training Too
by Eugene M. Johnson, DBA and Jack Dauner, Ph.D.

The authors note that successful salesmen frequently fail to convert successfully to management because it's assumed too often that the newly named manager has the unique tools required by the job, or that he can acquire them easily on his own.

Fifteen months ago Bob Leonard was a happy, productive salesman. For the six years he had been a salesman for Medix (fictitious name), a medium sized manufacturer of medical equipment, Bob had always exceeded his quota and had been in the top third of the company's sales force. During the two most recent years he had been the top salesman in his district. He was the ideal salesman — liked by customers, respected by competitors, always prompt and complete with his sales reports. Last month Bob quit in disgust to accept a position with a competitor.

What happened? Over a year ago Bob was promoted to sales manager and his life, and that of his salesmen, will never be the same.

Why Did Bob Fail?

On the surface, Bob's promotion to sales manager was obvious. He had proven himself in the field and was ready to move up. His promotion was popular with his peers, even his chief rival for the promotion recognized that Bob was the logical choice. Why, then, did Bob fail?

The cynic would say that Bob failed because he had reached his level of incompetence — the popular theory advanced by Lawrence J. Peter and Raymond Hull in *The Peter Principle*. But did Bob fail because he was *not qualified* to be a manager or because Medix failed in its responsibility to prepare Bob for management?

As so often happens, Bob made the transition from successful salesman to unsuccessful manager because his company *assumed* that a good salesman would become a good manager. The company failed in its obligation to help Bob make the difficult transition from salesman to sales manager. Although Medix had an extensive sales training program and would never put a new salesman in the field without adequate sales training, the company *expected* Bob to assume his new responsibilities as a sales manager without providing him with management training.

The Transition From Doer to Manager

Let's examine this difficult transition more closely. As a salesman, Bob was a doer. He was successful because he was able to meet goals which had been set for him. He had to solve problems related to his job (e.g., time management, self motivation, and learning new products), but these problems were mostly related to him and his customers. Bob, the successful salesman, depended upon *himself* to get things done.

As a sales manager, Bob was no longer strictly a doer. Rather, he became a manager of doers. As a manager, he was expected to get things done through others. His new situation was not unlike the former star quarterback who becomes a coach and has to stand on the sidelines while his rookie quarterback fumbles the handoff. Sure, Bob could show his salesmen how to call on an account, but he could not make every sale himself. Like the football coach, Bob had to recruit and select his men, provide training, motivate them, and then hope that they would be able to get the job done. Understanding this role change is critical if a new sales manager like Bob is to make the transition successfully from doer to manager.

Training To Reorder Priorities

Management training is the key to helping a salesman make the transition from salesman to sales manager. Most important, the new sales manager must understand how to reorder his priorities. A recent book suggests that most new sales managers fail because they don't have their priorities straight. The authors comment: "Knowing what to do first, and doing it, is the key we have found to successful sales management."[1]

Perhaps the most important shift in priorities is to have the new sales manager realize that his primary function is no longer personal selling. Even though he enjoys selling and does it well, the new sales manager cannot continue to devote a major portion of his time to selling. He must, as Albert H. Dunn wrote a number of years ago, "resist the natural temptation to flee the frustrating world of management to the old familiar world of selling."[2]

Our experience with new sales managers is that training will help them recognize the need to reorder their priorities. Case studies of new sales managers will stimulate discussion and help new sales managers recognize the difficulties of making the transition from selling to managing. Another successful technique is to have sales managers compile a job description. By analyzing the important components of his job, the new sales manager is able to recognize his priorities. Selling is usually not one of these.

Returning to Bob Leonard, it is not difficult to guess that he was unable to make the transition to sales manager. He continued to put his emphasis on selling because that is what he did best. By doing this, he neglected those important functions of sales management: planning, organizing, recruiting, selecting, training, motivating and controlling. He simply could not wear the hats of both salesman and sales manager at the same time. He worked long hours, his wife began to complain, he failed to meet deadlines, and his salesmen began to feel neglected. Finally, when he could take the pressure no longer, Bob quit.

Constructive Conclusion

Another good salesman and potentially good sales manager failed. Why? Because his company made too many assumptions about his experience and did not adequately prepare him for management responsibilities. Effective management training and development early in Bob's sales management career could have averted this failure.

[1] Mark Hanan, Howard Berrian, James Cribbin, and Jack Donis, *Take-Charge Sales Management*, New York, Amacom, 1976, p. 2.
[2] Albert H. Dunn, "Should You Cut Your Field Sales Manager Out of Selling?" *Sales Management* (October 1, 1965), p. 40.

Dauner — Johnson

Dear Mom and Dad

4 — MEDIA TIMES, SEPTEMBER 1981

Enrolments flooding in for marketing symposium

WHAT PROMISES to be the marketing symposium of the year, if not for many years, also looks like being deservedly one of the best attended.

The Sales and Marketing Executives national conference being held in Wellington on October 8, 9 and 10 is attracting wide interest among marketing, sales and advertising people nationally.

Mr James T.F. Francis (above), chairman of the S.M.E.I. Associations and president of the N.Z. Institute of Management, Wellinton Division, believes the October marketing symposium the most important to be held in New Zealand for many years. "Anyone competing in the tough market conditions that exist today — chief executives, marketing and sales people, advertisers — must find the S.M.E.I. convention invaluable."

Conference organiser, Mr Barry Manley says enrolments are flooding in and with the number that can be accommodated limited to about 200 people, the conference will most certainly be fully subscribed.

It's not surprising because for only $150 for S.M.E.I. members and $190 for non-members, the sheer quantity and quality of the speakers makes the conference amazingly good value.

"Rarely", Mr Manley claims, "have so many top-flight marketing experts been gathered together — both from business and academia — from overseas and New Zealand.

"We are determined", he said, "to provide marketers with much more than the usual convention."

"S.M.E.I. was set-up to foster more effective marketing. If that's our aim, then that's also what a national S.M.E.I. conference should do and do supremely well."

S.M.E.I. also felt that the knowledge and expertise it was bringing together shouldn't be limited to its own members. Consequently, for a small additional charge, non-members can attend all or any of the conference seminars and functions.

• Dr. J. Dauner

Speakes include Dr Jack Dauner, a leading American marketing consultant and university professor of marketing; Dr Guenther Mueller-Heumann, chairman of the Department of Marketing at the University of Otago; Renny Cunnack, chairman of Ogilvy & Mather Advertising, Australia; Bruce Perrott, an Australian marketing consultant; Steve Bridges, Professor of Marketing, Massey University; Richard Brookes, Victoria University and Ken Fink-Jensen from Heylen Research; Graeme Hunter, media director, Colenso Communications and Ralph Parsons, director — variety, Woolworths New Zealand Limited.

Post-War Academic and Professional Life

SELLING AND SALES MANAGEMENT

"Sell or Sell Out in the Eighties"

Selling—this word angers some bankers, frightens others, and confuses most. There is no single word within the financial community that is less understood. And yet, all signs point to selling as the key to successful financial marketing in the 1980s.

As we begin this series of columns for **Financial Marketing**, we shall start by emphasizing the importance of effective selling to the professional financial marketer, and then outline the broad scope of selling in a financial institution. Later columns will discuss selling techniques and the management of those persons who are responsible for solving customers' problems through the sale of financial services.

GROWING IMPORTANCE OF SELLING

Almost 20 years ago an article by Carl Rieser appeared in **Fortune** bearing the title, "The Salesman Isn't Dead—He's Different." The major point: less need for salespersons in those lower level selling activities which could be mechanized or automated and a greater need for sales consultants who could more adequately serve as problem solvers for identifying and satisfying buyers' needs.

The title of Rieser's article could be changed to reflect the evolution of financial marketing in the late 1970s and early 1980s: "The Banker Isn't Dead—He's Different." In fact, N. W. ("Red") Pope, Marketing Vice-President for Sun Banks of Orlando, Florida, aptly summarized the challenge of financial marketing for the 1980s when he wrote "It Will Be Sell or Surrender in the 1980s" for **The American Banker**. Pope stressed that bankers must become totally committed to selling, not just casually involved. The challenge to financial marketers in the eighties is the development of professional financial sales consultants. These professionals will help banks and savings institutions counter aggressive competition by providing personal, professional financial assistance to customers.

Pope and others are responding to three major forces which require banks to place more emphasis on personal selling. These are the unique nature of financial services, the importance of people in financial marketing, and the rapidly changing competitive structure of the financial community.

Financial services are different. Unlike most products, financial services do not have tangible features which appeal to a buyer's senses. This makes marketing more difficult. It is this intangibility of financial services that increases the need for personal selling to illustrate important customer benefits and differentiate them from services of competitive institutions.

The complexity and diversity of financial services add another dimension to the selling process. In the hierarchy of sales personnel, financial marketing requires a highly creative, knowledgeable, and well trained person to make business development calls. Such a salesperson will be able to adapt the extensive services of a financial institution to the individual needs and preferences of each customer. On the other hand, a salesperson without these qualifications will typically have a difficult time determining customers' needs and then developing a financial service "package" to meet those needs.

The relationship between seller and buyer in a financial transaction is like a doctor-patient relationship. Both require well trained professionals who are capable of sizing up and meeting the needs of their respective customers.

People are still important. Nothing is more important to financial marketing than the personal contacts between a bank's employees and its customers. Your customers are human beings, and they want to be treated as individuals with unique financial needs and problems. In fact, it is often personal relationships, rather than services, that lead to satisfaction or dissatisfaction with a bank.

Dear Mom and Dad

Banks and other financial institutions must be careful not to eliminate the desired personal contacts. In an effort to reduce labor costs and increase productivity, many financial institutions have begun to use machines and other nonpersonal methods to provide some basic services. Automatic teller machines and telephone transfer and bill paying services are examples. It is expected that machines will enable financial institutions to operate smaller offices with fewer employees. However, there will still be a major need for personal assistance and creative selling.

Banking and finance are changing. Perhaps no service industry is undergoing more rapid change than financial institutions. In 1979, Comptroller of the Currency, John G. Heimann observed: "Within the next three years, we could have a dramatically restructured financial system. And most of the change will be made by the market." Heimann's prediction has come true; the financial system of 1981 is vastly different from that of two years ago.

The most dramatic industry changes have come about because of deregulation and increased competition. The Depository Institutions Deregulation and Money Control Act, which was enacted by Congress in early 1980, and other regulatory changes have put commercial banks and savings institutions on an equal footing with respect to the services they can offer.

There is also much more competition from other financial intermediaries. As competition continues to grow, marketing, and especially personal selling, will move to the forefront as commercial banks and savings institutions react to the dynamic challenges of a free market. The successful financial institutions will be those that serve their customers best. To put it more succinctly—financial institutions will either have to learn to sell . . . or sell out to their more aggressive competitors.

SCOPE OF FINANCIAL SERVICE SELLING

Personal selling involves some form of interaction, usually face-to-face, between a financial institution's employee and a prospective customer for the purposes of assisting the customer and/or establishing an account relationship. From this definition it is clear that almost all bank employees engage is some sort of personal selling. Even security guards, whose major function is protection, should be able to answer questions, give directions, and provide other forms of assistance to customers.

There are various forms of selling in a modern financial institution. One framework for reviewing the forms of selling is a continuum of sales tasks developed for industrial selling by F. Robert Dodge. Based on the activities performed, salespeople in financial institutions can be divided into four categories: support, maintenance, missionary, and development salespeople.

Support salespeople assist in the selling process, but their major function is not to make sales. In a commercial bank or savings institution tellers, secretaries and platform personnel provide selling support. They assist customers, build and maintain goodwill, and sometimes help customers purchase additional financial services.

Maintenance salespeople are mainly concerned with increasing business from existing customers. They are also responsible for preserving long-lasting, satisfactory relationships with customers. Branch managers, assistant managers, and customer service representatives do a lot of maintenance selling. Tellers are also expected to perform maintenance selling tasks, especially when they are asked to cross-sell services.

Missionary salespeople provide assistance to "pull" products through marketing channels. In recent years banks and savings institutions have used missionary salespeople to help introduce automated teller machines and other related services. Customer service representatives are stationed in lobbies to demonstrate a machine's operation or give advice on other services which would strengthen the relationship between the customer and the financial institution.

Developmental salespeople have the most difficult task. They must sell the financial institutions's services to new customers or sell new services to existing customers. Sometimes branch managers and customer service representatives are expected to be creative salespeople, but most developmental selling in financial institutions is done by specialists. These are usually trust or corporate calling officers. They sell pension plans, retirement programs, trusts, certificates of deposit, and other specialized services to business, professional and other knowledgeable customers.

SELLING AND SALES MANAGEMENT

CONCLUSION

It has been our experience that most bank officers and employees can sell. However, they and their superiors must first be convinced that personal selling is consistent with their image of professionalism. This requires an understanding of the marketing concept and its focus on identifying and satisfying customers' needs. When bank and savings institution executives recognize this, they are

JACK R. DAUNER, Ph.D., has served as a professor of marketing and management at St. Louis University, the University of Detroit, University of Akron and Fayetteville State University. He is also president of his own consulting firm, Jack R. Dauner & Associates, Pinehurst, North Carolina, which specializes in sales, marketing and management development. As a consultant he has served a diversified list of clients ranging from those in banking, heavy equipment, recreation, food, airlines and many others. In 1976 Dr. Dauner was honored as Marketing Educator of the Year by Sales & Marketing Executives-International. He is author of the book Salesmen's Compensation: Plans Policies and Trends; and co-author of How to Plan an Evaluation Program, Readings in Marketing, and Conducting Sales Meetings. He is a frequent contributor to the business and trade press; and, is a frequent participant as a speaker for company, association and university programs.

… *Dear Mom and Dad*

Three Keys To Successful Financial Selling

By Eugene M. Johnson and Jack R. Dauner

SELLING AND SALES MANAGEMENT

In the last issue of **Financial Marketing** we discussed the importance of personal selling and outlined its scope in a financial institution. We now turn to a closer look at the selling process itself. Let's assume that you, a calling officer, have pinpointed a qualified prospect for a business development call. An appointment has been made to discuss your financial services.

The selling process chart was developed by sales trainer Sidney Carter. This chart illustrates the three distinct components of selling. They are: (1) the presentation; (2) the mental benchmarks of the buyer during the sale; and, (3) the major steps in the buying process. To be even more explicit the presentation is what the calling officer does; the mental steps represent what should be accomplished in the buyer's mind; and the buying process is what the calling officer ultimately gets the buyer to do.

THE PRESENTATION

The presentation involves five key steps. The first is the **approach**. This step includes those activities that must be done to actually see the prospect and the critical first few moments when the calling officer meets the prospect. It is essential that a cordial relationship and some interest in the financial service be established during this step.

The approach is followed by an **explanation** during which the calling officer shows the features and benefits of the financial services. The third step is where **proof** is given and claims are made in order to clearly demonstrate the value of the services.

If the previous steps have moved along smoothly, the time has now come to use the gentle art of **persuasion**. This is where the calling officer helps the prospect crystalize awareness of specific wants or needs and move toward a final purchase decision. The **close** should then be a normal culmination of the previous four steps, and the interview concludes with a commitment from the prospect.

THE MENTAL STEPS

Just like the presentation there are five steps involved in this facet of the chart, but this time they are in the form of actions which must be accomplished in the buyer's mind. First, a calling officer must gain the **attention** of the prospect. This can be accomplished in many different ways, but the most popular techniques are using a compliment, such as recognizing a promotion, appealing to the buyer's curiosity by asking a question, and offering a gift or special service.

Once the prospect's attention has been gained, the calling officer then takes the initiative to spark **interest** in the service. This can be done either through a series of questions, by talking about the client's problems, or by discussing those benefits which will give the client the greatest amount of satisfaction. The third step involves **conviction**. This is when the calling officer obtains agreement on the sales points. To do this, a calling officer must demonstrate a high level of knowledge and enthusiasm for the service and must use visuals and other forms of evidence to impress the prospect.

The effective use of evidence will create a **desire** in the prospect to make a positive decision to choose the service offered. Simply stated, this is the stage where the prospect feels so strongly that he or she is ready to say "yes" to the proposition. Finally, comes the **consent** or action step, when the calling officer obtains the commitment. This is accomplished through the use of trial closes, intuitively watching for buying signals, and then asking the prospect to make a commitment.

THE BUYING PROCESS

The third major area which is so critical in financial institution selling is a thorough knowledge of the buying process. A bank salesperson must be fully trained to understand exactly what he or she is attempting to get the buyer to do.

The first step involves the establishment of a

18 FINANCIAL MARKETING

feeling of **need-pressure**. If the calling officer has successfully approached the prospect, and then has gained his or her attention, it is only normal that these actions will culminate in some feeling of need-pressure within the prospect.

Further explanations of the service should generate additional interest and ultimately encourage the prospect to move through the second step of the buying process—namely, **seeking a solution to a problem**. The greater the pressure, the stronger becomes the desire on the part of the prospect to seek relief from that pressure and that leads to the next step.

The third step involves **finding a solution to the problem**. It is during this step that the prospect may present objections or ask questions in an effort to clarify his or her thinking about the proposition. If the calling officer has done a good job up to this point, the process will move to the fourth step, which is **wanting the proposition**. It is here that the prospect has been able to successfully remove the fears and any doubts about the proposition and is now ready to take action.

The final step is in the actual **purchase**. This may include the establishment of an account relationship or some other form of commitment.

IN CONCLUSION

Successful selling of financial services requires a logical plan in which the salesperson knows precisely which steps are to be followed during the presentation, what mental steps will be accomplished in the mind of the buyer, and what actions the prospect will ultimately take.

No financial institution calling officer can ever expect to make a sale on every business development call. On the other hand, a thorough understanding of the buying/selling process will enhance the potential for achieving a higher level of sales productivity. With competitive forces operating at the highest levels in the history of the financial community, knowledge and effective use of selling strategies is a pre-requisite for maintaining industry leadership.

The long overdue shift to a marketing orientation is starting to arrive. Many financial institutions have recognized that they are in the people business, and that their customers have multifaceted financial needs which can be met by an ever expanding list of competitive services.

To explain these services and attract more customers, more training should be provided for those persons who are responsible for business development activities. This means very simply that a greater amount of emphasis needs to be placed on all three of the critical factors of a sale: the presentation, the mental benchmarks used by the customer during the sale, and the phases of the buying process. □

JACK R. DAUNER, Ph.D., has served as a professor of marketing and management at St. Louis University, the University of Detroit, University of Akron and Fayetteville State University. He is also president of his own consulting firm, Jack R. Dauner & Associates, Pinehurst, North Carolina, which specializes in sales, marketing and management development. As a consultant he has served a diversified list of clients ranging from those in banking, heavy equipment, recreation, food, airlines and many others. In 1976 Dr. Dauner was honored as Marketing Educator of the Year by Sales & Marketing Executives-International. He is author of the book **Salesmen's Compensation: Plans Policies and Trends**; and co-author of **How to Plan an Evaluation Program, Readings in Marketing**, and **Conducting Sales Meetings**. He is a frequent contributor to the business and trade press; and, is a frequent participant as a speaker for company, association and university programs.

EUGENE M. JOHNSON, D.B.A., is Professor of Marketing at the University of Rhode Island. From 1971 to 1979 he served as Associate Dean and Director of the MBA Program, and during the 1976-77 academic year he was Acting Dean of the College of Business Administration. His present research and teaching interests include services marketing, sales management, and instructional techniques for selling and sales management. A frequent speaker at professional seminars and company training programs, Dr. Johnson has served as a consultant for a number of businesses and non-profit organizations. His research has been published in many marketing and business journals and he has written several books. His most recent book is **Managing Your Sales Team**.

Dear Mom and Dad

by
Eugene M. Johnson
and Jack R. Dauner

Sales Success Begins With Prospecting

Financial marketing has changed in many ways. Perhaps one of the most shocking changes has developed among bank officers and branch managers who no longer can sit behind their desks hoping that customers will come to them. Instead they, like most professional salespeople, must seek out customers. This crucial selling activity is known as prospecting.

WHY IS PROSPECTING SO IMPORTANT?

Finding qualified potential customers, or prospecting, is the first step in the selling process. This is an essential activity for two major reasons. First, lost customers must be replaced. People move, they die, they become unhappy and close their accounts, and businesses fail. It is estimated that a business loses approximately ten percent of its customer base every year for these and other reasons. Therefore, prospecting is vital if an organization wants to tread water and simply maintain the status quo.

But most financial institutions don't want to stand still. They want to grow. In fact, they **must** grow to survive. This is the second important reason for prospecting. A financial institution must be aggressive in its efforts to attract potential customers (prospects).

Once a financial institution has established the target markets from which prospects will be drawn, calling officers and branch managers must learn how to attract these customers. They must also learn to qualify the prospects to determine if they are valid potential customers.

BEGIN WITH CUSTOMERS

The successful financial salesperson knows that existing customers are the best sources for new sales. It is not unusual for 70 percent of the sales of a new financial service to come from existing customers. For this reason, bank customers should always be notified first when any new service is introduced. Further, cross-sell opportunities should be recognized and actively promoted when calling on customers. These are the people who have confidence in the calling officer and the financial institution. Typically they will be interested in new services and consequently more receptive to cross-sell efforts.

However, existing customers are more than a source of additional sales. Satisfied customers are also excellent sources for referrals. When you ask your customers for the names of friends and business associates who might be interested in similar services, they are flattered. Most likely, a request will result in several valid prospects. It is especially timely to ask for referrals just after an account relationship has been established since the customer will be in a positive frame of mind.

A successful prospecting technique which is based on customer referrals is known as the "endless chain" method. The process operates on the same basis as the familiar chain letter. For example, suppose the calling officer asks a customer for the names of two prospects. The office then calls on these prospects and during the sales call receives two more names from each. The four new prospects lead to eight more prospects and then sixteen, and so on. Of course, the "endless chain", like the chain letter, will not work perfectly. But by asking customers for referrals, an organization's prospect list will be greatly expanded.

Before turning to other sources of prospects, let's consider one other type of customer — the former customer. The approach here requires three simple steps. First, compile a list of former customers. Second, review this list and eliminate those that will be impossible to sell. Finally, consider the remaining names as prospects and place them on the Active List. In all too many cases the reason they left your financial institution is no longer relevant. Remember, in the dynamic environment where financial institutions operate there may have been important changes in customers' attitudes, financial situations, and personnel that will make them more receptive to a sales call.

OTHER PROSPECTING METHODS

In addition to calling on present and former customers when searching for prospects, there are a number of other new business sources. Those that most frequently pay the greatest dividends for experienced financial sales people are: advertising, directories and lists, direct mail, and personal contacts.

Advertising. Most banks and savings institutions spend a lot of money on advertising. If these advertisements are doing their job, they are attracting inquiries from potential customers. However, these inquiries, or "leads", must be followed up before the prospect loses interest. A formalized plan for collecting and disseminating customer inquiries will help the financial institution make sure this is done.

Directories and lists. There are a wide variety of directories which may furnish a financial institution with prospect lists. Sources of business prospects include, but are not limited to, state industrial directories, Dun & Bradstreet's directories, Thomas' Register of Manufacturers, and, of course, the classified telephone directory. For retail prospects membership directories of trade associations, professional societies, civic groups, and social organizations are fruitful prospect sources.

Direct mail. Mailing lists compiled by firms specializing in direct mail lists are a similar source of prospects. These lists may be more current and selective than directories, but they will also be more expensive to obtain. Before purchasing a list be sure to precisely identify the characteristics of the target market. Then go to a reputable list broker with your request for an estimate of the cost. Before buying any list be sure that the names on the list have the desired prospect characteristics. Like anything else a business buys, a list must provide an acceptable return on investment.

Personal contacts. Employees of a bank or savings institution have many contacts with members of the community. This involvement in civic, service and professional organizations provides a base of exceptionally good business development contacts. The people one meets may be prospects themselves or they may provide helpful leads.

In the search for prospects through personal contacts one must always be aware of "centers of influence". These are people who have information about other people or who could help a calling officer identify prospects. Those persons who are closely identified with financial services are: realtors, accountants, attorneys, local business leaders, and government officials. All are excellent centers of influence. Just like a calling officer or branch manager is a center of influence for many real estate, insurance, and other salespeople, calling officers can reverse the process and use the knowledge and contacts of these centers of influence to identify prospects.

QUALIFYING PROSPECTS

Once a person or organization has been identified as a potential customer, the prospect must be qualified. Even the best salesperson cannot sell to someone who is not a valid prospect. For example, the person who is just scraping by on a limited income is a poor prospect for a sophisticated savings plan. The only way to find out whether a prospect will make a good customer is to qualify him or her. There are three key questions for qualifying a prospect.
1. Does the prospect need the service? Unless one is convinced that the prospect can benefit from the financial service, there is no reason to waste the calling officer's time or the prospect's. Selling an automated payroll processing service to a small company with six employees would be foolish since this company can easily handle its payroll processing needs manually.

2. Does the prospect have the resources to buy? Unless the prospect has sufficient resources, or money, he or she is not a qualified prospect. A small business person may need a commercial loan, but that person may not have the cash flow or collateral to justify a loan.
3. Can the prospect make a commitment? This refers to the **authority** to make a binding decision. When dealing with corporations, foundations, and other organizations, the salesperson must be sure that the prospect can make a commitment for the organization. If not, then it will be necessary to determine who the key decision maker is and arrange for another opportunity to explain the program to that person who can say "Yes"!

CONCLUSION

The purpose of this article is to provide the reader with an introduction to and an understanding of what role prospecting plays in personal selling. With the impact of rapidly advancing technology, a dramatic increase of innovative financial services, and ever expanding markets, it is even more important that calling officers and branch managers remain alert to potential new customers. Sound prospecting will provide the flow of new customers who are so vital in minimizing normal attrition.

As described in this column, prospecting involves a three-step process. The first step requires the identification of the target market which the financial institution hopes to reach. The second step is its development and maintenance of a constant stream of prospects. Finally, these prospects should be qualified to determine if they have the need for the proposal, the resources to make the purchase, and the authority to buy. When these three criteria are met, prospecting has provided the first step toward a successful sale. □

Post-War Academic and Professional Life

MARKETING

As Exemplified By Today's Churches

The principles of marketing can be applied to any nonprofit organization. A marketing expert shows you how.

BY JACK R. DAUNER

The term "marketing" is frequently either totally overlooked or completely misunderstood by associations, organizations, churches, governmental agencies, and other nonprofit groups. Yet, if ever there was a group with a need for understanding and implementing sound marketing programs, it is the nonprofit organization.

In order to provide the proper perspective, a definition of the term *marketing* should be first on the list. According to the American Marketing Association, "marketing consists of the performance of business activities that direct the flow of goods and services from producer to consumer or user." In the case of nonprofit organizations, a slight modification should be made in the definition to encourage the sensing, serving, and satisfying of member needs within certain budget constraints.

Jack R. Dauner, Ph.D., is a product of two careers. For 16 years he served as a trade association executive and consultant with heavy emphasis on sales and marketing management. Since then he has served as a professor of marketing and/or management at St. Louis University, the University of Detroit, University of Akron, and Fayetteville State University, while at the same time heading his own consulting firm, Jack R. Dauner & Associates. Dr. Dauner is the author of Salesmen's Compensation: Plans, Policies, and Trends and co-author of How to Plan an Evaluation Program, Readings in Marketing, and Conducting Sales Meetings. He was a contributor to the Handbook of Modern Marketing as well as having numerous articles published in professional journals and the trade press. Dr. Dauner may be reached through Jack R. Dauner & Associates, P.O. Box 1828, Pinehurst, NC 28374, phone (919) 295-3208.

22 / NONPROFIT WORLD REPORT

The marketing concept, when applied to both the profit and nonprofit world, is simply a philosophy which is concerned with meeting needs and solving the problems of a person or an organization. The success or failure of the organization rests on four critical areas of marketing, commonly referred to as the marketing mix. They are (1) the products and services made available; (2) the pricing of those products and services; (3) the efficiency of distribution; and (4) the effectiveness of promotion, including advertising, personal selling, sales promotion, and public relations.

In viewing the services of a nonprofit organization, it is important that we consider its mission, or just what is to be achieved. In order to focus on a specific example, let's use the case of a church. Let us see how a church may use each of the four key factors in the marketing mix: services, pricing, distribution, and promotion.

SERVICES

Basically, a church should be a responsive organization which is dedicated to serving the wants and needs of its parishioners within its budgetary constraints. Through church programs, members should be offered need-satisfying activities that provide positive feelings of faith, hope, charity, and other solutions to personal problems.

What are some of the services a church may offer to meet members' needs? The worship service itself is a good starting point. The weekly service gives members the opportunity to get together in a common bond of worship, under the leadership of a trained person. Other services which a church may offer include: educational programs for persons of all ages; recreational programs; counseling of young and old alike to assist in overcoming stress-related conditions and personal problems; and

311

Dear Mom and Dad

Some of the greatest promotional strategies of modern times involve religion.

sponsorship of internal clubs or other organized groups to encourage a feeling of belonging.

PRICING

Seldom does the church give much thought to pricing of its services, and yet this marketing factor must be considered. Price is related to the value of the services provided and the satisfaction which the member receives in return.

The tangible aspects of pricing come into focus most frequently in church fundraising activities. These include church bazaars, ice cream socials, dinners, and concerts. Pricing is usually on a free-will contribution basis or is established with a minimum mark-up over cost so as to appeal to the greatest number of members.

On the other hand, the development, growth, and survival of a church depend heavily on the number of members. Natural attrition through death, relocation, and change in personal habits takes an annual toll on membership. In addition, costs are constantly increasing as a result of new programs to meet the needs of the congregation.

Therefore, the member canvass or annual drive to secure church pledges involves a pricing strategy. If the value of the church in meeting member needs has grown significantly, the task of securing increases in annual pledges is simplified. Building or modernization programs are also a part of this approach, since such activities are designed to enhance the physical facilities and thus increase the psychological values of the church. As distasteful as it may seem to ministers and lay leaders, the old adage of success breeding success still plays an important role in the impact which a church makes upon a community and its target market.

DISTRIBUTION

Effective distribution means having the right product or service at the right place, at the right time, and at the right price. Distribution is handled through various intermediaries in the world of consumer and industrial products. The services of the church, on the other hand, are usually administered through one central location—the specific church where members worship. Beyond the local church is the network of affiliated churches under the flag of a certain religion.

Thus, when people travel to other cities, their religious and other needs are often met through services performed in another church which adheres to the same doctrines. This is important not only to the church but to the participants in that religious group, because the door is opened to new friends and need satisfiers in communities other than their own.

PROMOTION

Some of the greatest promotional strategies of modern times involve religion. Without taking a position pro or con on these ministries, just consider the impact of Billy Graham, Oral Roberts, Jerry Falwell, and Robert Schuller, to name a few. Each week millions of people receive the televised messages of such ministers. Each week these ministers meet the needs of countless men and women. Through the effective use of mass communications beaming these televised services into millions of homes, through computerized direct mail programs with emotionally charged messages, and through carefully planned telemarketing programs, these merchants of religion are raising millions of dollars over and above the contributions made to local churches.

Modern promotional strategies offer the kind of technology which brings the church directly into the home and creates a new sense of value for religion and the church. Let's not forget that promotion is a key factor in the marketing mix. Promotion is that element which serves as the educational vehicle in satisfying needs.

The church as a nonprofit organization must still be concerned about finances. For a church to expand, its membership—the lifeblood of its financial well-being—must be in tune with those promotional strategies which will produce its fair share of contributions. These strategies include televising Sunday services or carrying the services on the radio, as well as advertising the services in

Post-War Academic and Professional Life

Marketing should provide the guiding light for all nonprofit organizations.

newspapers, mailing weekly bulletins to all members, establishing member committees to call on the sick, and providing community services which are well publicized. All such ideas can be beneficial as promotional strategies not only for a church but for many other organizations in the nonprofit sector.

ORGANIZATION LIFE CYCLE

Although the church might be considered a mature organization, each specific church might fit some other position in the life cycle pattern. A church, with its position in the community and array of services for its members, goes through a series of life cycle stages just as any product or service does. These include: the introductory stage, growth stage, maturity stage, and decline stage. Each stage provides new opportunities, new challenges, and a new set of problems.

Let's trace the life cycle of a church which might be located in Anytown USA. First, the church undergoes the pangs of organization. In these early *introductory* days, a small nucleus initiates activities in modest surroundings.

If the nucleus survives, the organization begins to expand and moves into the early stages of *growth*. During this period membership begins to expand, slowly at first, and then much more rapidly with increased geometric progression. Almost simultaneously, the church experiences marked financial growth and an over-all commitment to longer range goals. Often it is during this period that major capital improvements, such as a building program or new furniture and fixtures, are approved by the church trustees. The growth stage also provides a period in which many new programs and services are launched to meet the needs of church members. As these programs gain wider acceptance, the church increases its membership and assumes a position of leadership in the community.

As the years pass, the church moves into a stage of *maturity*. It is at this point that we begin to see the organization reach a plateau in membership expansion and program development. The church has achieved a solid share of its target market and a certain level of stability. Should poor leadership develop—and it frequently does

during the mature stage—the church will probably begin a downward turn and enter the stage of *decline*.

Initially the decline will be a slow process, but gradually the negative forces will take hold. The decline will then be expedited, with members ceasing to participate or moving on to other churches or alternative programs. Finally, unless drastic changes are made, the church will end up with only a small nucleus of diehards. When the decline reaches this point, the church either closes its doors or hangs on until a new nucleus of members bands together and offers a new mix of services geared to the needs of a different target market.

IN CONCLUSION

In recent years the full implications of the marketing concept have begun to penetrate the wall of ignorance which has surrounded it. Business has finally begun to appreciate the words of Peter Drucker when he said, "The aim of marketing is to make selling superfluous . . . to know and understand the customer so well that the product or service fits the person and sells itself. Ideally marketing should result in a customer who is ready to buy."

Nonprofit organizations have long been in business to satisfy needs of members. By fully utilizing the marketing concept, each has a better opportunity not only to survive but also to increase its share of the market.

This article has used the church as a prime example of a nonprofit organization. Churches need to recognize the impact of marketing on their own well-being if they expect to meet and deal with the competitive environment of the 1980s. If a local church hopes to survive, it must: (1) understand its target market and the various sub-groups within that target market; (2) recognize the needs of these sub-groups; and (3) use the full array of modern technology to satisfy those member needs.

Nonprofit organizations are in the people business. Marketing is understanding and meeting the needs of people through improved products and services. Therefore, marketing should provide the guiding light for *all* nonprofit organizations. In the days ahead, marketing will have to serve as the beacon for organizations in their efforts to better serve the needs of their members. ■

Chapter 24

Jack's Later Life and the Interment at Arlington

Jack, after losing Carolyn, met Denise. Denise was born in Dubuque, Iowa, in 1923. She attended the public schools in Dubuque, and graduated from Dubuque University in 1945 with a Bachelor of Science degree. She was also an accomplished pianist and a graduate of Dubuque Academy of Music. After a long-distance courtship, Denise married Jack on June 1995. Both graduated with honors in the class of 1941 at Dubuque Senior High School. Their families were very close friends and it was only logical that they return to St. Luke Methodist Episcopal Church in Dubuque to repeat their marriage vows. Following the ceremonies, Carolyn's brother, Richard J. Wells, and his wife Peg invited the wedding guests to a reception and dinner at Thunderbird Country Club. Jack and Denise enjoyed playing bridge and golf, and were active in these activities while members of both the Country Club of North Carolina and the Pinehurst Country Club. Jack loved golf and he even received a Hole-in-one Award. They also enjoyed cruising, and took about twenty cruises together till Denise passed away on February 2014.

Jack and Dick Wells at Pinehurst Country Club.

Jack's Later Life and the Interment at Arlington

On May 28, 2015, Jack, while flying to Dusseldorf, Germany, to attend the annual meet of the Sons and Daughters of World War II German and American soldiers, at Newark Airport met Natalie, who was visiting Miami as a keynote speaker in an international conference. Jack and Natalie exchanged business cards and Jack said, "It takes one to spot one," as Natalie also had a PhD, in economics. Natalie's mother, Prisca, is from India and her father, George, was half English. His father, Leo Renaurd West, moved to India from England in 1900 to

Natalie and Jack at their wedding.

work in the tea gardens in northeast India, and then later married Sophila. Natalie served as a professor, researcher and consultant for the Indian Institute of Management, Shillong, India, an institute of national importance, like the Ivy League in the United States. She has also lectured at Duke, Georgia State, and Oxford. One of her books was launched in St. Hugh's College, University of Oxford, on June 18, 2018. After exchanges of daily emails and phone calls, Jack and Natalie got to know each other well.

Natalie and Jack at the Taj Mahal.

In the month of September, Natalie got an invitation from Yale University for a Conference and Jack said to Natalie, fly via Raleigh-Durham and he would pick her up to take her to his house in Pinehurst and then fly with her to Connecticut. After arriving in Pinehurst, Natalie found Jack not doing so well as Jack had suffered an attack of Bell's palsy in December 2014. Hence, Natalie became Jack's caretaker. Natalie would then fly to visit Jack about four times a year, and Jack would also fly to Shillong, India, to spend time with Natalie's family about twice a year. Natalie married Jack on January 04, 2018, at Community Congregational Church, Southern Pines, NC, in the presence of Carolyn's family and Natalie's. Richard J. Wells, Carolyn's brother, who was the best man for Jack when he married Denise, was also the best man this time, and we heard him saying during the reception, "Jack, this should be the last."

Jack and Natalie got along very well despite their age and culture differences. They loved travelling and attended the 9th Infantry Division Reunion and the annual meet of the Sons and Daughters of the American and German Soldiers of WW II. Natalie took Jack to many

Jack's Later Life and the Interment at Arlington

Jack with Pete Stern, Ex-President, 9th Infantry Division Association, and Major General Christopher Donahue, last US soldier to board a plane out of Kabul Airport.

cities in India to witness the wonders of the country, including the Taj Mahal. Jack and Natalie also took cruises together. Jack loved planes and he would drive to the Moore County Airport every day to see the landings and takeoffs. Kathy, the lady who works at the airport customer service, is such a wonderful person and would make Jack's time at the airport so at home. He would enjoy watching the planes and a cup of coffee. Natalie would then take him to the airport every day when he couldn't drive anymore. His passion to be a pilot, which he failed to achieve

Jack at the Annual Meet of the Sons & Daughters of the American and German soldiers of World War II, Dusseldorf, Germany.

Dear Mom and Dad

Jack at the Annual Meet of the Sons and Daughters of the American and German soldiers of World War II, Dusseldorf, Germany.

Certificate presented to Jack at a Sons and Daughters of the American and German Soldiers event.

Jack's Later Life and the Interment at Arlington

Jack in the cockpit of an A–26 attack bomber after his *first flight*, 1945.

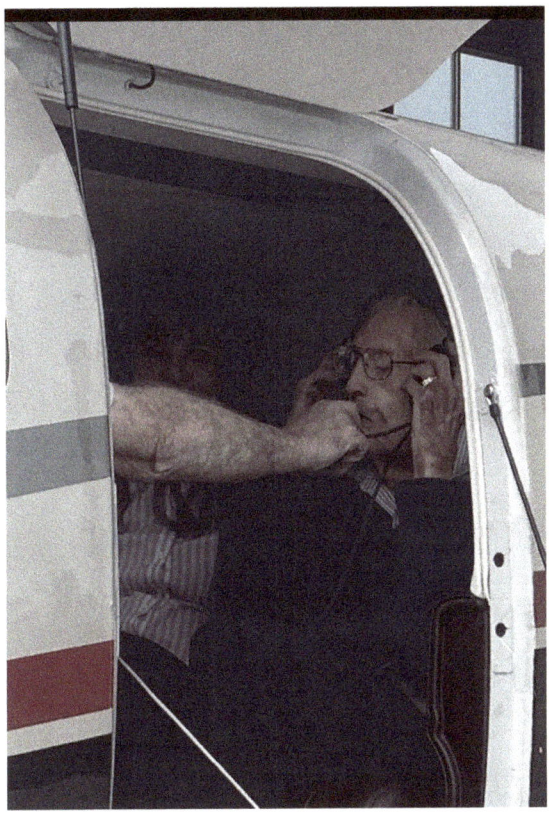

Jack's *last flight*, a 98th birthday surprise TBM ride flown by Ken Haenliein, Moore County Airport, March 22, 2022.

Dear Mom and Dad

due to his 20/30 vision, could be seen even in his later years, but he was happy to have in the family Ruth, Natalie's daughter, who is a pilot. After enjoying seeing the diverse types of aircrafts, Jack loved to go to Pete's restaurant to dine with his friends almost every evening.

On the morning of March 22, 2022, Jack was given a surprise 98th birthday celebration at the local airport, not only with tea, cake, and snacks but also with a special flight piloted by Ken Haenliein. "Jack jumped out of his seat when Kathy said, 'Jack, would you like to take a ride?'" Jack had a wonderful time and we could see the excitement and happiness on his face. That was to be his last ride in the air. In the evening, Jack threw a big dinner at Table on the Green, his favorite restaurant, and it was an unforgettable celebration attended by Carolyn's family, Natalie's family, and Jack's closest friends. Jack delivered a long speech right from his military days till he met Natalie at the airport, and that was his last speech.

Jack's 98th birthday cake, "Around the World," at Table on the Green, March 22, 2022.

Jack's Later Life and the Interment at Arlington

On June 01, 2022, Jack received France's highest tribute, the French Foreign Legion of Honor from the French Consul General, Mr. Vincent Hommeril. The award ceremony was held at The Community Congregational Church, Southern Pines, where Jack had been a member for about thirty years, and was presided over by the church pastor, Mike Dubbs. The ceremony was attended by Jack's family members, church members and friends. This award is bestowed upon both French citizens and foreign nationals who have demonstrated meritorious service to France. On this day, Jack asked Natalie to line up all his military medals, including the Purple Heart on his jacket. Natalie knew that it would be Jack's last event.

Jack's French Legion of Honor award, June 01, 2022..

Legion of Honor press release, *The Pilot*.

Jack's Later Life and the Interment at Arlington

Legion of Honor Ceremony for
Dr. Jack Dauner

June 1, 2022
1700 hours

Welcome and Introduction

Invocation

Republic of France National Anthem

United States of America National Anthem

Bestowing of Legion of Honor Award
                         Mr. Vincent Hommeril

Hymn—How Great Thou Art (back page)

Benediction

(Thank you for attending this Ceremony, please join us for a reception in the Fellowship Hall, with light refreshments.)

Jack Rhodes Dauner
(cover photo circa 1943)

Entered military service February 2, 1943
Combat: Co. K, 60th Infantry, 9th Division
Wounded: December 11, 1944, at Konzendorf, Germany
Reassigned to: 305th Bomb Group (B-17 bombers)
Chelveston, England and St. Trond, Belgium

Honorable Discharge: January 11, 1946

"The world must know what happened, and never forget."

Dwight D. Eisenhower

Legion of Honor ceremony program.

Jack took good care of Carolyn and Denise in their sick beds, and God blessed Jack with Natalie, who honored her marriage vows and left her job to take care of Jack till his last day. Jack's health deteriorated during the fall of 2022 and he passed away peacefully at the First Health Hospice Foundation on December 18, 2022, with Natalie by his side, along with Natalie's daughter, Ruth, and her husband, Hunter Phillips. The memorial service and the celebration of life were held on January 22, 2023. It was followed by a repast at Table on the Green. The service was attended by Carolyn's nephews and niece, Jack's cousin, Natalie's family, colleagues, friends and church members. On a beautiful day, a clear blue sky, July 01, 2024, Jack was laid to rest at Arlington National Cemetery after a breathtaking ceremony in the Old Post Chapel with military honors. As desired, Jack's life story ended with a funeral repast at Carlyle Restaurant, Arlington, for his beloved family and his dear friends. Jack never had children of his own, but he was blessed with a big family who love him dearly. God is good and faithful till the end.

Dear Mom and Dad

Jack's obituary.

Jack R. Dauner

Dr. Jack Rhodes Dauner, 98, of Pinehurst, passed away on Sunday, Dec. 18, 2022, at FirstHealth Hospice House, in Pinehurst.

Jack was born on March 22, 1924, to the late Wilson and Pauline Rhodes Dauner. Jack was a graduate of Dubuque Senior High School. He attended the University of Dubuque for one year before joining the Army to serve in World War II. He received a Purple Heart for a wound received in Hurtgen Forest, Germany. In 2022, Jack was awarded the French Legion of Honor medal for his service to the country during World War II.

DAUNER

VETERAN

After the war, Jack continued to pursue his education. He received a Bachelor of Science in commerce from the University of Iowa, Iowa City, Iowa; Master of Science in commerce from St. Louis University, St. Louis, Mo.; and a Ph.D. in business administration from St. Louis University, St. Louis, Mo.

From 1974-1975, he was president of the Sales Marketing Executives Association. Jack served on the faculty of many institutions of higher learning and was a consultant to many large companies and service organizations. He was a teacher and author in business, management and marketing. He received many awards for excellence in teaching. He authored more than 150 published articles and three books in marketing and sales.

Jack moved to Pinehurst in 1978, and was a member of the Country Club of North Carolina and Pinehurst Country Club. He was an avid and accomplished golfer into his 90s and stopped playing at the age of 95. He was a patient fisherman. Jack went after muskellunge (muskie), the so-called fish of 1,000 casts.

Jack loved to travel. He visited friends around the country, went on many cruises and often attended the 9th Infantry Division reunion and the annual meeting of the families of German and American Soldiers of World War II in Germany. He loved life and was a people person as evidenced by his many good friends. Jack spent most of his afternoons watching the airplanes at Moore County Airport and enjoyed the company of the pilots and the staff.

Dr. Dauner was preceded in death by his first wife, Carolyn Wells Dauner; and his second wife, Denise H. Dauner.

Jack is survived by his beloved wife, Dr. Natalie West Dauner; and her children, Ruth and her husband, Christian Hunter Phillips, Dannie and Dave; his cousins, John T. Dauner and Edward Rhodes; his nephews, Thomas G. Wells, David L. Wells, Jonathan J. Wells, R. Douglas Wells, Robert J. Wells and Steven J. Wells; his niece, Suzanne Wells Brooks; and his goddaughters, Linda Lapp Gravelle and Karen Lapp Schneider.

A memorial service will be held on Sunday, Jan. 22, at 2 p.m. at Community Congregational Church, 141 N. Bennett St., Southern Pines, NC 28387. The service will be followed by a memorial repast.

In lieu of flowers, memorials may be

Jack's Later Life and the Interment at Arlington

Jack's Celebration of Life, January 22, 2023.

Old Post Chapel, Arlington.

Jack's last journey.

Jack's Later Life and the Interment at Arlington

Jack at the altar.

Dear Mom and Dad

Family and friends paying last respects. GOODBYE, JACK!

Location: Arlington National Cemetery
Birth Date: 03/22/1924
Death Date: 12/18/2022
Interment Date: 07/01/2024
Branch of Service: US ARMY
Section: 64
Grave: 934

Jack's headstone, Arlington National Cemetery.

Jack's Later Life and the Interment at Arlington

Thank you to the loved ones at Jack's interment:

Pastor Mike Dubbs
R. Douglas Wells
Mr. and Mrs. Robert J. Wells
Suzanne Wells Brooks
Maggie Villafluentes
Edward Rhodes
C. Hacker Rhodes, III
Linda Lapp Gravelle
Karen Lapp Schneider
Mary Jean George
Steve Cano
Alec Cano
Mr. and Mrs. Joe Wilson
Mr. and Mrs. Mike Kline
Donna Myrick
Mr. and Mrs. Craig Phillips
Mr. and Mrs. Dan West
Dave West
Ruth and Hunter Phillips
Natalie West Dauner

In memory of Jack Dauner

By Mr. and Mrs. Thomas Beddow

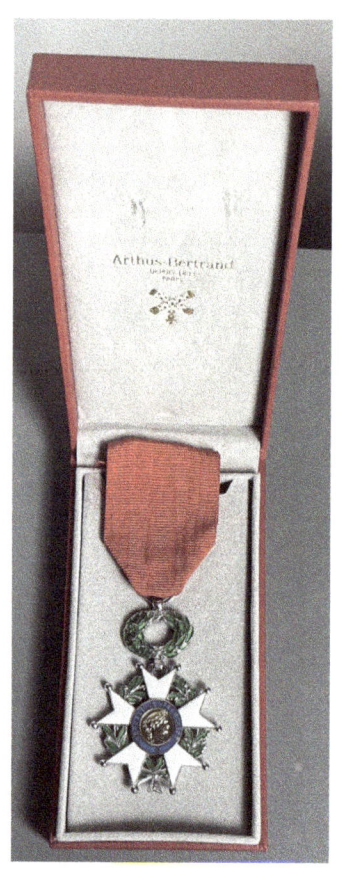

Jack's French Legion of Honor medal.

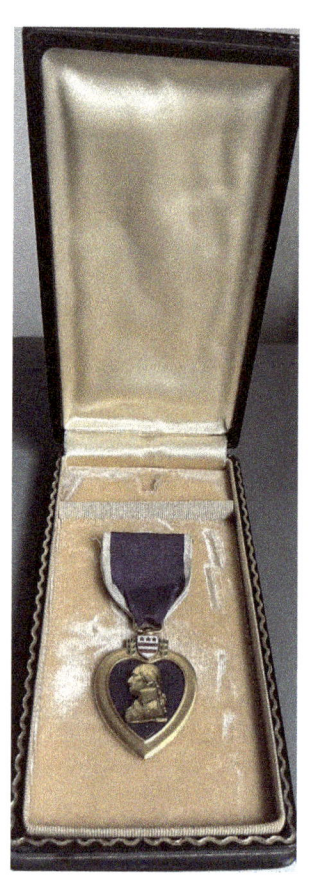

Jack's Purple Heart medal.

Jack's Later Life and the Interment at Arlington

US WW II 9th Infantry Division patch.

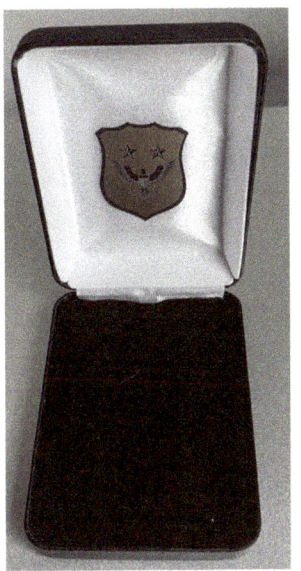

Jack's Military Shield of Honor

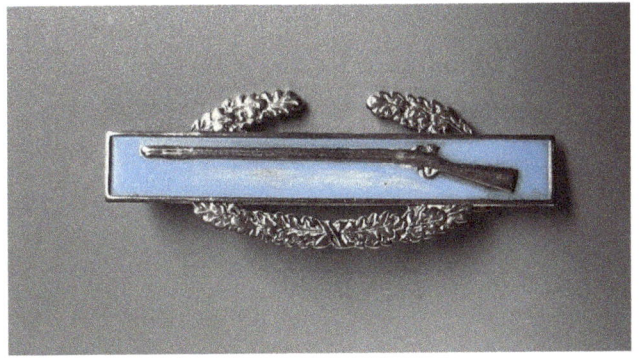

Jack's Army Combat Infantry Badge.

Dear Mom and Dad

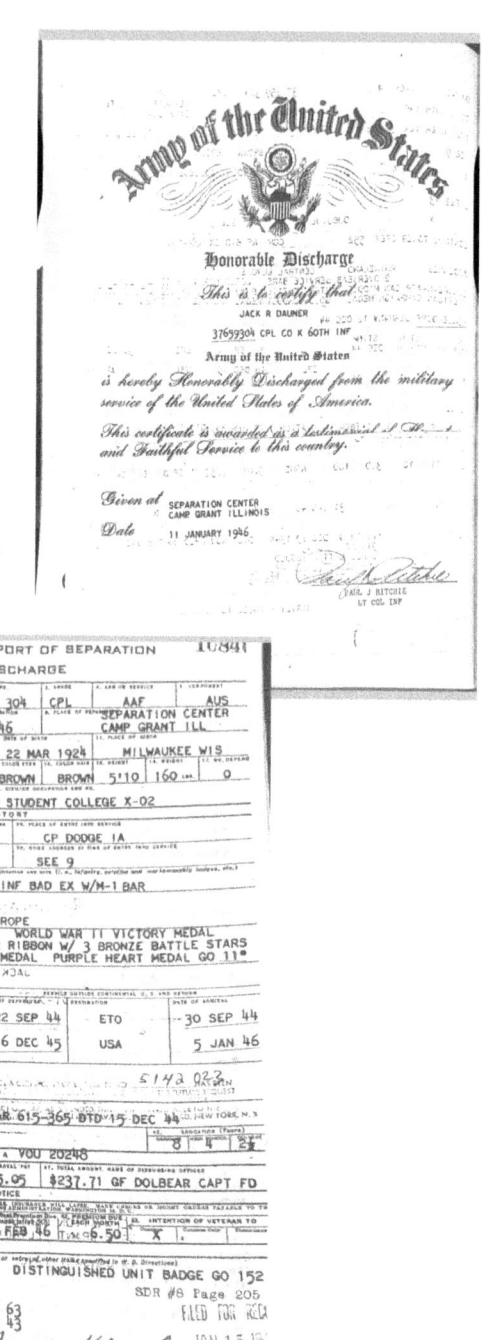

Jack's honorable discharge.

332

Acknowledgments

At the close of Jack's life, I would like to say thank you to the Wells family: Peg Wells, R. Douglas Wells Atty. and Ami Wells, Robert J. and Kim Wells, Steven J. and Kate Wells, Mike and Suzanne Wells Brooks, Thomas G. Wells MD and Bonnie Wells, David L. and Josey Wells, Jonathan J. and Lily Wells and all their children for their love shown to Jack during the happy and sad times. They have a special place in Jack's heart and gave Jack so much pride, happiness and contentment. My gratitude especially goes to Tom, Doug and Bob for their support and assistance given to me after Jack passed away.

I would also like to thank Jack's only paternal cousin, John Dauner, and his wife, Sue Dauner, Jack's maternal cousin, Dr. Edward Rhodes, and his family for all the good times spent with Jack over the phone as well as visits. Special thank you also goes to Linda Lapp Gravelle and Karen Lapp Sneighder, whom Jack loved dearly as his own daughters. They have brought lots of happiness to Jack and made Jack's life more enjoyable.

I would also like to thank my parents, (L)George West and Prisca Kharkongor, for allowing me to tie the knot with Jack in spite of the age difference. My thanks also go to my brothers, Gordon, Robert, Mark and Alan, and my sisters, Jean and Sherry, and my nephews and nieces for all the love shown to Jack when he was in India. The note is not complete without mentioning Mary Jean, my spiritual mother, who loves us as her own family and who is my companion, especially in my dark and sad days. My gratitude also goes to Angela and Craig Phillips for the happy moments together and for taking care of Jack in my absence. My love and care for Jack would not have been complete without the support of my sons, Dan and Dave, and especially Ruth

Dear Mom and Dad

and Hunter Phillips. Ruth and Hunter have gone beyond the call of duty to make Jack a happy and proud father, and gave Jack the best birthday party ever, which turned out to be the last. I would also thank my first husband, Balaph, who is with the Lord now, for giving me three beautiful children. I am blessed abundantly.

Good friendship was an integral part of Jack's life. In this regard, I would like to thank Pastor Mike Dubbs of Community Congregational Church, Southern Pines, and all the members of the church for the assistance, moral support and sweet fellowship that Jack always valued. I also thank Jack's doctor, Dr. Wyman T. Mcquirt, MD, for the care, jokes and love shown to Jack in the hospital and outside the hospital. My gratitude also goes to Tom and Kathy Beddow for loving Jack and for all the donations made by them in memory of Jack. I would also like to thank Kathy Priest for being so nice to Jack at the local airport and always treating him with respect. I thank Sharon and Richard, Gale and David, Janice and Lisa Morrison, JoAnn and Jim Hansz, and Kay and Jeff Beran for being lifetime friends. My thanks also go to Mike and Annie Kline for loving Jack and for taking care of Jack's wheels during his last days, and for remaining my close friends. Their wedding is the last wedding party in Jack's list.

A special thank you goes to the 9th Infantry Division Association: Mary Blann Cooper, President, Pete Stern, ex-president, Clare Irwin, Theda Ray and Cindy Melson, Dennis Bonkowski, JoAnn Bryant, Linda Jorden, Janet Schnall; and to the Germany Annual Meet Group: Albert and Sheila Trostorf, Rudi, Maren, Steve and Nina Cano, Joe and Cecilia Wilson, Yuri Beckers, Harry Stumpf; and to all the esteemed members of the 9th Infantry Division Association and the Germany Group, who have given Jack so much excitement, joy, pride and a spirit of fulfillment towards the country he fought for.

I want to extend my gratitude to the Arlington National Cemetery for conducting an honorable burial of Jack on July 01, 2024.

Last but not least, I would like to thank the Department of Veterans Affairs for all the diverse types of assistance and support provided

Acknowledgments

to Jack, especially during his later years. A special thank you goes to all the doctors and staff at the VA hospital who had taken good care of Jack with loving care.

Above all, the acknowledgment is incomplete without thanking God for the strength and wisdom that enables me to complete the editing of this book, and adding two more chapters as well. All my gratitude goes to Him for His grace and love and with this agape love, I could love Jack and be with him till his last breath on this earth. I would like to end by quoting from the Bible that "I can do all things through Christ who strengthens me" and "all things work together for good to those who love God." Amen.

—Natalie West Dauner